T0305455

Managing Conflict in Facility Siting

To Ysabel and Adrian and in memory of their loving grandfather, Sidney Ernest Lesbirel

To Showmei, May and Chenghao

Managing Conflict in Facility Siting

An International Comparison

Edited by

S. Hayden Lesbirel

Associate Professor of Political Science, James Cook University, Australia

Daigee Shaw

Research Fellow, Institute of Economics, Academia Sinica, Taipei, Taiwan, ROC

Edward Elgar

Cheltenham, UK · Northampton, MA, US

Published by
Edward Elgar Publishing Limited
Glensanda House
Montpellier Parade
Cheltenham
Glos GL50 1UA
UK

Edward Elgar Publishing, Inc.
136 West Street
Suite 202
Northampton
Massachusetts 01060
USA

A catalogue record for this book
is available from the British Library

Library of Congress Cataloguing in Publication Data

Managing conflict in facility siting : an international comparison / edited by S. Hayden Lesbirel, Daigee Shaw.
    p. cm.
    Includes index.
    1. Hazardous waste sites—Location—Decision making. 2. Nuclear facilities—Location—Decision making. 3. Industrial location—Decision making. 4. Conflict management. 5. Transaction costs. I. Lesbirel, S. Hayden (Sidney Hayden), 1957– II. Shaw, Daigee, 1951–
    TD1040.M36 2005
    658.2'1—dc22
                                     2004056381

ISBN 1 84376 523 3

Printed and bound in Great Britain by MPG Books Ltd, Bodmin, Cornwall

Contents

Figures

Tables

Contributors

Daniel P. Aldrich is a Ph.D. candidate in the Department of Government at Harvard University and an Affiliate of the Weatherhead Center for International Affairs. He has published articles in, among other journals, *Political Psychology*, *Social Science Japan*, the *Asian Journal of Political Science*, and the *Journal of East Asian Affairs*.

Yannick Barthe is a researcher at the Institute of Political Studies, Grenoble (part of the French National Center for Scientific Research, CNRS). He is co-author, with Michel Callon and Pierre Lascoumes, of *Agir dans un monde incertain. Essai sur la démocratie technique*, Paris: Le Seuil, 2001.

Hank C. Jenkins-Smith is the Joe and Teresa Long Professor of Business and Government at the George H.W. Bush School of Government and Public Service at Texas A&M University. He writes about environmental and security policy, and has recently had articles appearing in the *Journal of Politics*, the *Journal of Conflict Resolution*, the *Journal of Environmental Economic and Management*, and the *International Studies Quarterly*. He is the editor of the *Policy Studies Journal*, the official journal of both the APSA's Public Policy Section and the Policy Studies Organization.

Roger E. Kasperson is Professor at Clark University. He served as Director of the Stockholm Environment Institute from 1999 to 2004. He has written widely on issues connected with risk analysis, risk communication, global environmental change, risk and ethics, and environmental policy. Dr Kasperson has served on various committees of the National Research Council and is past president of the Society for Risk Analysis. He has been honored for his hazards research by the Association of American Geographers and the American Association for the Advancement of Science. He was elected to the National Academy of Sciences in 2003 and the American Academy of Arts and Sciences in 2004.

Aynsley Kellow is Professor of Government at the University of Tasmania in Australia and author of *Transforming Power: The Politics of Electricity Planning* (1996) and *International Toxic Risk Management: Ideals, Interests and Implementation* (1999) (both with Cambridge University Press), and *International Environmental Policy: Interests and the Failure of the Kyoto Process*, Northampton, UK: Edward Elgar, 2002.

Howard Kunreuther is the Cecilia Yen Koo Professor of Decision Sciences and Public Policy at the Wharton School, University of Pennsylvania as well as serving as Co-Director of the Wharton Risk Management and Decision Processes Center. He has a long-standing interest in ways that society can better manage low probability-high consequence events as they relate to technological and natural hazards. He has been concerned with the role that incentives, such as compensation, coupled with standards can play in siting noxious facilities. He has studied the socioeconomic impacts of siting the high level nuclear waste facility in Nevada and is co-author (with Doug Easterling) of *The Dilemma of Siting a High-Level Radioactive Waste Repository*, Boston: Kluwer Academic Publishers, 1995.

S. Hayden Lesbirel is an Associate Professor of Political Science at James Cook University in Australia. He is author of *NIMBY Politics in Japan: Energy Siting and the Management of Environmental Conflict*, Ithaca: Cornell University Press (1998), and has contributed articles to *Policy Sciences, Journal of Business Administration, Energy Policy, Pacific Affairs, Asian Journal of Political Science, Australian Journal of Political Science, Japanese Journal of Political Science* and other journals on Japanese energy and environmental affairs and policy.

Joanne Linnerooth-Bayer is leader of a program on Risk, Modeling and Society at the International Institute of Applied Systems Analysis (IIASA) in Laxenburg, Austria. She has published widely on issues of siting hazardous facilities, including a special issue of RISK: Health, Safety & Environment, 7:2 on Fairness and Siting (with R. Löfstedt). She addressed the transboundary problems of siting unwanted facilities in her book (with R. Löfstedt and G. Sjöstedt) titled *Transboundary Risk Management in Europe* London: Earthscan (2001). She is an associate editor of the *Journal for Risk Research* and on the editorial board of *Risk Analysis and Risk Abstracts*.

Claire Mays is a social psychologist at Institut Symlog, a private research consultancy in Cachan, France. She leads a working group on Implementing Local Democracy in the European Commission-sponsored action 'Communities and Waste Management' (COWAM, 2004–2006) and was part of the U.S. National Research Council group to author *Disposition of High-Level Waste and Spent Nuclear Fuel: The Continuing Societal and Technical Challenges*, Washington, DC: National Academy Press, 2001. The follow-on to events described in Barthe & Mays may be read in Claire's chapter in *Facility Siting: Risk, Power and Identity in Land-Use Planning* (Boholm & Löfstedt, eds), London: Earthscan, 2004.

Felix Oberholzer-Gee is the Andreas Andresen Associate Professor of Business Administration at Harvard Business School. His articles on siting issues have appeared in journals such as the *American Economic Review*, the *Journal of Political Economy* and the *Journal of Policy Analysis and Management*.

Bettina Oppermann, full Professor for Spatial Planning at the University of Hannover and co-director of the consulting company 'Komma-Plan'. She is co-author with E. Schneider, B. Oppermann and O. Renn: 'Experiences from Germany: Application of a Structured Model of Public Participation in Waste Management Planning', *Interact, Journal of Public Participation*, Vol. 4, No. 1 (July 1998), pp. 63–72.

Ortwin Renn, full Professor for Environmental Sociology at the University of Stuttgart and director of the non-profit institute 'DIALOGIK' for communication research. He is co-author of the book: O. Renn, Th. Webler and P. Wiedemann (eds): *Fairness and Competence in Citizen Participation. Evaluating New Models for Environmental Discourse.* Dordrecht and Boston (Kluwer 1995) and author of the publication 'The Challenge of Integrating Deliberation and Expertise: Participation and Discourse in Risk Management', in: T. L. MacDaniels and M.J. Small (eds), *Risk Analysis and Society: An Interdisciplinary Characterization of the Field*, Cambridge: Cambridge University Press, 2004.

Elke Schneider, scientific administrator of the department of infrastructure planning at the University of Stuttgart. She is co-author of the article: E. Schneider, B. Oppermann and O. Renn, 'Implementing Structured Participation for Regional Level Waste Management Planning', *Risk: Health, Safety & Environment,* Vol. 9 (Fall 1998), pp. 379–39.

Daigee Shaw is Research Fellow at the Institute of Economics, Academia Sinica. He has published widely on economic analysis and policy analysis related to natural resources and pollution control issues. Dr Shaw is co-editor of *Global Warming and the Asian Pacific* (2003) and *The Economics of Pollution Control in the Asia Pacific* (1996) (both with Edward Elgar), and editor of *Comparative Analysis of Siting Experience in Asia*, published by the Institute of Economics of Academia Sinica in 1996.

Acknowledgements

Chapter 4 was originally published in *Risk Analysis*, Blackwell Publishing Ltd., UK, 2001; Chapter 8 was originally published in *Journal of Risk Research*, Taylor & Francis Ltd., UK, 2001. Reprinted here by kind permission of Blackwell Publishing Ltd. and Taylor & Francis Ltd..

Preface

The siting or development of unwanted facilities has emerged as a major policy problem in all democratic countries. It has become increasingly difficult to find places to store radioactive waste, locate power plants or new industrial facilities, and identify local communities willing to accept solid waste facilities. Over the past decade and a half, there have been a growing number of case studies of siting, principally in single country contexts, reflecting the importance of this issue as a policy problem. These analyses have provided important insights into the factors that command support for and opposition to siting projects and the impact of those factors on resolving conflicts in an effective manner.

Many of the papers included in this volume were selected from those presented at an International Workshop on Challenges and Issues in Facility Siting, held at the Institute of Economics, Academia Sinica, in Taiwan in January 1999. Several other papers were commissioned by the editors to make the context of the book more complete and to ensure coverage of a broad range of siting experience. Each paper went through a rigorous review process. The papers were carefully reviewed by the editors and external reviewers.

The Workshop was designed to capitalize on the experience of practitioners and researchers concerned with facility siting problems by linking descriptive analyses with prescriptive guidelines. The objective of the workshop was to examine the factors which influence siting decisions and explore ways to improve siting processes by investigating actual case studies in democratic countries. A key conclusion was that existing policy approaches have not been effective in reducing the transaction costs of siting and that there is a need for institutional change which can deal with the public goods nature of democratic governance.

The editors would like to thank Taiwan Cement and Bayer (Taiwan) Companies in Taiwan and Tokyo Electric Power Company and the Central Research Institute of Electric Power Industry in Japan for their generous financial support in supporting the workshop and the production of this book. We are grateful to the Institute of Economics, Academia Sinica for support in organizing the workshop and in editing this book. We also want to thank the chapter authors for their full cooperation in the long process of workshop preparation and book editing.

1. Transaction Costs and Institutional Change

S. Hayden Lesbirel

The development or siting of unwanted facilities remains a major policy problem for industrialized countries around the world. Throughout Asia, Australia, Europe and North America, intense local opposition almost always greets attempts to site facilities that are perceived to be highly hazardous and risky, such as nuclear plants, high-level waste projects, and industrial projects. Local residents often view any local benefits as being small relative to the risks and burdens. These projects may be justified from a broader national perspective, but local communities often want them located somewhere else, a response often referred to as the 'not in my backyard' (NIMBY) syndrome (Popper, 1983). Such outcries generate political resistance, and makes siting a major policy challenge for both the private and public sectors in all democratic nations alike.

Securing agreement to house many types of projects perceived to be risky is difficult, complex and frequently protracted. In many cases, developers are unable to win approval to build projects in the face of concerted opposition. There will usually be high levels of uncertainty confronting stakeholders. Developers may be uncertain about the extent of future demand for outputs generated from projects. This may cause considerable concern about capital investment strategies, particularly given the lumpiness of many projects. Local communities may be unclear about the risks of accidents at projects and this may cause considerable anxiety about the potential health effects of projects. They often view that the risks are high in relation to any potential benefits accrued. Siting is a high stakes game for both developers and community interests.

The comparative evidence from a range of democratic nations, including Austria, Australia, France, Germany, Japan and the United States, strongly suggests that the transaction costs involved in securing community agreement to locate unwanted projects have increased. Democratic nations have adapted to this challenge and have developed new approaches to managing siting conflicts. Despite the development of innovative policy processes, instruments and strategies, these nations have been unable to manage the high transaction costs effectively because of the public goods nature of the democratic system of governance. This volume argues that institutions matter in managing high transaction costs (North, 1991; 1999). It suggests that dealing effectively with these transaction costs will require significant institutional change in terms of *who* participates in siting decisions and *how* those decisions are made.

This volume is about the management of legitimate and rational claims in siting decision processes where transaction costs are high. It seeks to analyze the extent to which the institutional and policy environment can assist in managing siting conflicts in a range of democratic nations. By exploring siting conflicts in the context of a transaction cost framework, the volume aims to further our understanding of this issue in two principal ways. The first is to enhance our theoretical and comparative knowledge of siting conflicts and their management. The second is to help in developing more robust and effective policies for managing this increasingly intractable problem.

1   CONFLICT AND TRANSACTION COSTS

In any siting conflict, there are a set of interested stakeholders, each of whom has its own interests, values and goals. There are groups who would like to see a project built because it may yield important benefits to them; others will have serious concerns about the facility. The key parties can be found at different jurisdictional levels. The applicant, normally a private firm or government agency, is generally supportive of the project. Local citizens groups and environmental organizations often oppose because of social and natural environmental concerns about the facility. Government regulatory agencies also become involved as they are responsible for developing and enforcing regulations. The general public, particularly at the local level, reflects a wide spectrum of attitudes about the facility, and has an interest in the project.

These interests get involved because project development imposes both positive and negative spillover effects, both monetary and non-monetary in nature, on them. There may be expected benefits from projects to local and national communities. Some interests in local may see the project as stimulating local economic growth and enhancing local development and employment opportunities. However, at the same time, other interests may see the project in terms of economic and financial losses, degradation to the natural environment, negative impacts on human health, and disruption to traditional community networks (Baram, 1976; Morell and Magorian, 1982). In contrast, the national community may see the project as beneficial for national security or other national policy priorities.

This volume assumes that these competing views about the benefits and costs of projects represent legitimate claims and are rational. It is legitimate for public and private developers alike to develop facilities to meet demand; it is also legitimate for some local interests to support projects while others vehemently oppose them. Furthermore, it assumes that these interests are acting rationally. It is rational for developers and national communities to wish to develop projects perceived to be in their interests. Equally, it is also equally rational for local community interests to oppose projects where they feel that there will be net negative spillover effects. A critical first step to managing siting controversies is to assume that both supporters and opponents, both within and across different jurisdictional levels, have legitimate and rational claims.

Siting conflicts arise where local community interests perceive a disproportionate allocation of burdens expected from the project development. Put differently, they occur where there are perceived inequities between who gets the benefits and who has to accept the adverse risks and burdens. The adverse costs of projects are often seen to be concentrated on the local level. In contrast, the benefits of projects are often more diffused; while local communities do receive benefits from projects, they share those benefits with the national community (O'Hare, Sanderson and Bacow, 1983). It is no wonder that resistance emerges to the siting of many types of facilities given views about the expected distribution of costs and benefits from the project.

Where local communities have legally recognized property or zoning rights or other forms of political power, as they often do in industrialized nations, the siting of unwanted facilities will involve a political process of deciding the allocation of costs and benefits expected to accrue from the project development. This will involve a process of deciding on how to decide about the project development. It will also involve a process of deciding which policy mechanisms to use in seeking a resolution of the conflict. For example, this might involve deciding on whether developers compensate for losses, whether developers will mitigate losses, or whether they will adopt a combination of both mechanisms. In short, the political process will involve deciding who wins and who looses (Lasswell, 1936) from project development, and in what forms the costs and benefits from projects will be reallocated.

The transaction costs involved in reaching political settlements are likely to be high where communities expect net negative spillover effects from the project and where they can mobilize political power to stall or block decision processes. Decision processes are inherently political. There are difficulties in measuring the attributes of projects. For instance, parties to siting conflicts almost always contest the expected social, economic and health effects on individuals and on local industry from both the construction and operation of projects. Given the high levels of conflict in siting processes, the negotiating costs of reaching agreements are very high. For instance, developers often have difficulties getting parties to reveal their preferences and even sit at the negotiating table. The uncertainties associated with enforcement of siting deals can be extremely high. For instance, local parties may decide to abrogate siting agreements; those costs can be extremely detrimental particularly when developers have sunk funds into the construction of capital-intensive projects (Bacow and Wheeler, 1991).

2   PERSPECTIVES

The increased transaction costs involved in facility siting is reflected in the increased difficulties involved in managing siting disputes. This volume in concerned with exploring the approaches, policy instruments, decision-making processes and institutions that have characterized the siting and development of unwanted projects comparatively. I explore each of these issues briefly.

The history of siting reveals significant change in **approaches** to managing environmental conflict. As Kasperson (Chapter 2) notes, democratic countries have adapted themselves in different ways to dealing with siting problems. Early attempts to site projects featured *DAD (decide- announce- defend)* and *technical screening techniques*. Developers either sought to ride out community opposition or to override community interests even when they sought to justify site selection using technical criteria. As Rabe (1994) demonstrates, such approaches have not worked for some time. The chapters in this volume reinforce that conclusion. In democratic countries, communities are generally powerful enough to delay or stop the development of projects that they perceive to be risky. Many states still have the legal and constitutional authority to impose environmental burdens on community interests (through the use, for example, of eminent domain). Yet, increased demands for more voluntary and democratic processes, power sharing, and transparency effectively mean that communities have veto power over project placement decisions.

In response to demands for more democratic siting processes, many countries have developed or experimented with more participatory and voluntary approaches. Comparatively, two approaches have emerged: *battered consent* and *voluntary/partnership siting*. Battered consent involves bargaining and compensation for negative spillover effects. Although this approach has been practised in Japan and Taiwan, and has been attempted in the U.S., there has been increasing opposition to the use of compensation, which is often seen as immoral, in resolving siting conflicts. Voluntary/partnership siting involves seeking to obtain greater voluntary acceptance of projects given expectations for greater public information, consultation and participation and to engage community interests in a partnership with developers in siting the project. This approach has been attempted on a wider scale in countries such as France, Germany, the U.K., and Canada. While these approaches seem to have worked marginally better than more traditional ones, they still have not have reduced transaction costs of siting in any meaningful way.

The continued failure of even these innovative approaches to siting reflects importantly different values about key elements of these approaches. Stakeholder values toward key siting issues, such as equity and fairness, are socially constructed (Stone, 1997). As such, they will have contested views about issues such as equity in both procedural and substantive terms (Rae, 1981). Stakeholders will have divergent views about such goals. These divergent values toward projects form an important basis of conflict and are an important determinant of the increased transaction costs associated with developing projects. Forging social agreements on projects, even if through highly participatory and voluntary approaches, will continue to be problematic where such contested values polarize the positions of key stakeholders.

Linnerooth-Bayer (Chapter 3) argues that siting failures are due to not taking into account competing views of fairness in the context of major forms of social organization (hierarchy, market and egalitarian). Hierarchical approaches stress authority and procedural rationality. Fairness is settled by administrative determination. In nations such as Austria and Australia, the right to impose facilities rests with the central government. Market approaches are distinguished by an emphasis on personal rights, freedoms and economic rationality. Distributive issues are settled by market interactions, as in nations such as Japan and Taiwan. Egalitarians reject the unequal social relations contained in both hierarchical and market views of fairness. They abhor morally any procedures that perpetuate social inequalities. This is reflected in demands that unwanted projects should be sited in wealthy communities on environmental justice grounds. The key strategy in designing an effective deliberative approach to siting is to consider the moral boundaries of each of these cultural solidarities and to compromise based on appeals to cultural pluralities in a deliberative process.

The nature and effectiveness of **policy instruments** will also be an important factor influencing the transaction costs involved in resolving siting conflicts. Economic theory posits that peoples' perceptions of facilities are related to their expected risk-benefit calculations. According to the potential Pareto Improvement criterion, compensation, whether in monetary or non-monetary forms, aims to facilitate siting processes by making communities at least as well off after the change as they were before it (Kunreuther and Easterling 1991). But compensation also has a political and strategic role. By increasing the benefits, or at least reducing the costs of projects to host communities, compensation has the potential to reduce or nullify political and other resistance (O'Hare, Sanderson and Bacow, 1983).

There has been growing evidence that compensation has not been as effective as a policy tool for resolving siting disputes as simple economic theory might posit (Kunreuther and Easterling, 1991; 1996). Several chapters of this volume explore the nature, scheduling and effectiveness of compensation. Smith and Kunreuther (Chapter 4) in their analysis of a U.S. case find evidence that compensation seems to work reasonably well in resolving conflicts for projects perceived as low risk or benign (prisons), but it rarely works for projects perceived to be highly risky (nuclear waste repositories). For high-risk projects, compensation is likely to be relatively more palatable where safety measures, such as regular inspections by independent inspectors, have the ability to shut down plants. Levels of support are likely to be higher where non-monetary compensation is offered first. Under these conditions, communities may not treat compensation so strongly as bribe or 'blood money', which can actually increase resistance to projects. (Gerrard, 1995 and Frey, Oberholzer-Gee and Eichenberger, 1996). The political acceptability of benefits packages is not likely to be independent of risks associated with projects. The commensurability of benefits in terms of the nature of risks may be more important than the absolute level of them in determining the effectiveness of compensation.

Compensating for spillover effects is inherently political. The extent to which social and political pressure keeps compensation off the agenda will influence importantly its strategic viability as a policy instrument in resolving siting disputes. Keeping issues off the agenda is a crucial form of political power in decision-making (Parry and Morris, 1982). Oberholzer-Gee and Kunreuther (Chapter 5) explore the relationship between compensation and social pressure in a U.S. case. They conclude that social pressure is a form of political power where private preferences hide behind a 'veil of silence' and leads to a preference for the *status quo*. The level of support is dependent on expectations about the level of support of other residents. Even high levels of compensation may not generate a site voluntarily as the minority who want compensation are reluctant to put the issue onto the negotiating table. Social pressure can be exceptionally high where morally objectionable forms of compensation are proposed.

Unlike the U.S. where the state has not played a significant role is siting, the state has played a more persuasive role in other nations such as Japan, Taiwan and France in facilitating the resolution of siting conflicts. Aldrich (Chapter 6) in a case study of Japanese experience, argues that the Japanese state has developed a range of policy instruments to alter citizens' preferences and increase the barriers to collective action against state supported projects. These have included a sophisticated interlocking array of authority, incentive, capacity, symbolic and learning instruments that have been modified and strengthened over time. For instance, in contrast to the U.S., Australia and several other European nations where compensation has been used more on an *ad hoc* basis, Japan has developed more institutionalized compensation mechanisms. While the comprehensiveness of this arsenal of policy tools has helped Japan manage transaction costs historically, their effectiveness seems to be waning in the light of increased safety concerns and an increasingly active citizenry.

The nature and structure of **decision-making processes** involved in deciding on whether and in what form facilities are developed is also a crucial aspect of managing transaction costs in siting. The unsuitability of coercive approaches to siting in democratic nations and social and political constraints to the use of compensation has led several nations to seek to develop more deliberative siting approaches. This has occurred at a time when there has been increasing concern about a lack of trust and accountability in both public and private institutions in democratic states. Stronger demands for more public participation, more democratic control, and more openness and transparency in siting processes, as reflected in all the chapters in this volume, has led to more deliberative decision processes (Kasperson, Golding and Tuler, 1992).

In such an environment, an important component of effective siting will be the nature of deliberative decision-making processes themselves. Schneider, Oppermann and Renn (Chapter 7) discuss the importance of public participation, paralleling more official technical decision-making processes, by applying a cooperative discourse model to a case in West Germany. The model involves three key steps: identifying concerns and evaluative criteria, evaluating consequences of alternative policy options, and rational discourse with citizens (jurors) and interest group representatives (witnesses) with citizens making the final site selection decision. Even with such a process, there were difficulties such as achieving broader public involvement and developing trust amongst stakeholders with different interests and values. Although exogenous factors led decision-makers to change the suite of candidate sites to an entirely different region, most participants found that the approach was fair, legitimate and transparent.

Open and consultative decision processes are inherently political with different stakeholders seeking to exert power over others. Barthe and Mays (Chapter 8) explore how the state, through local information commissions, can embed itself in local communities and seek to develop more dialogue over siting decisions with community interests in a French case. The state sought to shift the grounds for siting from scientific authority to procedural authority and to secure more democratic control by legislation. However, many participants saw state communicative processes as an attempt to exert political power in the site selection process by not only providing information *to* the public, but also *on* the public. The process opened up a forum for opposing voices or interests that generated different interpretations of risk. The commissions were not so much a vehicle for broad-based debate, but rather a vehicle to cajole parties who were perceived as being influential and to attempt to influence them over siting decisions. The terrain between voluntarism and coercion remains as grey as ever.

While open and participatory decision processes have increasingly been seen to lead to better processes, it is important to realize that they may not lead to better outcomes. Kellow (Chapter 9) highlights the potential dangers involved in such siting processes in Australia. In a relocation case, local environmental groups at the existing site formed a coalition with a broader-based movement at the proposed site for relocation. While this was a strategy to enhance their political power, it turned out to be a tactical error as it generated a political situation where the government could justify maintaining the *status quo* – which meant the project would not be relocated. The stronger and broader-based environmental movement at the proposed relocation site was able to amplify risk concerns more effectively than the smaller local groups at the existing site. The project remained at the existing site despite very strong evidence that the relocation would have imposed fewer environmental risks.

A comparative examination of siting highlights the responses of democratic nations to managing a common policy problem. Most nations generally have abandoned DAD approaches in favor of more democratic approaches to locating unwanted facilities. While important differences remain, siting remains an intractable policy problem in Austria (even with strong hierarchical traditions), France (even when the state tries to embed itself in local communities), Japan (even with a sophisticated arsenal of compensatory and other policy tools), the U.S. (even when it seeks to use compensation), Australia (even when it tries to be more open and consultative) and Germany (even with attempts at a highly participatory and transparent decision process). It is not surprising that no single deliberative model of siting has emerged from the comparative experience.

The most sophisticated set of explicit policy guidelines, which has reflected the emergence of deliberative siting processes in democratic nations can be found in the *Facility Siting Credo*. It comprises a host of guidelines to facilitate the siting of new waste facilities, although they are applicable to all types of projects (Kunreuther, Susskind and Aarts, 1993). The guidelines are grouped into three areas: The first relates to goals and objectives such as instituting a wide participatory process. The second set concerns appropriate outcomes such as guaranteeing stringent safety standards will be met. The third relates to steps in the process such as using a volunteer process and keeping a range of options open at all times.

While Kasperson (see Chapter 2) has taken the *Credo* further in a very useful analysis of the strategic imperatives, the comparative evidence strongly suggests inadequate attention has been paid to the **institutions** which govern siting processes. Where transaction costs are high and where settlement processes are highly politicized, institutions will matter in determining whether or not stakeholders can reach agreements. Institutions comprise both formal and informal rules. Formal rules include things such as legislation, while informal rules include things such as rules of thumb, social customs and moral rules (Stone, 1997). Whether official or non-official, rules govern political, economic and social interactions between developers and community interests in the siting of projects. They are crucial in creating some form of order in negotiating processes through a system of government or law. Institutions can therefore help in establishing regular, stable and predictable forms of behavior and interactions between stakeholders in decision processes (North, 1991; 1993; 1999).

Institutions are crucial in the management of legitimate claims over the siting of contentious facilities in several ways. First, they influence the nature of decision and negotiating rules and processes involved in reaching agreements over facility siting. Second, they determine the allocation of property rights and the distribution of power in siting disputes. Third, they help in ensuring that agreements made will be upheld and reduce uncertainty over such things as enforcement costs. Finally, they have an important bearing on the legitimate use of inducement structures, such as increasing benefits or reducing costs (including risks), for managing siting controversies. In sum, institutions are crucial for lowering the transaction costs involved in bargaining processes (Lesbirel, 2003).

Shaw (Chapter 10) concludes this volume by arguing that revising policy tools or strategies in themselves is not likely to be effective in managing the increasingly high transaction costs of siting. What will be more fruitful is the search for appropriate institutional forms which legitimize *who* makes decisions and *how* decisions are made. Such institutional change should involve the participation of both host and benefiting communities, the latter being those communities which benefit from having the project located in a particular host community. It should be facilitated by a federal system of governments formed by functional, overlapping and competing jurisdictions. Finally, it should institute decision-making rules based on the principle of Interest-Pay-Participation in order to manage the public good problem of democratic governance.

3   IMPLICATIONS

The conclusions of this volume have important analytic, comparative and policy implications.

There have been numerous attempts to model siting processes and outcomes in the literature. These have included a range of models of risk-benefit trade-offs, negotiation, collective action, networking, discourse, culture, and the state. Furthermore, there have been competing methodolo-gical approaches, including quantitative and qualitative methods, employed in revealing siting processes and outcomes. Each of these theoretical and methodological approaches yield important insights into different aspects of the nature and management of siting conflicts. While the chapters contained in this volume reflect a diversity of approaches, collectively they suggest the importance of more dialogue between those who adopt different ontological and epistemological approaches to examining siting problems. Differences in approach remain fundamental and fusion is not always possible. Yet, this volume shows that acknowledging competing approaches to examining siting issues is not only possible, but also highly beneficial.

Much of the siting literature originated in the United States. Over time, we have witnessed the growth of siting studies in a range of other countries in Europe and in the Asia Pacific (Vari, Reagan-Cirincione and Mumpower, 1994; Shaw, 1996; Lesbirel, 1998). This volume builds on this research and highlights the diversity of approaches, policy instruments and decision-making processes used in democratic nations to address a common problem. It stresses the importance of testing our propositions about siting processes and outcomes comparatively in the context of different institutions and socio-cultural experiences. We hope that this study will encourage further attempts at more rigorous and comprehensive comparative analyses of siting problems.

A more theoretically and comparatively informed study of siting assists in developing more rigorous policy framework for the management of siting conflicts. The analysis contained in this volume suggests considerable learning and adaptability to dealing with the siting dilemma. While existing approaches, policy instruments and decision processes offer important starting points to dealing with the siting problem in democratic nations, they are not likely in themselves be adequate for dealing comprehensively with the siting dilemma. Even the most sophisticated set of policy guidelines has not been effective in managing the increasing transaction costs of siting projects perceived to be risky. Institutional change will be required to legitimize policy approaches, instruments and processes. The challenge for policy makers in democratic nations will be twofold. The first will be to assess what institutions seem to facilitate siting comparatively and to assess the extent to which they can be transplanted given different historical and socio-cultural foundations. The second will be to design and structure institutions in ways that yield legitimate decision-making processes in specific country contexts.

REFERENCES

Bacow, Lawrence S. and Michael Wheeler (1991), 'Binding Parties to Agreements in Environmental Disputes', *The Villanova Environmental Law Journal*, **2**(1), 99–109.
Baram, Michael (1976), *Environmental Law and the Siting of Facilities: Issues in Land Use and Coastal Zone Management*, Cambridge, Mass.: Ballinger.
Frey, Bruno, Oberholzer-Gee, Felix and Eichenberger, Reiner (1996), 'The Old Lady Visits Your Backyard: A Tale of Morals and Markets', *Journal of Political Economy*, **104**, 1297–313.
Gerrard, Michael B (1995), *Whose Backyard, Whose Risk: Fear and Fairness in Toxic and Nuclear Waste Siting*, Cambridge: MIT Press.
Kasperson, Roger E., Dominic Golding and Seth Tuler (1992), 'Social Distrust as a Factor in Siting Hazardous Facilities and Communicating Risks', *Journal of Social Issues*, **48** (4), 161–87.
Kunreuther, Howard and Douglas Easterling (1991), 'Are Risk-Benefit Tradeoffs Possible in Siting Hazardous Facilities?', *American Economic Review*, **33**, 252–56.
Kunreuther, Howard and Douglas Easterling (1996), 'The Role of Compensation in Siting Hazardous Facilities', in Daigee Shaw (ed.), *Comparative Analysis of Siting Experience in Asia*, Taipei: Academia Sinica.
Kunreuther, Howard, Lawrence Susskind and Thomas Aarts (1993), 'The Facility Siting Credo: Guidelines for an Effective Facility Siting Process', Philadelphia: University of Pennsylvania, Wharton School, Risk and Decision Processes Center.
Lasswell, Harold (1936), *Politics: Who Gets What, When, How*, New York: McGraw Hill.
Lesbirel, S. Hayden (1998), *NIMBY Politics in Japan: Energy Siting and the Management of Environmental Conflict*, Ithaca: Cornell University Press.
Lesbirel, S. Hayden (2003), 'Markets, Transaction Costs and Institutions: Compensating for Nuclear Risk in Japan', *Australian Journal of Political Science*, **38** (1), 5–23.
Morell, David and Christopher Magorian (1982), *Siting Hazardous Waste Facilities: Local Opposition and the Myth of Preemption*, Cambridge: Ballinger Publishing Company.
North, Douglass C. (1991), 'Institutions', *Journal of Economic Perspectives*, **5**(1), 97–112.
North, Douglass C. (1993), *Economic Performance through Time*, Lecture in Economic Science in memory of Alfred Nobel (mimeo).
North, Douglass C. (1999), 'Dealing with a Non-Ergodic World: Institutional Economics, Property Rights, and the Global Market', *Duke Environmental Law & Policy Forum*, **X** (1), 1–12.
O'Hare, Michael, Debra Sanderson and Lawrence Bacow (1983), *Facility Siting and Public Opposition*, New York: Van Nostrand-Reinhold.
Parry, G. and P. Morris (1982), 'When is a decision not a decision?', in A. McGrew and M. Wilson (eds), *Decision-Making: Approaches and Analysis*, Manchester: Manchester University Press.

Popper, F. (1983), 'LP/HC and LULU's: The Political Uses of Risk Analysis in Land Use Planning', *Risk Analysis*, **3** (4), 255–63.

Rabe, Barry G. (1994), *Beyond Nimby: Hazardous Waste Siting in Canada and the United States*, Washington: The Brookings Institute.

Rae, Douglas, Douglas T. Yates, Jr., Jennifer L. Hochschild, Joseph Morone and Carol Fessler (1981), *Equalities*, Cambridge, Mass.: Harvard University Press.

Shaw, Daigee, ed. (1996), *Comparative Analysis of Siting Experience in Asia*, Taipei: The Institute of Economics, Academia Sinica.

Stone, Deborah (1997), *Policy Paradox: The Art of Political Decision Making*, New York and London: W. W. Norton & Company.

Vari, A., P. Reagan-Cirincione and J.L. Mumpower (1994*), LLRW Disposal Facility Siting: Successes and Failures in Six Countries*, Dordrecht, The Netherlands: Kluwer.

2. Siting Hazardous Facilities: Searching for Effective Institutions and Processes

Roger E. Kasperson

In the unfolding technological advances and economic growth of advanced industrial societies, few problems have proven more contentious or perplexing than the siting of hazardous facilities. The extent to which these problems have been shared across diverse societies differing in industrial structures, political cultures and social institutions is quite remarkable. Obviously the issues that underlie public concerns and opposition are sufficiently deeply seated to create policy impasses in varying social and political settings. This fact in itself should signal that these challenges are likely to be durable over time and unlikely to be readily resolved without major rethinking and significant redirections in responsible institutions and siting processes.

This discussion considers lessons apparent in siting experience over the past two decades and explores implications for improved institutional approaches. It begins with an assessment of the siting problem – why has it proven so difficult? It then reviews major approaches that have been taken to siting hazardous facilities, suggesting constraints and limits that circumscribe each. Lessons from comparative experience are noted. Finally, considerations are set forth for elements that must be addressed in order to achieve greater siting success.

1 SITING HAZARDOUS FACILITIES: WHY IS IT SO DIFFICULT?

Although many specific issues can contribute to any given siting situation, comparative experiences and post-mortems on them suggest a number of key problems that can greatly complicate and impede siting efforts. These include unclear need, lack of a systems approach, risks and risk perceptions, inequities, social distrust and amplification-driven impacts.

Although the need for a particular industrial or public facility is usually abundantly apparent to the advocates or sponsors of the facility, it is often not so to the community leaders and publics who are being asked to act as hosts. If the need for the facility is not clearly established, there is often little prospect that local communities will be willing to take on the burdens or risks that such a facility may entail. Establishing need can, of course, be disputed and sometimes for good reason. So public resistance to siting solid waste landfills in U.S. communities, for example, was eventually successful in forcing greater waste minimization and recycling. Similarly, public concerns over waste disposal have driven substantial gains in waste reduction in nuclear and chemical plants in a variety of countries. In their review of low-level radioactive waste disposal facility siting in six countries, Vari et al. (1994) identify four major factors necessary for siting success, of which clarity of program goals and process – and particularly the need for a repository – is the first. In many cases, however, siting sponsors have simply failed to address adequately the need to create a broad-based understanding among government officials and publics of facility need and this lack of agreement has then ultimately sabotaged the siting process as a whole.

Facility siting is typically viewed as a single-case process rather than through a systems approach. Yet facilities are always part of much broader production systems, be they the complex of energy facilities found in the coal production cycle, the nuclear power industry, or chemical waste processing and disposal. The deployment of a waste-management system, for example, requires a network of processing, storage and disposal facilities, interconnected by waste transportation links. This network may be designed in ways that minimize overall system risk, lower associated costs and reduce potential inequities. Alternatively, a myopic fixation on a single facility in this network can unintentionally exacerbate many of these problems and lead to sub-optimal solutions. Unfortunately, most siting processes across various countries have yet to recognize facility siting as a system problem and most parliamentary, agency, or policy stipulations have repeated this failure in the institutional structures that have been established.

Although considerable consensus may be achieved in the expert community, including informed critics and opponents, that a well-designed and well-managed modern industrial waste-disposal facility poses only limited risks to host communities and publics, acceptance of such risks by those who must bear the burdens has proven difficult to achieve across various societies. Oftentimes, this has to do with public perceptions of high risks – chemicals, radioactive materials and genetically altered materials are known to elicit particular concerns. Incinerators that put waste emissions into the atmosphere or waste disposal plants that threaten groundwater also typically generate fears over the ultimate effects of hazardous materials that disappear from public view into highly valued ecological components (such as groundwater) of the environment. Such risks have qualitative properties, such as newness, dread, or involuntary risk, that are known from past psychometric research to result in public perceptions of high risk (Slovic, 1987).

At a time when societies may be becoming more risk averse, it is apparent that risk avoidance is taking on greater weight in many communities in the balancing of risks and benefits. And, thus far, quantitative risk assessments and risk-communication efforts intended to assure local publics that the risks are minimal and will be well managed have generally not been persuasive. Ironically, the greater flow of information and discussion of risk intended to reassure publics that the risks will be minimal may actually, when taken up by local activists and media, contribute to a strong social amplification of the risk (Kasperson and Kasperson, 1996), feeding public opposition and heightening controversy. And even higher knowledge, according to at least one Swedish study (Biel and Dahlstrand, 1991), does not appear to explain risk perception or public resistance to a repository.

Exacerbating risk concerns are inequities, or mismatches between the concentration of risk in the host community and the diffuse distribution of benefits. In one of the few thorough empirical analyses of distributional equity at a hazardous waste site, associated with the nuclear waste reprocessing facility at West Valley, New York, Kates and Braine (1983) painted a complex picture of gains and losses over more than a dozen locations stretching across the United States and a concentration of losses in the host community and region. The degree of mismatch can reach quite dramatic proportions, as is evident in the distributional pattern of nuclear high-level waste generation in relation to their potential disposal sites across a number of countries. This lack of concordance between benefits and burden is compounded by the opportunism frequently exhibited in the past by those involved in siting facilities in 'down and out' communities where high unemployment rates and limited access to political power undermined and limited community opposition and the ability of local opponents to challenge decisions. These equity problems have been the primary focus of an emergent environmental justice movement in the United States. They have also become an important aspect of siting in many European countries (Linnerooth and Fitzgerald, 1996) and have also been very evident in a number of Asian countries as well (Shaw, 1996). Indeed, Japan has perhaps the most elaborated set of principles for guiding compensation to remove or reduce inequities (Lesbirel, 1998; Tanaka, 1999).

Assessing equity in siting cases, it needs to be appreciated, is a complex matter. Multiple equity problems may exist simultaneously, such as 'geographical or distributional inequity' in the choice of a site, the issues relating to intergenerational equity, the 'cumulative inequity' problem arising from past siting and other actions that have created a legacy of risk-bearing in the community and region, tradeoffs between protecting workers and protecting publics and 'procedural inequity' if fairness in the site consideration and selection process has been violated. Elsewhere (Kasperson and Dow, 1991), we have proposed an analytic framework for a comprehensive approach to assessing such diverse equity problems.

The complexity of the risk and equity problems points to the need for high levels of public trust and confidence in the institutions and people responsible for siting hazardous facilities and managing the risks. It is quite apparent, however, that the requisite social trust often does not exist. Where prospective risk-bearers harbor suspicions over the fairness of the siting process and doubt the trustworthiness of those responsible for protecting them, the conditions exist for intense conflict and impasse. Studies in Sweden (Biel and Dahlstrand, 1991; Sjöberg and Drott-Sjöberg, 1994) have documented the low level of trust in government in nuclear waste decisions and its importance in public attitudes. At the proposed high-level radioactive waste disposal facility at Yucca Mountain, the U.S. Secretary of Energy (1993) saw the need to commission a far-reaching study of the deep-seated distrust in the U.S. Department of Energy. But distrust problems occur widely throughout North America, Europe and Asia. Past inequities, meanwhile, exacerbate the distrust and anchor it more deeply in accumulated negative experiences.

Assessing trust and distrust and the sources responsible for them is no less complicated than equity analysis. Previously, Kasperson et al. (1992) identified four dimensions that may contribute to or erode social trust.

The first is commitment. To trust implies a certain degree of vulnerability of one individual to another or others, to an institution, or to the broader social and political system. Thus, trust relies on perceptions of uncompromised commitment to a mission or goal (such as protection of the public health) and fulfillment of fiduciary obligations or other social norms. Perceptions of commitment rest on perceptions of objectivity and fairness in decision processes and the provision of accurate information. Commitment, however, does not entail blind progress toward predefined goals, nor insufficient awareness of and response to changing circumstances.

The second concerns competence. Trust is gained only when the individual or institution in a social relationship is judged to be reasonably competent in its actions over time. While expectations may not be violated if these individuals or institutions are occasionally wrong, consistent failures and discoveries of unexpected incompetence and inadequacies can lead to a loss of trust. In particular, risk managers and institutions must show that they are technically competent in their mandated area of responsibility.

The third relates to caring. Perceptions that an individual or institution will act in a way that shows concern for and beneficence to trusting individuals are critical. Perceptions of a caring attitude are an especially important ingredient where dependent individuals are critical. Perceptions of a caring attitude are important where dependent individuals rely upon others with greater control or authority over the situation and the individual' s opportunities and well-being.

The fourth involves predictability. Trust rests on the fulfillment of expectations and faith. Consistent violations of expectations nearly always result in distrust. It should be noted, however, that predictability does not necessarily require consistency of behavior. Complete consistency of behavior would require unchanging actions or beliefs, even in the face of contradictory information and also more consistency in values and related behavior than most individuals, groups, or institutions possess.

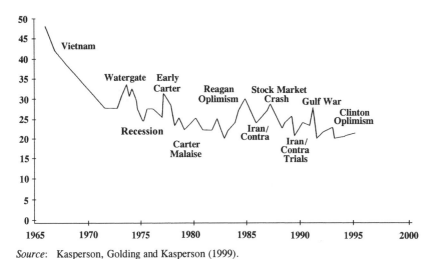

Source: Kasperson, Golding and Kasperson (1999).

Figure 2.1   Trend line of confidence in U.S. institutions

Here, too, a system perspective is important. Trust is a primary property of the social capital that exists in society, as Putnam (1993) has persuasively argued and it is built over time in the socialization of individuals into the political culture and in their encounters with others and the political system. It is likely, as we note elsewhere (Kasperson et al., 1999), that trust exists at different levels of the political system, including the most basic level of the political community, the regime of norms and basic authority structures, at specific institutions (often doing the siting) and most superficially in the particular representatives of the institutions. Since patterns of trust in institutions and representatives appears, as Figure 2.1 indicates for the United States, to be quite stable over time, changing levels of distrust over the short-time frame of most siting encounters may be unrealistic in most cases.

*Table 2.1	Public images of a nuclear waste repository: totals for four
surveys, 1988–1990 (percent of 10,000 images recorded)*

	Image	% of images
Negative consequences	Dangerous/toxic	16.83
	Death/sickness	7.83
	Environmental damage	6.92
	Leakage	2.16
	Destruction	1.33
	Pain and suffering	0.18
	Uninhabitable	0.07
	Local repository area consequences	0.06
	Negative consequences – other	0.08
	Subtotal	35.46%
Negative concepts	Bad/negative	6.81
	Scary	4.01
	Unnecessary/opposed	2.96
	Not near me	2.73
	War/annihilation	1.26
	Socially unpopular	0.41
	Crime and corruption	0.40
	Decay/slime/smell	0.39
	Darkness/emptiness	0.37
	Negative toward decision-makers and process	0.32
	Commands to not build or to eliminate them	0.24
	Wrong or bad solution	0.19
	No nuclear, stop producing	0.15
	Unjust	0.14
	Violence	0.10
	Prohibited	0.05
	Negative – other	0.15
	Subtotal	20.68%

Source: Flynn, Slovic and Mertz (1993), p. 648.

Nonetheless, siting institutions and their representatives persist in seeking to enlarge trust as a key part of the siting strategy and usually are destined to disappointment and unpleasant outcomes. And, of course, little is known of the processes by which trust is lost and regained. Such unrealistic goals have the unfortunate effect of diverting siting officials from the search for institutional processes that are *geared to conditions of high social distrust.*

When the siting of a facility becomes controversial, opposition groups tend to arise, extant distrust becomes mobilized, prior injustices are revisited and media coverage expands. The result is a process that we have described elsewhere as the *social amplification of risk* (Kasperson et al., 1988; Kasperson and Kasperson, 1996; Pidgeon et al., 2003). The social processes for depicting and debating the risk can provide strong signals to society that the risks may be more serious, more inequitable and more difficult to manage than earlier thought. These signals, in turn, drive greater concerns about the proposed facility. Eventually, this process of alarm and controversy can contribute to secondary impacts of the risk – and what we term 'risk ripples' – including conflicts within the community, the stigmatization of the facility and the community, the possible out-migration of residents and a loss in property values. A telling example of such stigmatization is the negative imagery that has grown up around the proposed Yucca Mountain nuclear waste repository (Table 2.1). What is striking is that, for certain risk problems, the amplification-driven impacts may be the dominant adverse effects, exceeding the direct public-health or environmental impacts. This suggests the need for a very different approach to environmental impact assessment than has evolved over the past several decades in nearly all industrialized countries and is now well embedded in established institutional processes. Facility siting appears to be a prominent example of a case where amplification-driven impacts are the primary risk problem and where, accordingly, extraordinary attention to perceptions, inequities, trust and social processes generally is required.

The problems described above constitute a phalanx of issues for assessing siting institutions and processes. To what extent are existing siting approaches well adapted to these problems? How do we best move forward with innovations in siting approaches that will be more effective and robust in addressing these issues? How may new approaches best be adapted to different political cultures? What level of success can realistically be expected?

2   APPROACHES TO SITING FACILITIES

Various institutional approaches have evolved over time for siting facilities. There is some time dimension to how they have been employed, as contexts have changed and as siting processes have become more contentious. We begin with the earlier, more technocratic approaches and work toward more recent voluntary siting models.

Decide, Announce and Defend

Historically, facilities have often been sited by a developer who has surveyed the candidate sites and, once having met various substantive locational needs (available land, accessibility, physical site properties, etc.), has sought those places where sites are available, where land and labor are cheap and where the ability of the targeted community to resist is minimal. These have often been communities that were rural and small and where unemployment was high and income low. Residents of such places were more likely to trade safety or environmental quality for material gain – through jobs, increased tax revenues and improved services. Communities with high standards of living, for whose residents new jobs associated with a waste facility had less appeal, where safety and environmental quality were more highly valued and where a strong capacity to resist the siting existed, were places to be avoided.

The process utilized for siting typically involved quietly exploring, often through agents, alternative sites until an appropriate one was found. Oftentimes there were closed discussions with political officials or business interests within the community. Applications for permits than proceeded and it was only then that word leaked out or a public announcement of the siting would be made. If controversy or opposition occurred, the strategy was to ride it out, since the site and perhaps even the needed permits were already in hand.

Such a siting process was a creature of its time when siting decisions were private economic matters and expectations for public consultation and involvement were minimal or nonexistent. It is apparent that the process is objectionable on both distributive and procedural equity grounds, since burdens are disproportionately allocated either to poor communities that usually share little in the benefits of waste generation or to localities already so contaminated that additional health burdens are viewed passively. The process itself is almost always objectionable: developers tend to withhold information or create intentional ambiguity, the capacity for community participation tends to be minimal and the means of redress are few. The opportunism involved in such a siting approach carries a large potential for eroding the technical criteria necessary to ensure the safety and the economic efficiency of the system. More fundamentally, this kind of covert approach no longer works in a radically altered political setting where public expectations for consultation and involvement and capability to force their use have grown dramatically in many countries (see, for example, experience in Australia, as described by Kellow, 1996).

Technically-Based Site Screening and Selection

Over the past two decades, the siting of controversial facilities in Europe,

North America and Asia, such as radioactive waste disposal plants, has typically employed a technically based process of identifying a large array of prospective sites, evaluating them according to technical criteria, gradually reducing the candidate options and eventually selecting the one that best meets these criteria. This approach was also the preferred one until recently in most European countries, where it has often been combined with a hierarchical institutional approach that still commands significant public support (Linnerooth-Bayer, 1999). The rationale for such a siting approach is that the general well-being of society requires overriding individual (or local) interests and the principal issues are the technical qualities of the site. Selection may be done with or without compensation arrangements for redressing inequities and with varying degrees of local participation. The actual selection process frequently includes provisions intended to ensure that the decision is analytically sound and unbiased, guided by technical criteria aimed at protecting health and safety.

The key assumptions of site search and selection through technical appraisal by some siting agencies are that the siting of controversial facilities is not fundamentally different from siting any other industrial facility on a rural area; local concern over risk can be abated through an unbiased, technically oriented siting process, using established means, such as public hearings and information meetings; authorities responsible for the siting and protecting of public health possess sufficient legitimacy and credibility to win eventual local acceptance of the siting decision; and committed opponents will not succeed in generating sufficient political resources to resist the siting decision.

Although special cases may exist in which these assumptions hold, they are generally problematic. The public perception of risk, as we note above, evokes substantial fear of sites and this cannot be allayed by institutions that command little trust (Rabe, 1994). In the absence of special efforts to achieve fairness, the chosen site almost invariably views itself as victimized. The use of preemptive actions to overcome the opposition usually succeeds only in escalating the intensity of the opposition and broadening its scope. For these reasons, as broad experience in Europe, North America and Asia attests, the power of government authority to override local concerns tends to be illusory.

Bartered Consent

The evident problems with the two preceding siting approaches produced a search for alternative siting strategies and for institutions capable of dealing with public distrust, value conflicts and local controversy. One siting approach that emerged has aimed at achieving greater local acceptance of siting through the proffering of compensation and bargaining. This is the case in Japan, for example, where compensation, negotiation and local acceptance are all required (Lesbirel, 1998;

Ohkawara, 1996). The central problems of siting, as viewed in this approach, are the geographical dissociation of benefits and harms and the inability of the host area to share in the siting decision. This conception of the siting problem has led to a clear solution – provide compensation to the residents of a prospective host site and give them the means to bargain for the appropriate amount. Compensation and incentives, in this approach, have been intended to serve four purposes: to reduce local opposition; to help redress inequities; to increase the overall efficiency of the siting process and to promote negotiation instead of conflict. Kunreuther and Easterling (1996) have provided a searching assessment of the potential and limits to compensation-based siting approaches.

Compensation arrangements and negotiation in siting are sophisticated and extensively developed in Japan, growing out of earlier practices in managing common pool resources for agricultural and fishing cooperatives (Lesbirel, 1998, p. 21). A wide array of legally acceptable means exist for negotiating siting agreements with communities and property owners. Tanaka (1999) identifies four such types of compensation: fishing rights compensation, regional development cooperation funds, 'Dengen Sanpo' community siting grants and fixed property taxes. Despite this compensation and incentives, opposition to facility siting in Japan has grown (Tanaka, 1999).

In the United States, an innovative market-bargaining approach emerged in the state of Massachusetts in the 1980s. The key ingredients of this approach were: primary siting roles for the developer and the host community; a required negotiated or arbitrated settlement between the two; impact mitigation and compensation to the host community as key features of the siting agreement; a tightly specified basis on which the community could exclude the facility; and impasses between the developer and host community to be submitted to an arbitrator (O'Hare et al., 1983).

In practice, the U.S. approach ran into a number of problems. Communities tended to view the prospect of compensation as a bribe rather than a means for redressing inequity. Also, it was quickly apparent that communities were unwilling to accept compensation as a tradeoff for facility risks and burdens. The intense social amplification of risk in communities also undermined the processes of bartering and negotiation, making such activities appear as immoral. While the bargaining process was intended to facilitate the development of community consensus, a spiral of growing polarization and conflict was often the unintended result. But the use of compensation and public responses to it appear to vary significantly with political culture. Sweden and Switzerland, for example, do not permit compensation in siting, whereas its use in Japan and Taiwan in siting contexts is well established.

Voluntary/Partnership Siting

Over the past 15 years, in the face of determined local resistance to facility siting in many countries, interest has grown in a process capable of achieving greater voluntary acceptance of a facility by a local community. In large part, this has reflected a judgment, based on much contentious experience, that strategies of preemption or coercion are unlikely in the end to be successful. With changing expectations for high levels of public information, consultation and participation and with societies apparently growing more risk averse, it seems clear that a viable siting process will need to address public concerns over the risk; redress inequities to the extent possible; to empower local communities in the siting process; to win broad-based consent or acceptance of the facility by the host community; and engage in negotiation to win greater local acceptance.

A noteworthy example of such a process has occurred with the siting of a low-level radioactive waste facility in Canada. In 1988, the Canadian federal government appointed a Low-Level Waste Siting Task Force with a mandate to implement a siting process based on voluntarism and partnership (Frech, 1998). This Task Force sent invitations to all municipalities in Ontario to attend regional information meetings and 400 community representatives did turn out. Twenty-six communities discussed the process for volunteering to be a site and 14 community liaison groups were appointed to examine issues in detail. The process allowed a community to negotiate the terms under which it would be willing to act as a site. In the case of the finalist community, the Town of Deep River, the dormitory community for Atomic Energy of Canada Limited's Chalk River Laboratories, its negotiated agreement included an $8.75 million economic package and employment guarantees for 15 years. In 1995, the community held a referendum in which 72 percent of those casting ballots voted in favor of the facility. Negotiations eventually broke down, however, during implementation. Another site, the Town of Port Hope, remained a prospective volunteer community until the end of the process and apparently would have accepted the site but for the unnecessary rigidity in the technical solutions mandated by the Task Force (Frech, 1998). Nonetheless, after 10 years, $20 million and extraordinary efforts in public consultation and participation, an ambitious national siting program failed to deliver an approved site.

The experience in the United Kingdom considering the use of the Sellafield site for intermediate radioactive waste storage suggests the move ment occurring in many countries for greater transparency. Nuclear authorities proceeded with a public inquiry in well-established manner, seeking to build a technical and governmental consensus about the site. The multidimensional controversy that occurred and the ultimate failure of the effort have led to a

Table 2.2   Elements of the New Jersey voluntary siting approach

Protection of Health, Safety and the Environment	Any proposed site must: • meet the Board's siting criteria • protect public health, safety and the environment • meet state and federal regulations A community can establish additional measures to satisfy its particular concerns.
Voluntary Participation	• A community's request for information and its participation in the process is entirely voluntary and will not be regarded as a commitment to host a facility. • An interested community chooses how far to proceed in its consideration and can withdraw from the voluntary siting process at any time; prior to its decision to volunteer.
Shared Decision-Making	• Any interested community undertakes careful examination of the merits and impacts of hosting a low-level radioactive waste disposal facility. • To aid a community in making informed decisions the Siting Board will provide information and assistance. • The municipal governing body acts as the decision-maker of record on matters that are of community interest. • Community-wide dialogue and citizen involvement is central to the voluntary process throughout the consideration and decision-making. • Municipalities are encouraged to work with neighbors who may be affected by its decision to propose a site. • The voluntary approach is intended to be truly interactive and cooperative among the interested community, the Siting Board and the facility operator. • Ultimately, the municipal governing body must pass a resolution if it wishes to propose a site to the Board.

Table 2.2   Elements of the New Jersey voluntary siting approach (cont.)

Compensation/ Resources	• The Siting Board will support interested communities with resources so each can develop its own community education program. • All out-of-pocket expenses related to examining environmental, health, economic and social impacts can be compensated.
Benefits/Incentives	NJ Siting Law guarantees certain benefits to a host community. In addition, the voluntary siting process allows a community to establish added measures to meet its local needs and to improve quality of life, such as: • preserving open space • upgrading recreational and park areas • tax and monetary incentives
Facility Development Agreement	• The host community, Siting Board and facility operator agree upon protection, compensation and incentives related to facility design and operation. • These measure are represented in a Facility Development Agreement.

Source:
New Jersey Radioactive Waste Advisory Committee, Proposed Voluntary Siting Plan for Locating a Low-Level Radioactive Waste Disposal Facility in New Jersey (1994).

major turnaround in the U.K. institutional approach, one emphasizing transparency, extensive information sharing, consultation with publics and efforts at trust-building. Similar changes have occurred in the French nuclear waste program as well.

   In the U.S., various states and regional compacts have initiated siting efforts for low-level radioactive waste and other hazardous wastes. A number of these siting processes have developed extensive mechanisms aimed at partnership arrangements and voluntary acceptance, as indicated by the abortive New Jersey example (Table 2.2). Generally these processes have not been successful although the experience is difficult to judge since this species of siting processes is still very new. But some elements of the various programs have been successful and nearly all have faced the difficult legacy of proceeding in social contexts already highly polarized by earlier siting failures. For example, both the Ontario and New Jersey voluntary siting processes were viewed by their managers as potentially workable if some things had been done differently (in the New Jersey case, for example, by having the compensation package up front in the process). A very advanced siting process in the state of Connecticut found it difficult to surmount the polarization remaining from the legacy of earlier conflicts associated with a technically based siting effort.

The New Jersey experience is instructive for what were and what were not problems. The program managers felt that money was not a problem as the program provided for a generous award of $2 million per year to a host community; that the anti-nuclear and environmental groups were not a dominant opposition as in many siting disputes; local coverage by the press was fair and accurate; and that the local political leadership was generally very capable and willing to lead. In contrast, Weingart (1998) identifies several major obstacles which included the public fear of radiation; public distrust in all levels of government, including local officials; a high discomfort with local controversy, especially the 'grief' local leaders experienced 'every time we went out for a quart of milk'; very few people displaying a willingness to invest the time to become knowledgeable about the project; and circular arguments: 'you say the facility is safe; then why are you willing to give us so much money?'.

An extensive Canadian assessment of nuclear waste management in 1998 reached a series of conclusions highly instructive to siting efforts generally. The first was that broad public support is necessary in Canada to ensure the acceptability of a concept for managing nuclear fuel wastes. The second is that safety is a key part, but only one part, of acceptability. Safety must be viewed from two complementary perspectives: technical and social. To be considered *acceptable*, a concept for managing nuclear fuel wastes in Canada must have broad support including that of aboriginal people; be safe from both a technical and social perspective; have been developed within a sound ethical and social framework; be selected after comparisons with the risks, costs, and benefits of other options; and be advanced by a stable and trustworthy proponent and overseen by a trustworthy regulator (Nuclear Fuel Waste Management and Disposal Concept Environmental Assessment Panel, 1998).

Obviously, cross-national experience is yet too early with these more voluntary siting approaches to assess how their elements may be best developed in different national contexts. But experience suggests that no single voluntary/partnering siting model has yet emerged that incorporates all the elements that would contribute consistently to success. On the other hand, there are indications of the changes and modifications needed and enough encouraging progress, to suggest how a more resilient and effective voluntary siting model might be designed.

3   TOWARD GREATER SITING SUCCESS

A variety of specific institutional and process mechanisms can contribute to more effective siting outcomes, many of which are specific in detail to the situation, historical context, or political culture. The 'facility siting credo' (Table 2.3) authored by Kunreuther et al. (1993) provides a good list of more generic considerations. Here we continue this search for what may be considered as 'strategic imperatives' for improved siting approaches, setting aside for this discussion the issue of which tactical or site-specific measures are likely to be most helpful in what specific national or sub-national contexts.

Table 2.3   The facility siting credo

When planning and building Locally Unwanted Land Uses (LULUs), every effort ought to be made to meet the following objectives:

---

1. Seek consensus through a broad-based participatory process

2. Work to develop trust

3. Achieve agreement that the status quo is unacceptable

4. Choose the facility design that best addresses a solution to the problem

5. Fully address all negative aspects of the facility

6. Seek acceptable sites through a volunteer process

7. Consider a competitive siting process

8. Work for geographic fairness

9. Keep multiple options on the table at all times

10. Guarantee that stringent safety standards will be met

11. Fully compensate all negative impacts of a facility

12. Make the host community better off

13. Use contingent agreements

14. Set realistic timetables

Source: Kunreuther, Susskind and Aarts (1993).

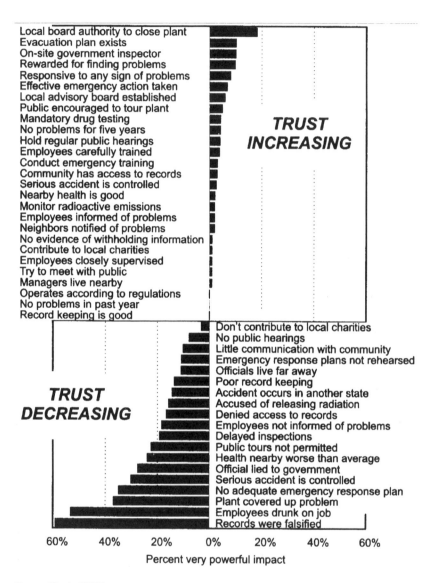

Source: Slovic (1993).
Note: Only percentages of Category 7 ratings (very powerful impact) are shown here.

Figure 2.2   Differential impact of trust-increasing and trust-decreasing events

Establish Need

As noted above, very little can move forward in any siting case of a controversial or risky facility if the societal need for the facility is not apparent.
The controversies over low-level radioactive waste facilities in a variety of
countries, it must be appreciated, have driven dramatic reductions in waste
generation. In doing so, siting conflicts have greatly simplified the siting task
since fewer sites must be found. Assuming that a clear need for the facility
can be demonstrated, substantial efforts are needed *in advance of the siting
process* to establish a widespread recognition and consensus that the proposed siting is in the general public interest and that non-siting alternatives
have been duly considered and rejected for appropriate cause.

Experience from Canada underlines this point (Frech, 1988). In successful
voluntary siting experiences of waste facilities in the provinces of Alberta
and Manitoba, the need for the facility was an important issue. Extensive
discussions were begun over the need question well in advance of initiating
the siting processes. And the siting agencies viewed the siting process as a
search for willing communities, not for potential technically qualified sites
and the relationship between the developer and the prospective host community as akin to courtship. The federal process, although ultimately unsuccessful, did address the need part of the process well, allocating a
two-year discussion of need to precede actual siting initiatives. A social
consensus on facility need, in short, is an essential base on which to build, a
recognition supported both by cross-national studies in Europe (Vari et al.,
1994) and North America (Gerrard, 1994).

Narrow the Risk Debate

In most technical or engineered systems, the safety goal is to optimize investment. This is embodied in notions such as ALARA (as low as reasonably
achievable) where investments are required to lower the risk so long as the
gain registered can be justified economically. In routine risk management,
such an approach makes eminent sense in balancing risks and benefits and
choosing most cost-effective risk reduction strategies.

But in situations of polarized risk debate over a proposed facility, or what
the author would term highly amplified risks, the failure to win a consensus
that a high level of safety will be achieved is usually fatal. There is little
prospect that the siting process can move forward if local concerns over
safety cannot be assuaged. Accordingly, there is much to be said for the
approach used in siting nuclear facilities in Sweden to resolve risk controversies wherever possible and to narrow the risk debate where such opportunities exist. This will require, not infrequently, *overbuilding the safety*

function. If the vantage point is optimizing the siting process rather than optimizing the cost of technical safety at the facility, then such an approach and the additional marginal investments may be very sensible. Involving the host community leaders in negotiations about the safety level and design of the facility is also a means of local empowerment and the development of a negotiating climate may encourage public involvement and help to build trust. Additional mechanisms that can be employed include: funding for technical consultants for the community so that they conduct their independent evaluations and participate in negotiations in an informed and effective way and provision for the host community to monitor facility performance and to have the means, under prescribed procedures, to initiate a review to shut down the facility if standards are violated.

Assume Trust Does Not Exist; Act to Deserve It

As noted earlier, many siting processes are initiated under conditions of high social distrust in the siting agencies. The automatic response by developers in such cases is to resolve to change the trust context, usually by seeking to demonstrate that this particular siting agency, unlike others the community may have encountered, is trustworthy. Currently our knowledge of the conditions under which trust may be recovered or strengthened is very limited. Slovic (1993) has demonstrated that a series of actions or events that might be expected to either build or erode trust do not appear to have equal effects on individuals. Rather an asymmetry principle appears to prevail for trust, as indicated in Figure 2.2, in which trust is more easily lost than it is gained by comparable events and actions. Moreover, we know from siting experience that efforts predicated upon regaining trust within the time frame of siting decisions have generally been unsuccessful (English, 1992). Worse still, they may encourage siting advocates to employ the wrong institutional mechanisms and processes, those predicated on assumptions of trust, consensus and cooperation that may not exist.

By contrast, the siting agency could assess that the reality is that a climate of social distrust exists and is likely, despite the best of the agency's efforts, to continue during much of the siting process. Such a determination would encourage institutional approaches that afford prospects of success in the absence of trust or confidence in the siting agency. Strategies of partnership, power sharing, collaboration and negotiation allow a host community to proceed with a siting process that relies less on judgements of the reliability of some external group than upon the host community's own capabilities and evaluation. Specific mechanisms involved in such an approach include community participation in all phases of the siting process, support for independent consultants, community review of facility design and safety systems, monitoring of facility performance, property value protection and right to initiate shutdown if health and safety standards are violated.

Maintain a Systems View

There are clear opportunities for taking a broader view of facility siting, in which it is recognized that public agencies and jurisdictions will need to site a multitude of potentially controversial facilities over time. Strategies could be developed that aim at an equitable sharing of the burden among communities within the jurisdiction over time. So if one area, for example, hosts a waste disposal plant, it might be excepted from (or ineligible in) the next round of siting involving an incinerator. Or the political officials of a jurisdiction could examine the overall pattern and risk implications involved in a network of facilities, treating efficiency, risk reduction and risk sharing and equity as relevant considerations in making decisions. It is clear that we need to get beyond the myopia associated with single-facility siting processes and to view siting in system terms.

Compensate for Irreducible Inequities

The preferred ethical base for siting should be to avoid or reduce risk rather than to compensate for it. Indeed, any approach that does not proceed from this principle may exacerbate problems involving risk perception and trust. The strategy of narrowing the risk debate and erring on the side of safety noted above is consistent with this ethical imperative.

But, of course, residual risks and uncertainty will remain that cannot feasibly be eliminated. A compensation or benefit-sharing package should be available, intended to restore the original condition before facility-related risk and burden were introduced; to reward the community for contributing to resolving one of society's difficult problems (finding facility sites) and for allowing a needed industrial sector to operate; and to provide an additional flow of benefits to the host community (and nearby region) as compensation for irreducible uncertainty and potential amplification-driven impacts (Easterling and Kunreuther, 1995). Such a compensation package should be negotiated with the host community and region so as to deliver a package of benefits, usually not a cash award, most relevant to local needs and development goals.

Build a Constituency of Support

The institutional aspects of a successful siting process will need to address the development of a constituency of support for the facility. A number of major interests must be convinced that they cannot stay out of the fire and in the background if a successful political coalition is to be created. The make-up of such a coalition or concert of support will vary from country to country and with the particular facility involved. In the United States, industry must commit to support of the siting process early and assume a visible leadership role. The political head of the jurisdiction, be that a governor of a state or a mayor of a city, will need to be a firm supporter, even when the debate becomes acrimonious. A coalition of local officials who are knowledgeable about and open to the siting process needs to be created. Effective contacts with local media will be essential. And dialogues should be opened with prospective critics and opponents so that they are kept well informed and their concerns, where appropriate, are addressed.

Adaptive Institutions and Processes

Finally, comparative experience suggests that, because of the strong intermingling of social and technical issues and the high political volatility involved in facility siting, highly adaptive institutions and approaches are needed. Siting facilities, it is clear, is not a highly predictive process that can be mounted in the programmed way that many developmental programs or projects can. Issues change dramatically, unlikely opponents enter the fray, participants change over the course of the controversy, the debate links to other agenda and concerns in unpredictable ways, the media may frame debates in ways beyond the control over the siting agency and the routes to conflict resolution are often unclear. Accordingly, the siting agency and process need to be highly flexible, able to respond rapidly to surprise, open and attentive to the external environment and to have a strong capability to gather and assess diverse information.

In other words, the siting and the siting agency need to be smart. Such an institution needs not only high technical expertise but strong capabilities in political diagnosis, communications, constituency building and political analysis. It must be able to work collaboratively with communities and the elected officials and informal leaders that may enter the debate. The siting process may need to be reinvented multiple times over the course of achieving a successful site and, as we have argued elsewhere (Cook et al., 1990), the siting agency should regard the siting and management task as experimental. One need only look at the radioactive waste facility siting experience in countries such as France, the United Kingdom, Canada and the United States to see how extensively established processes and institutions have changed in the search for siting models and how altered approaches better geared to the challenging problems posed in facility siting have evolved.

4   CONCLUSIONS

While the facility siting experience across countries has proven a rocky road over the past two decades, important social learning has occurred which may presage more effective approaches and outcomes in the coming years. There is now a broad recognition in many societies about the nature of the siting challenge and that announce-and-defend or technically oriented approaches are unlikely to be successful. In particular, it is apparent to most that a set of interlocking social transformations are in process that are shaping the nexus of problems involved in hazardous facility siting. First, the publics in many societies appear to be more preoccupied with and perhaps more averse to, risks than at earlier times, especially if the risks are involuntary in nature and imposed on concerned communities. Second, it is also clear that hazardous facility siting carries with it an intermingling of difficult intra- and inter-generational equity problems that interact with, and greatly complicate, the prospects for achieving a consensus that procedures and outcomes are fair. Third, many countries have experienced a loss of trust in governmental and social institutions that have placed new demands on and erected obstacles for, siting institutions. Finally, a wave of democratization is now apparent that entails heightened responsibilities for consultation, involvement and more explicit forms of consent from communities and publics hosting hazardous facilities.

A full realization of the depth of these changes is yet to come but increasingly those responsible for siting facilities are grasping the general outline of changed conditions. This was remarkably in evidence recently at an international symposium on high-level radioactive waste management sponsored by the U.S. National Research Council (1999) held in Irvine, California in the U.S. Representatives from various countries repeatedly acknowledged the centrality of social issues to the siting task and indicated adaptations and innovations under way to address them. Although no single approach is yet to emerge in this siting arena, new departures show some common emphasis in elements of more voluntary and democratic procedures, namely greater transparency, early and sustained involvement with prospective host communities, power sharing and negotiation, greater burden of proof on the siting authority and its experts and more open acknowledgement of uncertainties and surprises.

Just as siting processes are in metamorphosis, so are the institutions. A wide range of siting institutions is still apparent, with a continuum from those emerging from military models to those aligned to the new emphasis upon power sharing, collaboration and negotiation. But the shifts in process are forcing changes in institutional designs and cultures, with new capabilities required in information gathering and dissemination, conflict resolution, appraisal of value issues and social impact analysis. This path of institutional adaptation will certainly continue to step into potholes and run down cul-de-sacs. But current trends are encouraging that the siting problem is being reconceptualized and approaches are being recentered in better accord with the actual sociopolitical impediments that have thwarted progress to now.

REFERENCES

Biel, A. and U. Dahlstrand (1991), 'Riskupplevelser I samband med lokalisering av ett slutfövar för använt kärnbränsle,' SKN Rapport No. 46, Stockholm: Statens Kärnbränslenämnd.
Cook, Brian J., Jacque L. Emel and Roger E. Kasperson (1990), 'Organizing and Managing Radioactive Waste Disposal as an Experiment,' *Journal of Policy Analysis and Management*, **9** (3), 339–66.
Easterling, Douglas and Howard Kunreuther (1995), *The Dilemma of Siting a High-Level Nuclear Waste Repository*, Dordrecht: Kluwer.
English, Mary R. (1992), *Siting Low-Level Radioactive Waste Disposal Facilities*, New York: Quorum Books.
Flynn, James, Paul Slovic and C.K. Mertz (1993), 'Decidedly Different: Expert and Public Views of Risks from a Radioactive Waste Repository,' *Risk Analysis*, **13** (6), 647–52.
Frech, Egon (1998), 'Low-Level Radioactive Waste Siting Process in Canada: Then and Now,' Paper presented to the National Low-level Waste Symposium on Under- standing Community Decision Making, March 4–5, Philadelphia.
Gerrard, Michael B. (1994), *Whose Backyard, Whose Risk? Fear and Fairness in Toxic and Nuclear Waste Siting*, Cambridge, MA: MIT Press.
Kasperson, Roger E. and Jeanne X. Kasperson (1996), 'The Social Amplification and Attenuation of Risk,' *Annals of the American Academy of Political and Social Sciences*, May, **545**, 95–105.
Kasperson, Roger E. and Kirstin Dow (1991), 'Developmental and Geographical Equity in Global Environmental Change: A Framework for Analysis,' *Evaluation Review*, February, **15** (1), 47–69.
Kasperson, Roger E., Dominic Golding and Jeanne X. Kasperson (1999), 'Trust, Risk and Democratic Theory,' in George Cvetkovich and Ragnar E. Löfstedt (eds), *Social Trust and the Management of Risk*, London: Earthscan, 22–44.
Kasperson, Roger E., Dominic Golding and Seth Tuler (1992), 'Social Distrust as a Factor in Siting Hazardous Facilities and Communicating Risks,' *Journal of Social Issues*, **48** (4), 161–87.
Kasperson, Roger E., Ortwin Renn, Paul Slovic, Halina Brown, Jacque Emel, Robert Goble, Jeanne X. Kasperson and Samuel J. Ratick (1988), 'The Social Amplification of Risk: A Conceptual Framework,' *Risk Analysis*, June, **8** (2), 177–87.
Kates, Robert W. and Bonnie Braine (1983), 'Locus, Equity and the West Valley Nuclear Wastes,' in Roger E. Kasperson (ed.), *Equity Issues in Radioactive Waste Management*, Cambridge, MA: Oelgeschlager, Gunn and Hain, 94–117.
Kellow, Aynsley (1996), 'The Politics of Place: Siting Experience in Australia,' in Daigee Shaw (ed.), *Comparative Analysis of Siting Experience in Asia*, Taipei: The Institute of Economics, Academia Sinica.
Kunreuther, Howard and Doug Easterling (1996), 'The Role of Compensation in Siting Hazardous Facilities,' *Journal of Policy Analysis and Management*, **15**,

601–22.

Kunreuther, Howard, Lawrence Susskind and Thomas Aarts (1993), 'The Facility Siting Credo: Guidelines for an Effective Facility Siting Process,' Philadelphia: University of Pennsylvania, Wharton School, Risk and Decision Processes Center.

Lesbirel, S. Hayden (1998), *NIMBY Politics in Japan: Energy Siting and the Manage- ment of Environmental Conflict*, Ithaca, NY: Cornell University Press.

Linnerooth-Bayer, Joanne (1999), 'Fair Strategies for Siting Hazardous Waste Facilities,' in *Proceedings of the International Workshop: Challenges and Issues in Facility Siting*, January 7–9, 1999, Taipei: The Institute of Economics, Academia Sinica.

Linnerooth, Joanne and Kevin B. Fitzgerald (1996), 'Conflicting Views on Fair Siting Processes,' *Risk: Health, Safety and Environment*, **7** (2), 119–34.

Nuclear Fuel Waste Management and Disposal Concept Environmental Assessment Panel (1998), Canadian Environmental Assessment Agency, Nuclear Fuel Waste Management and Disposal Concept, Hull, Quebec: The Agency.

O'Hare, Michael, Lawrence Bacow and Debra Sanderson (1983), *Facility Siting and Public Opposition*, New York: Van Nostrand Reinhold.

Ohkawara, Toru (1996), 'Siting of Nuclear Power Plants in Japan: Issues and Institutional Schemes,' in Diagee Shaw (ed.), *Comparative Analysis of Siting Experience in Asia*, Taipei: Institute of Economics, Academia Sinica, 51–73.

Pidgeon, Nick, Roger E. Kasperson and Paul Slovic (2003), *The Social Amplification of Risk*, Cambridge: Cambridge University Press.

Putnam, Robert D. (1993), *Making Democracy Work: Civic Traditions in Modern Italy*, Princeton, NJ: Princeton University Press.

Rabe, Barry G. (1994), *Beyond Nimby: Hazardous Waste Siting in Canada and the United States*, Washington: The Brookings Institute.

Shaw, Daigee (ed.) (1996), *Comparative Analysis of Siting Experience in Asia*, Taipei: The Institute of Economics, Academia Sinica.

Sjöberg, Lennart and Britt-Marie Drottz-Sjöberg (1994), 'Risk Perception of Nuclear Waste: Experts and the Public,' *RHIZIKON: Risk Research Report*, No. 16, Stockholm: Center for Risk Research, Stockholm School of Economics.

Slovic, Paul (1987), 'Perception of Risk,' *Science*, **236**, 280–85.

Slovic, Paul (1993), 'Perceived Risk, Trust and Democracy: A Systems Perspective,' *Risk Analysis*, **13**, 675–82.

Tanaka, Yasamusa (1999), 'Is the Nimby Syndrome a Universal Phenomenon: Symptoms and Remedies,' Proceedings of the International Workshop: Challenges and Issues in Facility Siting, January 7–9, 1999, Taipei: The Institute of Economics, Academia Sinica.

U.S. National Research Council (1999), 'Disposition of High-Level Radioactive Waste Through Geologic Isolation: Development, Current Status and Technical and Policy Challenges,' Discussion paper prepared for the November 4–5, 1999 Workshop, Washington: National Academy Press.

U.S. Secretary of Energy (1993), Earning Public Trust and Confidence: Requisites for Managing Radioactive Waste, Washington: The Department.

Vari, A., P. Reagan-Cirincione and J.L. Mumpower (1994), *LLRW Disposal Facility Siting: Successes and Failures in Six Countries*, Dordrecht, The Netherlands: Kluwer.

Weingart, R. (1998), Comments presented at the Symposium on Understanding Community Decision Making: Engaging the Public in Constructive Dialogue, Philadelphia, March 4–5.

3. Fair Strategies for Siting Hazardous Waste Facilities

Joanne Linnerooth-Bayer[1]

---

1 INTRODUCTION

In most industrialized countries the siting of facilities from prisons to AIDS treatment centres, and especially hazardous and nuclear waste disposal plants, continues to face public opposition, delay, and in many cases, abandonment. Numerous case studies in North America, Europe and Asia document the failures and few successes in siting facilities (Kasperson, 1986; Shaw, 1996a; Rabe, 1994). From these cases, there is now general agreement on the requisites of a successful siting process, which include widespread agreement that the facility is needed and that it addresses the long-term problem at hand, early discourse and involvement of the public, recognition that the facility will not impose unacceptable health and safety risks or violate other community values, and a view that the siting process and outcome are fair (Kunreuther et al., 1993).

There is less agreement on how to design a siting process that meets these requisites. Throughout the industrialized world, many innovative processes have been suggested and implemented, but with little success in terms of reaching an agreement that all or most of the interested and affected parties view as fair and legitimate. Most of these innovations have sought alternatives to traditional siting processes in which the government or industry selects a site and imposes it on an unwilling community. These alternatives range from including the public in hierarchical decision structures to voluntary siting rules that solicit the consent of the community with offers of compensation. While these innovations have often proven successful in siting facilities such as solid waste treatment and disposal plants, with few exceptions (and mainly in Japan) they have failed to provide procedures for successfully siting more controversial hazardous and nuclear waste facilities.

This paper argues that the impasse in siting needed hazardous waste facilities can be attributed to the failure of most siting initiatives to take adequate account of the diverse views held by the public and other stakeholders on a fair siting process and outcome. The public is not homogeneous with regard to its views on what is fair, and basing a siting process on one view of fairness inevitably encounters resistance from those who hold opposing views. Hierarchical, authoritarian approaches, which appeal to those who trust their government and its network of experts to make choices in the social interest, are opposed by those who desire more personal influence and responsibility for the siting decision. Yet, voluntary, market approaches to siting facilities are vehemently opposed by those who believe that market approaches will further widen the gulf between the rich and the poor by siting facilities in poor communities. These three views of a fair process and outcome – the hierarchical, market and egalitarian – must be reconciled to build a social consensus for a successful siting approach.

Siting controversies, therefore, go beyond the not-in-my-backyard (NIMBY) syndrome (or beyond a clash of interests) and involve a clash of social views on a fair and legitimate process and outcome. Views on fairness, in turn, are closely related to forms of social organization and social solidarities, in other words, they are socially determined. In this paper, I describe these three different views of fairness in siting hazardous waste facilities and show that they correspond to three forms of social solidarity and organization identified by cultural theorists (Thompson et al., 1990). These descriptions, however, represent only general characteristics of generic approaches and cannot be used to describe wholly any one approach in actual experience. After identifying the extremes, I will discuss hybrid siting approaches that combine different views of fairness, and I will illustrate each with actual siting processes drawn from the U.S., Canada, Austria, Japan and Taiwan. Finally, I will suggest some extensions of current siting innovations to render them more 'robust' or more acceptable to the diverse and contending values held by the interested and affected parties in siting debates.

2 NORMATIVE VIEWS

According to an institutional perspective on risk perception, whatever hazards may be present in the world, social organizations will select for attention those that help to maintain their solidarity and cohesion (Douglas and Wildavsky, 1982). Similarly, views on fairness can be said to be socially and culturally determined, and thus they cannot be separated from ideas about community and social organization or the need to establish shared values for the conduct of community procedures and the distribution of rights, goods and burdens (Rayner, 1994; Thompson and Rayner, 1997).

Two well-documented forms of social organization that coexist, as well as compete, are *hierarchy* and *market* (Lindblom, 1977; Williamson, 1975; Thompson, et al., 1990). Hierarchy is characterized by positional authority, inequality, and procedural rationality and, therefore, stands in sharp contrast to market forms of social organization with their emphasis on personal rights and freedoms and a more substantive form of rationality. In hierarchies, people accept their rank and station (and inequality), as well as tightly administered rules and procedures, for the harmonious functioning and overall welfare of the society in which they live. Fairness and distributive issues are settled by administrative determination based on such considerations as the rank of the recipients, their needs or their contributions (Rayner, 1994). The market form of social solidarity, by contrast, enshrines individual rights and initiative, negotiation, and competition (Thompson, et al., 1990). Once the initial endowments of individuals are set, distributive issues are settled by market interactions.

Cultural theorists have added a third mode of social organization, the *egalitarian*, to the cultural policy space (Thompson, et al., 1990). Egalitarians, as their name suggests, reject both the unequal social relations of hierarchy and the competitive outcomes of markets. Their rationality is more critical, and generally they reject siting efforts for hazardous waste facilities on the strongly held moral basis that the wastes necessitating the facilities should not be produced in the first place (Thompson, 1996). Egalitarian solidarity is strengthened by appeals to a shared morality, and it is their moral imperative to reject siting procedures that perpetuate social inequality.

Of course, no country's or state's siting procedures can be characterized as singularly hierarchical, individualistic or egalitarian. Most siting procedures combine governmental and expert authority with participatory mechanisms that empower the communities, formally or informally, to negotiate or bargain for a siting contract of some sort. Still, viewing these procedures as embedded in and negotiated between those with different social solidarities is helpful in explaining the contradictory views on fair process and outcome that are observed in siting controversies. This cultural analysis is also helpful in designing 'robust' siting strategies that have a good chance of commanding support from the interested parties who hold different views of what is fair and legitimate.

3 THE HIERARCHICAL APPROACH TO SITING

In most European countries the right to impose a facility on a community has rested solidly with the central government. In Austria, for example, a constitutional amendment gave the federal government authority to overrule local zoning restrictions and other local impediments in identifying and designating suitable sites for hazardous waste facilities.[2] In the U.S., a major effect of the RCRA legislation was to transfer decision authority from the developer to state governments in the form of strict and complex permitting requirements and to the citizens in the form of more formal public participation. It is the latter that radically changed siting dynamics. The historical intransigence of the developers was met with intransigence on the part of the local citizens who stood in firm opposition to hazardous waste facilities. While the citizens did not formally possess the right to reject or accept a facility, they vested considerable control by using the legislation to impose crippling litigation and delay (O'Hare, 1977).

In hierarchical siting processes, central governments and public representatives act as trustees for the interests of the larger society. A crucial condition for the public legitimacy of a hierarchical approach is public trust in the responsible institutions and persons. As Roger Kasperson points out in Chapter 2, trust exists (or does not exist) at different levels of the political system, including the institutions and persons responsible for the siting decision, but also more generally in the norms and basic authority structures. Interestingly, Kasperson shows that trust in government institutions in the U.S. has declined, but not erratically so, over the past decades, meaning that a relatively constant proportion of the population retains trust in the authority and procedures of their governmental institutions.The responsible institutions and persons at the central level generally have responsibility for ensuring that minimum safety requirements of the facility are met, but in contrast to local governments they usually have a strong interest in seeing that a facility is sited somewhere. Whereas traditional site selection processes have often been justified on technical grounds, central governments can and do take account of other considerations. For example, they might ask if the local population is already burdened by other noxious facilities, or whether the local population needs the development. The government may also consult with the local authorities and even involve the public. Because public resistance in most countries has proven to be well organized and effective, governments have tried to gain the co-operation of their citizens by instituting sweeping reforms in public participation. The legal procedures in Europe and North America are quite varied, but usually include complex and multi-tiered site-screening, licensing and permitting requirements with varied forms of public involvement. The important point is that hierarchical siting processes may be consultative and even innovative in involving the public, but the final decision authority rests ultimately with the licensing and approval authorities at the state or federal level. Government thus retains the right to pre-empt local decisions.

An Example of a Hierarchical Siting Process in Austria

In the late 80s, the governor of the state of Lower Austria initiated a two-stage process to site and construct two hazardous waste disposal facilities. First, a team of experts selected by the government selected the towns of Blumau and

Enzersdorf as the potential hosts. Enzersdorf is an industrial town of about 2500 inhabitants and lies 20 km. to the east of Vienna. In contrast, Blumau is a farming town of about 400 inhabitants and lies close to the Czech border. This screening and selection process was conducted secretly with no public input or access to the information.

Once the two sites of Blumau and Enzersdorf were designated and announced, an innovative public participation process was put into train in order to determine if the sights were environmentally acceptable. This process gave broad authority to public representatives in co-operation with the public authorities in setting the frame for the environmental investigations, choosing the experts, and monitoring the investigative process. Interestingly, the residents of each of the communities, through their elected Citizens' Council, agreed that if they could participate in this environmental assessment process, they would accept the expert assessments and raise no further objections if the technical and social conditions proved satisfactory. At first glance, it appears that the Citizens' Councils willingly relinquished their rights to object to the facility on other grounds, for example, if it appeared unfair to put a facility in the poor, farming community of Blumau or the already heavily burdened community of Enzersdorf. This seems remarkable until it is recognized that the citizens, under the legislation at that time, had no legal rights to object to the facility if it met the legal requirements. The consensual approach, therefore, offered them a unique chance to participate in the most decisive aspect of the process – assessing the appropriateness of the site from an environmental and public health perspective.

Although the citizens had no legal right to block an unwanted facility, the authorities recognized that siting efforts would be politically untenable without the general co-operation of the community. Conspicuously absent from the negotiations, however, was mention of compensation to the community, such as tax reductions, investments in roads, sewerage, public safety, education or public health, employment guarantees, tipping fees or free garbage collection. Apparently, compensation for this kind of a facility is not considered an appropriate topic for political discourse in Austria. It is also noteworthy that participants at Blumau and Enzersdorf frequently expressed frustration at being asked to participate at a late stage. Siting experience in other countries has shown that efforts to involve the public are more likely to retain credibility if they involve the public from the very beginning; that is, if the public is asked to assess the need for the facility and to set criteria for an early site-screening and selection process.

This approach reflects the political culture in Austria, and one of its strengths is that it can accommodate recent public demands for more direct participation. The process resulted in the citizens of Enzersdorf accepting the facility, but it failed in reaching an agreement in Blumau. The approach was opposed by groups that demand less hierarchical procedures and more local autonomy as well as by groups who demand more direct consideration of equity and distribution.

Public Acceptance

Already in 1986, Kasperson identified the key social conditions for this hierarchical siting process to be acceptable to the affected and interested public as follows:

- Local concern over risk can be abated through an unbiased, technically oriented process using established means of public involvement;
- Higher authorities responsible for siting and the protection of public health possess sufficient credibility to command local trust; and,
- Committed opponents will not succeed in producing lower government use of institutional means to resist the siting decision.

In Enzersdorf, if not Blumau, these conditions appear to have been met. Indeed, in a survey of Austrian opinion on siting hazardous waste facilities, over half of the respondents expressed support of their expert-government dominated siting process (Linnerooth-Bayer and Fitzgerald, 1996). This appears to be true in many European countries and perhaps also partly the case in Canada. In his comparative study of U.S. and Canadian siting experience, Rabe (1994) notes that Canada 'remains more respectful of authority, more willing to use the state, and more supportive of a group basis of rights than its neighbour' (p. 23). This does not mean that everyone accepts hierarchical procedures in these countries. To the contrary, Rabe observes that in every Canadian province in which serious efforts have been made to site waste facilities, *nimby*-type reactions have emerged to block proposals. Likewise, in most European countries the central government authority to site waste facilities that are opposed by local citizens is waning (Kemp, 1990).

View of Fairness

To appreciate both the support that hierarchical, technocratic siting procedures enjoy, as well as the opposition, it is important to understand the utilitarian view of fairness on which many centralized, 'regulatory' siting procedures are based. Utilitarianism, which features strongly in many national constitutions, is concerned with the consequences of policies or actions on social welfare or the public interest. It is thus both consequentialist and welfarist. The overriding principle is to enhance public welfare even if it means restricting private activities and rights. Of course, no country's legal tradition is utilitarianism in its purest form. The public interest cannot be fully determined by adding benefits of the winners and costs of the losers, for example, by balancing the interests of a murderer and the interests of the victim. Even in the most hierarchical governing systems, the utilitarian spirit is curbed by constitutional protection of individual rights. Regardless of the costs and benefits (or the consequences) of the government's actions, certain rights and principles may take absolute priority. Hierarchical organizations can therefore embrace both consequentialist as well as deontological values.

Classical utilitarianism is based on a form of equality of treatment in that each person is regarded as equally deserving of benefits or burdens (Mac-Lean, 1993). These benefits and burdens can be compared among individuals, and the fairness of an action derives from our ability to aggregate the net gain to society. By purporting to find the most technically suitable site, or the site which imposes the lowest risk and costs on any one community in the interests of the overall society, most traditional siting approaches have found their justification in this classical utilitarian principle, or 'welfarism'. Their legitimization lies in the notion that the government can impose burdens on the citizenry without their direct consent.

Government imposed burdens are commonplace, and include highway rights of way, jury duty, military service, and taxes. No government can operate without imposing burdens on some for the benefit of others, although in some notable cases, cohersive procedures have been replaced by voluntary ones (for example, military duty in the United States). Almost all societies have well defined, accepted, and for the most part, hierarchical institutions and procedures for allocating many types of social burdens (see Elster, 1992; Young, 1994). The popular concept of cost-benefit analysis, for instance, does not ask for the consent of the losers in summing the benefits of those who gain to those who lose.

One frequently proposed way to make the distribution of the costs and benefits politically and morally acceptable is to require compensation from those who benefit to those who lose. If there is full compensation, then the policy analyst can use the appeal of the Pareto criterion to justify the policy – that there are only gainers and no losers. Thus for the benefit-cost analyst, compensation is an appealing but (contrary to the libertarian) not a necessary condition for recommending the choice of a particular site for a hazardous waste facility.

The welfare economist therefore accepts that the government can legitimately distribute social burdens, that there can be losers if the benefits justify them. For those who advocate more individual rights in making siting and other policy decisions, cost-benefit analysis is viewed as an illegitimate use of government power, even 'socialist'. A key figure in the development of cost-benefit analysis, Alan Kneese (1991), has responded to this criticism: (A) major, if not decisive, problem with using concepts placing overriding emphasis on individual rights for public policy is that they would paralyse the policy making and implementation process. The provision of public goods, or the control of public bads, inevitably involves some redistribution of income and/or risk. Such criteria, especially the Pareto criterion, tend to enshrine the status quo.

Although there are strong critics of government pre-emption in siting hazardous waste facilities, it is a mistake to assume that hierarchical systems do not still command a great deal of support. In the survey of Austrian citizens (Linnerooth-Bayer and Fitzgerald, 1996), it was asked whether the potential communities for hosting a hazardous waste facility should have the right to say 'no' to the facility. This would mean that the siting process is on a voluntary basis, and the communities can decide if the benefits of the facility justify the risks. Nearly *40 percent* of the respondents answered 'no' to this question and thus rejected the notion of voluntary siting. Interestingly, an even higher percentage of student respondents (nearly *65 percent)* responded negatively to this question. As noted above, almost *70 percent* of the respondents thought that the decision should be based solely on the expert estimates of the suitability of the site. A large number of Austrians, thus, support their traditional, hierarchical procedures for siting hazardous waste facilities.

The appeal of a hierarchical siting process appears to lie in the fact that it:

- offers expert assurances that the most efficient or least risky site is selected;
- appeals to the notion of equal treatment of all citizens in the society and the goal of increasing human welfare;
- enables the government to balance off the burdens of hosting a hazardous waste site with other benefits and burdens in society;
- may be psychologically preferable for some people to have a burden imposed on them than to accept a burden for monetary or other compensation.

4 THE VOLUNTARY, MARKET APPROACH

In spite of their appeal, siting processes based on technical assessments of risk (and attempts to win over the public confidence) have been mainly destined to failure. Increasingly in the U.S. and more recently in Europe, the experts can no longer rely on public trust in their assessments. As many siting controversies have shown, the debates are almost always characterized by competing expertise, and the available data are often insufficient, and always insufficient in the case of low-probability events, to determine whether a certain scientific statement is true or false. Reassurances about the risk burden of a facility in a climate of social distrust are unlikely to be convincing (Kasperson, et al., 1992).

Declining public trust in the experts is not the only reason for the dearth of hierarchical siting procedures. According to Whitehead (1991), since the citizens are only asked to participate, and not decide, this has often engendered a sense of powerlessness and hostility. Many observers argue that if genuine co-operation on the part of the public is desired, the control and decision authority should rest more firmly on the affected communities and their citizens (O'Hare et al., 1983; Mitchell and Carson, 1986; Kunreuther et al., 1987). Many proposals for siting facilities, therefore, have advocated *voluntary* approaches in which the local communities have a right to veto the facility (Laws and Susskind, 1991).

An underlying assumption of this approach is that communities will agree to hosting a facility if the residents view their personal benefits from the facility to outweigh their risks and costs. This assumption invokes the *nimby* syndrome by ruling out altruistic behaviour and a willingness to sacrifice personal interests for the overall good of the society. It follows that *compensation* is viewed by advocates of the voluntary approach as the key to community consent and thus reaching mutually agreed solutions to the siting impasse. Compensation can take the form of improved safety requirements, employment, in-kind reductions in risk, e.g. a hospital for the community, direct payments to the community or the citizens, or even assurances that other facilities will not be built in the community. Without mechanisms for transfers from the developer to the community, it is argued, siting is essentially a zero-sum game with clearly defined winners and losers. Unless the losers can be compensated for bearing the risks, few joint gains are possible and public participation forums will likely not be successful in securing public endorsement for a facility.

In the U.S., there have been many procedural innovations that award limited decision authority to the local communities. The earliest experiment with a form of voluntary siting was the 1980 Massachusetts Hazardous Waste Facility Siting Act. This Act gave the developer the right to construct a facility on land zoned for industrial use but only with a negotiated siting agreement with the community. Limitations were placed on the eligible communities, however, since they could reject the facility only if they showed it posed special risks. The Act provided for financial assistance to promote participation and also for compensation to neighbouring communities. This Act radically shifted property rights from the state government to the local communities and developers. However, it failed in that the communities refused to co-operate and negotiate siting deals with private industry.

Some observers have attributed this and other failures of voluntary siting approaches to the fact that the local government and not the citizens have the decision authority. The negotiation process is thus hampered by the lack of direct involvement with the residents, who do not always trust their elected representatives to act in their best interests. Trust in the agent controlling the risk is a critical element in promoting public confidence in the process. For all these reasons, many commentators advocate a process where the citizens vote directly on the siting package offered by the developer (Whitehead, 1991; Mitchell and Carson, 1986). Given a number of technically feasible sites set out by the government, the developer would contact the community and negotiate a siting package that includes technological safeguards, other types of risk mitigation measures, community control and monitoring, and compensation. Strong incentives exist that this package be attractive to the community since it serves then as the basis for the popular referendum.

The experience in Japan with voluntary siting is significantly different from that of the U.S. especially with regard to siting nuclear power plants. Not unlike the U.S., power plants in Japan are privately owned and operated, so siting is formally in the hands of the private companies. Given the hier-archical nature of Japanese society, it is remarkable however that private power companies have initiated a voluntary, market approach for siting. This approach, which has had mixed success, depends heavily on compensation to the host communities. The voluntary approach appears to have worked in those cases where the local population trusts its local officials and power brokers to negotiate agreements in their interest. Paradoxically, the hier-chical nature of Japanese society may be key to the past success of voluntary, market mechanisms for siting facilities since the public has trusted their local officials to act in their best interests This trust may be waning, however, and recent attempts at local referenda for siting approval of nuclear power plants indicate more resistance to compensated deals.

Examples of the Market Approach

An example of a siting process with explicit use of market mechanisms is a solid waste facility in New York State. Browning Ferris Industries (BFI) made an offer to virtually every municipality in New York State that they consider hosting a solid waste landfill in return for a share of the benefits from its operation. One community, Eagle (with 1300 residents), agreed to this process and eventually held a referendum in which the facility was rejected. However, after BFI (true to its word) withdrew from the town, a second referendum was held in which the facility was accepted by the residents. Note, however, that this example concerns solid wastes and not hazardous wastes. There are many examples in the U.S. where market mechanisms have been tried in siting hazardous waste facilities, for example, in Massachusetts and in Maine (Gerrard, 1994). However, to date, none has been successful.

The situation is different in Japan. As Lesbirel (1996) points out, a key feature of the Japanese voluntary approach is the extensive use of institutionalized compensation or redistributive mechanisms. However, the success of this approach has been declining, some of the reasons for which Lesbirel discusses in two recent cases of siting nuclear power plants in Ashihama and Hamaoka. The Ashihama attempt failed completely after fishing interests blocked the negotiated process between the private power company and the local power brokers. The situation was different in Hamaoka, where fishing interests formed an alliance with 'leftist' political groups and local residents, including lawyers, shopkeepers, schoolteachers, housewives and some local farmers. Presumably this leftist movement had strong elements of egalitarianism with grave concerns about the safety of the plant and little interest in negotiated compensation (unlike the fishing coalition). Indeed, the plant was eventually approved by the political leadership, but only by instituting a split between the leftist movement and the fishing interests and thereby preventing the former from hampering negotiations between the power company and regional officials over compensation and property rights transfer arrangements (Lesbirel, 1996, p. 88). While the power plant was approved, this procedure may have disenfranchised many of the local opposition, decreasing trust in the hierarchical-market siting procedure and ultimately in the democratic process. This and other cases have led to demands for more direct local decision authority with the use of referenda.

The market approach has encountered opposition not only in the U.S. and Japan, but also in Taiwan. There is a Taiwanese experience in siting a low-level radioactive waste repository. From the start, the responsible power authority, Taipower, opted for a voluntary siting process. The carrot was a very generous financial compensation package if their community should eventually be selected. Nine communities initially volunteered for the process, from which five were considered qualified. A majority of local residents accepted this approach. Predictably, however, anti-nuclear and local political groups blocked the process. Presumably these groups had very different worldviews from the local residents accepting this market approach. After the failure of this market process, Taipower took a different approach. The company selected a remote island (with only 19 residents!) for consideration, but assured the residents that the repository would be built on their island only with their consent. Again, a generous compensation package was offered. At first, the residents strongly resisted any investigations on their island, however, their resistance has declined, probably due to a strong public information campaign. Interestingly, however, in a referendum to allow Taipower to investigate one of the two small islands, 80 percent of the residents of Big-chiu agreed and only 25 percent of those on Small-chiu, where the repository would be located. The residents do not view the compensation package as a bribe, but rather as just payment for their motherland. The moral issue is not whether a community can be compensated for accepting risks to their health, but whether a community can legitimately sell the motherland to host a nuclear waste facility.

The Market View of Fairness

Supporters of the market approach to siting facilities consider negotiated compensation as the logical and fair way out of the siting impasse. In the words of Whitehead, 'It would appear that a combination of local decision making authority and negotiated compensation would produce the 'Coasean ideal' and siting would no longer be an issue' (1991, p. 14). The well-known Coase theorem in microeconomics suggests that if a facility has large overall benefits for society, but imposes a (lesser) negative externality on identifiable groups, then private negotiation can lead to a Pareto superior outcome where all members of society consider themselves better off with the facility than without it (Coase, 1960). Indeed, this Pareto superior outcome is the economist's view of fairness. In the words of Shaw (1996b), 'a process is fair when it will not take something from anyone without justly compensating them for it' (p. 181).

Important distinguishing features of the market approach are the acceptance of negotiated compensation in the siting process and a conviction that respect of individual rights is an appropriate foundation for public burden sharing (Frey et al., 1996). The local rights approach thus finds its support among liberals who believe the government should be limited in its role in redistributing goods and burdens. A fair and just policy is one that protects individuals in the exercise of their freedom over their property and entitlement. Since people have a right to their health and safety, activities such as siting hazardous waste facilities that impose personal risks should not be carried out without the consent of those affected.

As Maclean (1993) notes, it is unclear how this liberal view of fair allocation deals with risk-imposing activities. As Kneese (1991) remarked earlier, if all such activities are restricted unless they have the consent of the victim, this would paralyse our industrial societies. Like utilitarianism, it seems that the libertarian view has an appeal in certain situations, but that no one would try to apply it universally. Libertarians also have little to say about the distribution of the initial rights in society. Thus, voluntary siting approaches are not fully libertarian since they specify that the property right should be relocated from industry/government to the local community, a markedly egalitarian position.

According to Maclean, libertarianism shares one thing in common with utilitarianism: both are equal-treatment views of fairness. However, they believe in equal treatment for different reasons:

> Both subscribe to equal treatment of all people, but they have very different views of how to reason about or justify moral claims. The utilitarian takes the interests of all people, considered equally, and puts them together to determine what is right and wrong. He reasons from an impersonal perspective, where the interests of the majority will carry considerable moral weight. The libertarian reasons from the personal perspective or the point of view of each person. He treats people equally by taking their claims individually and aiming at unanimity instead of majority. A basic division in the philosophical discussions of equity is over which kind of justification is appropriate. (MacLean, 1993, p. 12)

This individualistic approach to siting hazardous facilities finds its support among those who oppose paternalistic, hierarchical approaches and who value personal authority and responsibility. The appeal of the individualistic market approach thus appears to be that it:

- guarantees a Pareto superior outcome such that the host community and the waste generators consider themselves better off with the deal than without it;
- resolves the siting problem without force;
- places responsibility on the developer to propose an acceptable technology and benefit package;
- places responsibility on the citizens to assess and approve the technology and monitor its performance.

5   THE EGALITARIAN SITING APPROACH

Proponents of voluntary, market siting approaches argue that the outcome is Pareto efficient. If the host community receives compensation such that its citizens feel in a better position with (rather than without) the facility, then all parties are better off. However appealing this solution is, it is not universally considered to be a fair process or outcome. The market approach leads inevitably to siting facilities in poor and otherwise disadvantaged areas (Bullard, 1993). The reason is that the poor, because of their economic circumstances, will likely have a lower 'reservation price' for lost amenity and exposure to health risks than the wealthy. That is, they will be willing to pay less to avoid a facility and willing to accept a facility for lower compensation. Therefore, it is less costly for developers and more efficient in the Pareto sense to locate waste facilities in poor areas. To the extent that minority populations, people with poor health, and other disadvantaged or vulnerable groups live in poor areas, the process may be viewed as discriminatory since there will be a predominance of hazardous and otherwise undesirable facilities close to these communities.

Not only is the vulnerability of the community important to the egalitarians, but other factors may also play a role. For instance, the extent to which the community has contributed to the hazardous waste problem may be important, and might lead to a preference for putting hazardous facilities where the wastes are produced. Alternatively, if the general population is viewed as the contributors through consumptive life styles, this criterion would lead instead to placing the facilities throughout the society.

The key element of this egalitarian ethic is that it is personal in the sense that the characteristics of the community and its citizens should count, and significantly so, in the selection of a hazardous facility site. This stands in contrast to the utilitarian and the rights-based ethics, where the numbers of people and their rights are important, respectively, but not *who* they are. In the individualistic, liberal ethic of the market approach, each person (community) has equal rights and deserves equal treatment, and justice is derived from respecting these rights. Because the liberal enshrines the status quo, there is no direct concern with the distribution of rights, property or risks; nor is any particular value attached to the distribution of the burdens or benefits. The same is true for utilitarians, who are also committed to equal treatment of interests – the interests of each to be happy – but this does not extend to the distribution of outcomes *per se*. 'Morality is strictly about maximising the good, according to utilitarians, and the distribution of the good (or burden) cannot count, because the distribution is not itself an effect on any conscious individual's experience' (Maclean, 1993, p. 7).

This is not the case for the egalitarian who is concerned primarily about the way goods and burdens are distributed in society. It is definitely not fair to locate a hazardous waste facility in a poor community, *even if this community gives its consent*. The egalitarian might even prefer an outcome where each community felt itself to be worse off if this decreased inequality. Thus, locating a facility in a wealthy community is morally superior to locating it in a poorer one, even if the wealthy community could negotiate to pay a poorer community to take the burden. The egalitarian would reject negotiated Pareto deals if they did not serve to reduce inequality.

In contrast to those who value choice, individual rights, and market mechanisms for distributing goods and burdens, egalitarians are extremely sceptical of market mechanisms and negotiated compensation. Not only might negotiated compensation lead to placing facilities in poor communities, it also does not assign significance to values such as the sacredness of life. Some things should not be explicitly placed on the market and traded for benefits. While economists point out that these kinds of trades are made in the context of hazardous jobs and other activities, ample evidence now exists that many citizens are reluctant to negotiate a price for accepting a hazardous facility (Portney, 1985), and many view compensation as nothing less than a bribe. For example, in a study of attitudes to compensation in both Hungary and New York, Vari (1993) noted a marked reluctance to accept this quasi-market approach. Typical comments were: 'Human life cannot be compensated'; 'Compensation is bribery'; and 'We cannot be bought'.

These responses have been notably absent in Asian cases of compensation for accepting hazardous facilities. In Japan, this may be explained by trust in the authorities to maintain high safety standards of the facilities, in which case the local population would not view monetary payments as compensating for an unacceptable risk. In addition, as was shown in the Hamaoka case, these egalitarian concerns are often effectively barred from the more hierarchical democratic process of local approval. Also in Taiwan, the residents did not view compensation as a bribe, but rather as the cost of their land. Indeed, the moral issue was that of selling off their motherland, and not selling off the health of their children.

Economists are quick to point out that with compensation, the victims can purchase greater health and safety by reducing more serious risks to them and their families. Yet, the egalitarian moral stance rejects this consequentialist reasoning, since even the Pareto efficient point will likely be an unequal one. In other words, the market transaction benefits both sides but it will not necessarily reduce the inequality. Egalitarians are therefore morally opposed to market-based processes for siting hazardous facilities, and this opposition is grounded in fundamental differences in the underlying moral principles.

Not only is the egalitarian opposed to the outcome of market solutions, but also the process of negotiation with the developer is unacceptable, as are the authoritarian procedures of the regulatory or hierarchical solution. As political scientist Ostrom (1990, p. 14) has observed with respect to 'common pool' resources, both advocates of centralization and privatization accept as a central tenet that institutional change must come from outside and be imposed on the individual affected. Thus the communities must accept that either the state makes the decision or that the decision is bargained with the developer. In neither case are the citizens responsible for designing the process by which the decision will be made. As Rabe argues, this leads to an initial showdown: 'In provinces and states with diverse political cultures, communities unexpectedly faced with the prospect of hosting a major disposal facility feel unfairly singled out ... despite the theoretical elegance of pure market or pure regulatory approaches to determining the distribution of siting responsibility, in practice such approaches simply fail to achieve the intended outcome. Over time, they make a difficult situation worse as distrust and adversarialism mount' (1994, p. 7).

In contrast to the procedural rationality of hierarchical organization and the substantive rationality of individualistic market organization, the rationality of the egalitarians is more holistic and critical (Thompson et al., 1990). Egalitarian discourse is critical of solutions that do not address the broader social issues responsible for the waste problem, pointing out that with more recycling and less waste the facility might not be needed at all. In the words of Thompson (1996), 'those who favour the egalitarian solution, and who wish to radically transform the production and consumption system that is all the time generating these hazardous wastes will see both markets and hierarchies as inevitably perpetuating rich-poor divides, on the one hand, and exploitative and unsustainable technologies, on the other' (p. 169).

Examples of Egalitarian Siting Processes

With a critical eye to the whole siting enterprise, it is not surprising that there are no certifiable egalitarian approaches that have yielded examples of siting hazardous waste facilities. Still, in some cases egalitarian groups, convinced that a facility is needed, have participated constructively in siting processes. Typically, they demand that the siting deal include plans for waste reduction, that it not further disadvantage already disadvantaged groups, that the community participates directly in its management and control, and that all the affected and interested parties are involved in the decision process. A more extreme position sometimes found in egalitarian discourse is that waste facilities should be sited in wealthy neighbourhoods, since the wealthy have benefited more from the production processes generating the waste (and it will make the siting process more difficult leading inevitably to less waste generation).

The appeal of the egalitarian approach appears to be that it:

- leads to more social and economic equality;
- discourages the generation of waste by making siting attempts expensive or blocking them altogether; and,
- involves the citizens in the process from the beginning.

6   ROBUST SITING APPROACHES

The three culturally based approaches to siting locally unwanted facilities and the arguments of their proponents and opponents are summarized in Table 3.1. The question we explore in this section is how to design siting approaches that will have more general appeal to culturally diverse, potential host communities.

There have been several recent proposals to design more robust strategies for siting hazardous waste facilities, but unfortunately these proposals have not taken account of cultural plurality. Gerrard (1994), following many others, argues persuasively for (i) assuring that every state takes its share and thus responsibility for disposing of hazardous wastes, (ii) siting a few integrated facilities on already contaminated land, (iii) finding voluntary communities through offering compensation, and (iv) obtaining consent through a referendum. He concedes that not everyone in a community will accept bargaining for compensation. 'In those communities that fear the facilities will endanger their children's health, offers of compensation and negotiation are ineffective and offensive' (p. 170). He rightly notes, however, that the cultural mix of communities can be quite different and some may be more receptive to bargaining than others, particularly if the dominant personalities in the community are more receptive to taking risks. In Richland, Washington, where the local basketball team is called 'the bombers', there is strong support for radioactive waste management (p. 110).

The key according to Gerrard is to identify those communities that are culturally inclined to accept the market procedures: 'The determinative issues in the success or failure of facility siting attempts seem to be (i) the culture of the local community and (ii) the host state's sense of national fairness ... There are some communities whose culture of risk perception does not lead them to fear (or at least to loathe) HW/RW facilities; in these communities, compensation and negotiations, as well as some degree of local control, can achieve local acceptance' (Gerrard, 1994, p. 170). Of course, no community is culturally monolithic, so we would not expect complete agreement in a community even if a referendum supports the facility. Those who are not satisfied with the bargained outcome, according to Gerrard, can take their compensation and move.

The difficulty with Gerrard's siting formula is that experience shows that residents who do not share their community's hegemonic culture will not only reject the outcome, but also the process. In Massachusetts, where legislation set a process of negotiation between candidate communities and waste facility developers, vocal groups in the communities blocked the negotiations. This has repeated itself in many other attempts at using market approaches, for example, in North Carolina and British Columbia (Rabe, 1994, p. 44). So rather than the minority culture accepting the outcome and moving out of the community, they may block the procedures.

Therefore, rather than uncompromisingly supporting one approach and seeking a community where the dominant culture is receptive to this approach, it may be preferable to find siting strategies that appeal to the plurality of cultural views. Perhaps more than the plurality of interests, these worldviews are key to understanding the siting impasse that most countries face. While interests no doubt play a role – *nimbyism* in its many forms is a factor in most siting debates – combating *nimbyism* in the narrow sense has proven insufficient for siting facilities. Even with regard to Japanese siting experience, Lesbirel (1996)

Table 3.1   *Proponents and opponents arguments for and against three siting approaches*

	Hierarchical Approach	Market Approach	Egalitarian Approach
Proponents argue that this approach:			
	offers expert assurances that the most efficient or least risky site is selected	guarantees a Pareto superior outcome	leads to more social and economic equality
	appeals to the notion of equal treatment of all citizens and increasing human welfare	resolves the siting problem without force	discourages the activity generating the need for an unwanted facility
	enables the government to balance off the burdens with other benefits and burdens in society	places responsibility on the developer to propose an acceptable technology and benefit package	involves the citizens in the process from the beginning
	imposed burdens may be preferred to accepting burdens for monetary or other compensation	places responsibility on the citizens to assess and approve the technology and monitor its performance	

Table 3.1   Proponents and opponents arguments for and against three siting approaches (cont.)

	Hierarchical Approach	Market Approach	Egalitarian Approach
Opponents argue that this approach:			
	is too authoritarian and paternalistic	Will lead to siting facilities in poor communities	Will paralyze industrial economies with too many demands for changes in the system
	Excludes viewpoints of citizens	Will force citizens to trade off health and other burdens for monetary reward	
		Gives too little credence to expert judgement	

argues that compensation alone is not sufficient to site hazardous facilities: 'Politics matters in market approaches to siting' (p. 76). As Rabe (1994) discusses, a growing trend in public opinion research rejects traditional perceptions of the citizenry as disengaged and preoccupied with its immediate and narrow self-interest. In the Austrian siting questionnaire, as a case in point, a surprising number of the residents of Enzersdorf and Blumau ranked as important siting criteria that went against their direct interests. In the country village of Blumau many residents thought that facilities should be sited in the pristine countryside, and many living in the industrial town of Enzersdorf thought that facilities should be sited in industrial areas (Linnerooth-Bayer and Fitzgerald, 1996).

This does not mean that changing the interest politics (with compensation) cannot play a role in a siting process, but it does mean that egalitarian concerns about compensation must be taken into account. Nor does it mean that expert authority should not play an important role, but it does mean that individualistic and egalitarian concerns about authoritarian systems must also

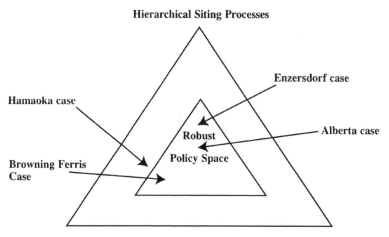

Figure 3.1   The policy triangle

be taken into account. The key is to design siting processes that yield outcomes that are considered fair within the moral boundaries of each of the
cultural solidarities, which means that each view of fairness deserves respect
and standing. Thompson and Rayner (1997) illustrate this cultural landscape
by the triangle shown in Figure 3.1, where each corner represents one form
of social solidarity and organization – in our case, each corner represents one
of our three approaches to siting. A siting approach that is considered fair in
the context of one cultural solidarity (and that solidifies this solidarity) will
be opposed by those whose moral positions lie in the direction of the other
two corners.

If each of the social solidarities has equal standing in the siting arena, then
a robust siting strategy will lie somewhere in the center of the triangle, represented by the 'robust policy space' in Figure 3.1. Robust solutions will
compromise each 'corner' view of fairness, but at the same time, they will
have features that make them attractive to each. An example of one such
criterion is the notion of *responsibility* – those who produce wastes or who
benefit from waste generation have primary responsibility for their disposal
(Linnerooth-Bayer and Fitzgerald, 1996). This concept appeals to each of the
social solidarities, but for different reasons. In hierarchical organizations,
responsibility is appealed to in solidifying the role of the state; in individualistic institutions, responsibility clearly rests on those who take the offend-
ing actions or benefit from them; for egalitarians, responsibility on the waste
generators and those who benefit from their generation is a way of putting

the burden on industry and the privileged public.

Similarly, *compensation* appeals to each of the cultural solidarities, but again in different forms and for different reasons. According to hierarchical argumentation, compensation is legitimately awarded to the victims of state policies *by the government* to set the ledger straight and in so doing to avoid social unrest and disruption; individualist discourse promotes compensation as the key component of a fair and efficient siting process since it can assure that no one will be worse off and it internalizes the externalities of the project; and compensation to the egalitarian rationality is a way of setting things right by reallocating to the victims. Note, however, that the hierarchical and egalitarian views of compensation would explicitly reject market, bargaining procedures. Yet, once the community has been victimized from a decision (by the state) to host a facility, then the victims deserve compensation. This is fundamentally different from the notion that the community will use compensation as a bargaining instrument, which the egalitarian ethic would reject as illegitimately buying and selling the health and safety of the children of the community and the hierarchical ethic would reject as decreasing the control of the state. There is, therefore, an important distinction between *ex ante*, negotiated compensation and *ex post*, non-negotiated compensation. The latter may be far more robust.

Indeed, this latter form of *ex post* compensation appeared to be key in the siting of the hazardous waste facility in Enzersdorf, Austria. During the heated debate on this facility, no mention was made of compensation to the community. Yet, quite surprisingly, after the experts had pronounced the site acceptable and the local citizens had relinquished their opposition, it was taken for granted that a compensation package would be negotiated. This package included more green areas, bicycle trails and other amenities to the community. Note, however, that the community did not give its consent to the facility, let alone bargain a deal for consent. Yet, apparently throughout the process there was a tacit assumption that the 'victimized' community would be compensated *ex post* – but the citizens' consent could not be bargained.

What explains, then, the quasi-success of compensation in Japan? Although it appears that *ex ante* compensation has been key to the voluntary process, the hierarchical nature of this process may have contributed to its seeming success in some cases. Generally, the acceptance of industrial facilities in Japan has been framed as an economic issue, where economic success and growth has dominated the value geography of the country. In promoting this growth, political representatives have focused primarily on issues of regional development in awarding their consent. Because the Japanese appear to have a great deal of trust in their local politicians, there has been surprisingly little opposition from more egalitarian groups who would tend to view compensation as a political bribe.

Whereas concepts of responsibility and *ex post* compensation appeal to each of the cultural solidarities, other criteria may find support in a liaison between two solidarities, sometimes in exclusion of the third. For example, local control and monitoring is a battle cry found in both individualistic and egalitarian discourse, but decreases the control of state hierarchy. Using siting strategies as a way to redress past inequalities in the society can be a strategy on the part of a state welfare system and also on the part of the egalitarians, but does not appeal to individualists who would prefer separate state measures to redress inequalities.

Examples of Robust Siting Strategies

It is instructive to examine the cases of siting discussed in this chapter with regard to their 'robustness' or their appeal to the plural cultural discourses of the siting debate. The hazardous waste facility in Enzersdorf and the Browning Ferris solid waste facility in Eagle are siting solutions located close to the two corners in Figure 3.1; yet, each proved to be robust. The Enzersdorf case, although not voluntary, had elements that appealed to the egalitarians, notably a broad based citizen participatory forum. However, it owes its success mainly to the constitutionally mandated, authoritarian siting process in Austria that has effectively ruled out a pluralistic process where the interested parties have legal influence on the final decision (Linnerooth-Bayer and Davy, 1994). The Browning Ferris process, alternatively, was pluralistic but did not involve what the citizens perceived as a significant risk to their health, which made bargaining more acceptable to a wide range of interested and affected persons irrespective of their social solidarities.

In Alberta, Canada, where a hazardous waste facility was successfully sited at Swan Hills, the innovative siting process was less hierarchical than in Austria, but more so than in many U.S. cases. *Responsibility* and *compensation* played important roles in the Alberta siting process. The public information campaign created a sense of responsibility to deal with the wastes within the province. Recently a town councillor has remarked, 'We're the future ... if it wasn't for us, where would all these other communities be, what would they do with their waste?' (Rabe, 1994, p. 77). The promise of economic benefits to the depressed region was also a contributing factor in Swan Hills' willingness to host the facility (Rabe, 1994, p. 76). Notably, however, the idea of bargaining with the developers for *explicit* compensation prior to the referendums was not a part of the process. The Alberta case is distinguished for its success with a *voluntary* process, but not an explicitly *market* process. As political sociologist Seymour Martin Lipset has observed, 'Canada remains more respectful of authority, more willing to use the state, and more supportive of a group basis of rights than its neighbours'

(Quoted in Rabe, 1994, p. 23). Though more hierarchical than the U.S., Rabe also notes the cultural plurality in Canada has led to adamant and successful protests against prior siting attempts. Any approach, therefore, based on only one concept of fairness will likely encounter strong opposition in Canada.

In this cultural context, Japan's exclusive use of market bargaining procedures in a predominantly hierarchical culture may at first appear as an anomaly. However, the tendency of the Japanese to accept the decisions of their political authorities, and the dominance of economic policy objectives, may have smoothed the path for market bargaining. As shown in Figure 3.1, the Haonoke case was an interesting mix of a hierarchical-market procedure, which, however, owes its success to the exclusion of the more egalitarian viewpoint. Since it did not grant legitimacy to the egalitarian 'corner', this process may not however be robust in the longer term.

A Deliberative Process

Having identified some of the key criteria for a robust siting process, the question is how the process will be designed and implemented. This implementation process can be rather traditional through political representatives. Indeed, politicians are generally ingenious at balancing different interests and worldviews of their constituents and at negotiating siting processes that take account of the competing views on fairness. In Japan, we even see the introduction of compensation into the traditional political negotiating procedures. Rabe (1994), however, shows through many case studies that communities in North America often resent the imposition of a decision process that does not allow them a chance to directly deliberate the issues. The Alberta case, for instance, involved the citizens in a deliberative process early on. Deliberation, which is any process for communication and for raising and collectively considering issues, has been recently emphasized by the U.S. National Research Council (Stern and Fineberg, 1996) as a key ingredient for controversial risk management processes. A central assumption behind this approach is that the citizenry, writ large, can evaluate policy options and welcomes and supports the creation of serious participatory opportunities.

A pluralistic, deliberative process may be key to identifying robust strategies. As such, the siting process would begin with public involvement to consider whether the facility is needed, a plan for equitable burden sharing among communities, alternative waste management technologies, and long-term, intergenerational burdens. Significant evidence is now available that citizens are capable of engaging in collective deliberation and making reasonable decisions about facility siting and waste management. Renn and his colleagues have developed a deliberative process for structuring national

policy debates and informing government decisions about siting waste disposal facilities (Renn et al., 1993). Their process is both analytical, involving
the expert community, and deliberative in that the citizenry ultimately de-
cides how to evaluate the technical evidence and the different views of a fair
outcome. However, elected, public representatives ultimately make the decision (and some view this as more democratic than decisions made by randomly selected citizens[3]). There is, of course, no guarantee that such a
process will lead to a robust siting policy that commands support from the
different cultural solidarities involved. But, the process, itself, should appeal
to the egalitarian views given its involvement of environmental and other
egalitarian groups in the beginning and its recourse to randomly selected
citizens. It should appeal to hierarchical interests in its acceptance of expert
authority and that the government ultimately takes the decision. It should also
appeal to market advocates in so far as it places more responsibility on the
individual citizen for providing input into the choices, and a deliberative
process does not rule out a voluntary process or even a 'robust' notion of
compensation.

7 CONCLUSIONS

Because each of the three siting approaches – the hierarchical, market and
egalitarian – represents only one view of what is fair and legitimate, each is
inevitably opposed by persons and groups who hold a contending view.
Hierarchical, authoritarian approaches appeal to those who trust their government and its network of experts to make choices in societies' best interests,
but are opposed as paternalistic and authoritarian by those who have lost trust
in governments and who desire more personal influence and responsibility for
the siting decision. An alternative view advocates more individualistic,
voluntary approaches and even bargaining procedures for compensation and
local control of the operation. Yet, market approaches to siting facilities are
vehemently opposed by those who view bargaining for health and safety as
illegitimate and who see markets as inevitably perpetuating rich-poor divides
and supporting exploitative and unsustainable technologies. The important
point is that there are no universal norms on which to base a siting strategy.
The interested and affected parties hold different views of what is fair, legitimate and morally correct, and in many respects these views are mutually
incompatible.

Community interests in the narrow sense, or the *nimby* syndrome, play a
role in the impasse many countries face in siting needed hazardous waste
facilities. Yet, the failure of compensatory processes shows that *nimbyism*
alone cannot fully explain this impasse. In addition, it is important to recognize the failure of most siting initiatives to take adequate account of the

diverse and mutually incompatible values of those affected. Basing a siting process on one view of fairness or legitimacy inevitably encounters resistance from those who hold opposing views. These competing views of a fair process and outcome must be reconciled to build a social consensus for a robust siting approach. Based on siting experience in the U.S. and Europe, it appears that important elements of a robust policy space are *responsibility* and *non-negotiated compensation*. Numerous studies have shown that taking responsibility by the residents for the wastes produced in their country or region is a strong motivating factor for siting a hazardous waste facility that appeals to many, if not all, of the actors in the policy space. Although experience shows that market approaches that require communities to explicitly negotiate compensation are not robust, a concept of non-negotiated, *ex post* compensation appears more promising.

Finally, it is important that the process is not imposed on a community, but that the citizens of a region deliberate the broad issue of waste management strategy for their region and decide themselves on how to select appropriate sites for needed facilities. There has been some limited experience in broadly based, deliberative processes for siting hazardous waste facilities in North America and Europe, and the challenge is to build on this experience in designing an open and flexible process for citizen participation. This participation goes beyond citizens giving their input to a siting decision, but involves them from the beginning in deciding how to decide. With the involvement of a culturally diverse group of citizens, there is promise that a robust siting strategy that reflects the local cultural plurality will emerge.

NOTES

1. International Institute for Applied Systems Analysis, Laxenburg, Austria.
2. Bundes-Verfassungsgesetz-Novelle 1988, BGBl 1988/685.
3. Discussions with Roger Kasperson, December, 1997.

REFERENCES

Bullard, Robert D. (1993), 'Waste and Racism: A Stacked Deck?', *Forum for Applied Research and Public Policy*, Spring, 29–35.
Coase, Ronald A. (1960), 'The Problem of Social Costs', *Journal of Law and Economics*, **3** (1).
Douglas, Mary and Aaron Wildavsky (1982), *Risk and Culture*, New York: Russell Sage.
Elster, Jon (1992), *Local Justice: How Institutions Allocate Scarce Goods and Necessary Burdens*, New York: Russell Sage.
Frey, Bruno, S., Felix Oberholzer-Gee and Reiner Eichenberger (1996), 'The Old Lady Visits Your Backyard: A Tale of Morals and Markets', *Journal of Political Economy*, **104** (6), 1297–313.

Gerrard, Michael B. (1994), *Whose Backyard, Whose Risk: Fear and Fairness in Toxic and Nuclear Waste Siting*, Cambridge: MIT Press.

Kasperson, Roger E. (1986), 'Hazardous Waste Facility Siting: Community, Firm, and Governmental Perspectives', in *Hazards: Technology and Fairness*, National Academy of Engineering, Washington, DC: National Academy Press.

Kasperson, Roger E., Dominic Golding and S. Tuler (1992), 'Siting Hazardous Facilities and Communicating Risks under Conditions of High Social Distrust', Article submitted to *Journal of Social Issues*.

Kemp, Ray (1990), 'Why not in my backyard? A Radical Interpretation of Public Opposition to the Deep Disposal of Radioactive Waste in the United Kingdom', *Environment and Planning*, **22**, 1239–58.

Kneese, Alan (1991), 'Reflections on Cost-Benefit Analysis', Unpublished Draft Paper, Resources for the Future, Washington, DC.

Kunreuther, Howard, Kevin Fitzgerald and Thomas D. Aarts (1993), 'Siting Noxious Facilities: A Test of the Facility Siting Credo', *Risk Analysis*, **13**, 301–18.

Kunreuther, Howard, Paul Kleindorfer, Peter J. Knez and Rudy Yaksick (1987), 'A Compensation Mechanism for Siting Noxious Facilities: Theory and Experimental Design', *Journal of Environmental Economics and Management*, **14** (4), 371–83.

Laws, David and Lawrence Susskind (1991), 'Changing Perspectives on the Facility Siting Process', Draft Paper, Massachusetts Institute of Technology, Boston.

Lesbirel, Hayden (1996), 'Power Plant Siting in Japan: The Role and Effectiveness of Compensation', in Daigee Shaw (ed.), *Comparative Analysis of Siting Experience in Asia*, Taipei: The Institute of Economics, 51–74.

Lindblom, Charles E. (1977), *Politics and Markets*, New York: Basic Books.

Linnerooth-Bayer and Kevin Fitzgerald (1996), 'Conflicting Views on Fair Siting Processes', *Risk: Health Safety & Environment*, **7**, 119–35.

Linnerooth-Bayer, Joanne and Benjamin Davy (1994), 'Hazardous Waste Cleanup and Facility Siting in Central Europe: The Austrian Case', Report to the Bundesministerium Fuer Wissenschaft und Forschung, IIASA Contract No. 93-105, International Institute for Applied Systems Analysis, Laxenburg, Austria.

MacLean, Douglas (1993), 'Variations on Fairness', Paper presented at the Workshop on Risk and Fairness, International Institute for Applied Systems Analysis, June 20–22, Laxenburg, Austria.

Mitchell, Robert Cameron and Richard T. Carson (1986), 'Property Rights, Protest, and the Siting of Hazardous Waste Facilities', *AEA Papers and Proceedings*, **76**, 285–90.

O'Hare, Michael (1977), 'Not On My Block You Don't: Facility Siting and the Strategic Importance of Compensation', *Public Policy*, **25**, 409–58.

O'Hare, Michael, Lawrence Bacow and Debra Sanderson (1983), *Facility Siting and Public Opposition*, New York: Van Nostrand.

Ostrom, Elinor (1990), *Governing the Commons: The Evolution of Institutions for Collective Action*, Cambridge: Cambridge University Press.

Portney, Kent E. (1985), 'The Potential of the Theory of Compensation for Mitigating Public Opposition to Hazardous Waste Treatment Facility Siting: Some Evidence from Five Massachusetts Communities', *Policy Studies Journal*, **14**, 81–9.

Rabe, Barry G. (1994), *Beyond NIMBY: Hazardous Waste Siting in Canada and the United States*, Washington, DC: The Brookings Institute.

Rayner, Steve (1994), 'A Conceptual Map of Human Values for Climate Change Decision Making', Paper presented at the Workshop on Equity an Social Considerations, IPCC Working Group III, Nairobi, Kenya.

Renn, Ortwin, T. Webler, H. Rakel, P. Dienel and B. Johnson (1993), 'Public

Participation in Decision Making: A Three Step Procedure', *Policy Sciences*, **26**, 189–214.

Shaw, Daigee (1996a), *Comparative Analysis of Siting Experience in Asia*, Institute of Economics, Academica Sinica: Teipei.

Shaw, Daigee (1996b), 'An Economic Framework for Analyzing Facility Siting Policies in Taiwan and Japan', in Paul Kleindorfer, Howard Kunreuther and David Hung (eds), *Energy, Environment and the Economy: Asian Perspectives*, Aldershot, UK: Edward Elgar.

Stern, Paul, C. and Harvey V. Fineberg (eds) (1996), *Understanding Risk: Informing Decisions in a Democratic Society*, Washington, DC: National Academy Press.

Thompson, Michael and Steve Rayner (1997), 'Cultural Discourses', in Steve Rayner and Elizabeth L. Malone (eds), *Human Choice and Climate Change*, Columbus: Battelle Press.

Thompson, Michael, Richard Ellis and Aaron Wildavsky (1990), *Cultural Theory*, Boulder and Oxford: West View.

Thompson, Michael (1996), 'Unsiteability: What Should It Tell Us?', *Risk: Health Safety & Environment*, **7**, 169–81.

Vari, Anna (1993), 'Public Perceptions about Equity and Fairness: Siting Low-Level Radioactive Waste Disposal Facilities in the United States and Hungary', Paper presented at the Workshop on Risk and Fairness, June 20–22, International Institute of Applied Systems Analysis, Laxenburg, Austria.

Whitehead, Bradley (1991), 'Who Gave You the Right? Property Rights and the Potential for Locally Binding Referenda in the Siting of Hazardous Waste Facilities', Draft Paper, Boston: John F. Kennedy School of Government, Harvard University.

Williamson, Oliver E. (1975), *Markets and Hierarchies*, New York: Free Press.

Young, Peyton (1994), *Equity in Theory and Practice*, Princeton: Princeton University Press.

4. Mitigation and Benefits Measures as Policy Tools for Siting Potentially Hazardous Facilities: Determinants of Effectiveness and Appropriateness

Hank C. Jenkins-Smith and Howard Kunreuther

1 INTRODUCTION

A key challenge in siting a prison, landfill, incinerator or radioactive waste disposal plant is to find a package of compensating benefits so that residents of the potential host community feel that they are better off having the facility than maintaining the status quo. Recent empirical studies reveal that a benefits package is likely to have some positive impact on the percentage of the residents of a potential host community who would support the facility (Kunreuther and Easterling, 1996). A radioactive waste repository appears to be an exception, where offers of compensation either do not change the percentage of individuals supporting the repository (Kunreuther and Easterling, 1996; Herzik, 1993) or may even decrease the fraction supporting the facility (Dunlap and Baxter, 1988; Frey et al., 1996). These studies also suggest that a facility has to be perceived as sufficiently safe for most of the affected public to even consider accepting some form of compensation. Otherwise it is likely to be considered as a bribe for taking the facility and an illegitimate form of trade in the marketplace (Gerrard, 1994).

This paper systematically examines the role that different safety measures coupled with economic benefits are likely to have in creating public support to site four different facilities – a prison, landfill, incinerator and radioactive waste repository. It is the first study that we are aware of which examines the significance of specific factors in improving the chances that a facility will be sited. Using the results of a nation-wide telephone survey, our analysis sheds light on the fraction of the population that has already made up its mind on whether or not to vote for the facility and those whose attitudes could be influenced by the nature of the benefit/safety package.

The data reveal that for all the facilities, including the repository, the majority of respondents are likely to view the facility more positively when presented with a benefits/safety package. The challenge for developers is how to design such a package to convince enough residents of the community or region to support the proposed prison, landfill, incinerator or repository.

In a number of ways, the public has been given an increasingly important role in determining whether or not a facility will be sited in their backyard. Those affected by decisions to locate potentially hazardous public programs appear to respond in important ways to levels of trust in program officials (Flynn et al., 1992; Williams et al., 1999). But trust across different kinds of public officials may not be homogeneous and the perception of *appropriate* roles for different officials may weigh heavily in decisions to accept a program or facility (O'Connor et al., 1994; Jenkins-Smith and Stewart, 1998). In that spirit, our survey sheds light on the impact of giving greater authority to local officials on public acceptance of these four different facilities.

The next section of the paper develops a simple theoretical model as to the role that compensation could play in siting facilities and the practical challenges in using this policy tool. Section 3 then describes the nature of the telephone survey design and how it combined the use of safety measures with compensation to address some of the issues raised by earlier empirical siting studies. Section 4 then examines the factors influencing the public's reaction to having each of the four facilities in their backyard when neither a benefits package and/or inspection procedures are explicitly introduced into the picture. The importance of specific safety measures and compensation packages in changing resident's attitudes toward the facility is explored in Sections 5 and 6. The concluding section proposes a set of policy recommendations and suggests directions for future research.

2 THE ROLE OF COMPENSATION IN SITING FACILITIES

The use of compensation to resolve a siting dilemma begins with the recognition that the proposed facility might impose certain negative impacts on the host community. Gregory et al. (1991) classifies these impacts into four broad categories: economic losses, impacts to human health, decrease in quality of life and degradation of the physical environment. At a theoretical level, one can illustrate the role that compensation can play in the decision. Consider a simple two-period model such as the one developed in Kunreuther and Easterling (1990) where the utility associated with having the facility in one's community is given by the following additive utility function:

$$U(y,F) = U_1(y_1,F_1) + U_2(y_2,F_2) \qquad (4.1)$$

Where y_t denotes the individual's income in period t (either 1 or 2),
F_t denotes the consequences of the facility during period t.
U_t represents a von Neumann-Morgenstern utility function for period t.

The expected utility model allows one to specify the level of benefits B^* where an individual is indifferent between the status quo and having the facility in his or her backyard. The a priori expected consequences of accepting the facility will be that there is some perceived probability (p) that some expected loss (L) will be realized in the community. In particular, B^* is defined as the level of benefits where the utility associated with the facility is equal to the utility of the status quo:

$$U_1(y_1,0) + U_2(y_2,0) = U_1(y_1,B^*) + (1-p)U_2(y_2,0) + pU_2(y_2,L) \quad (4.2)$$

If we rearrange the terms, we obtain the following equation:

$$U_1(y_1,B^*) - U_1(y_1,0) = p[U_2(y_2,0) - U_2(y_2,L)] \qquad (4.3)$$

This equation allows us to define B^* as the level of benefits that produces an improvement in an individual's utility during period 1 that just offsets his or her expected loss from the siting of the facility during period 2. An individual is assumed to vote for the facility if B is equal to or greater than B^*. Otherwise the individual will vote against the community hosting the facility.

In practice, residents may view the facility as sufficiently hazardous that they treat the benefits package B as a bribe and will not favor the facility no matter how large B is. A siting situation in Grants County, North Dakota graphically illustrates this point. In 1990 three country commissions in this sparsely populated county applied for a *non-binding grant* to study the possibility of hosting a monitored retrievable storage (MRS) facility for temporarily storing high level radioactive waste. The three commissioners who initiated the process were all voted out of office in a recall election because they accepted the grant even though they knew it was not binding in any way (Kunreuther et al., 1996).

Even if residents in the host community are willing to accept compensation, it may provoke very strong negative reactions by others because it is viewed as morally wrong. Elster (1992) suggests that people may view health and safety as inherent rights that should never be traded off for material goods. For example, articles in the German press have objected to the willingness of the citizens of Bergkamen, Germany to accept a power plant in exchange for money. One article in on a leading newspaper claimed that this exchange created incentives for groups to protest a facility under the expectation that they will eventually be bought off by the developer. Since that time direct monetary compensation has not been utilized in Germany in connection with the siting of any noxious facility (Kunreuther and Easterling, 1996).

Taiwan offers a second example of a negative response by others to monetary compensation. In this case, villagers forced 23 petro-chemical firms in an industrial park to close in 1988 after an overflow of wastewater from the treatment plant polluted nearby streams and adversely affected fishing in the area. The Minister of Economic Affairs responded by offering substantial amounts of monetary compensation to residents of the area who accepted the funds in return for reopening the facilities.[1] This action produced an outcry throughout the country and led the legislature to pass the Pollution Conflicts Resolution Act, which explicitly prohibits this kind of individual compensation in the future (Shaw, 1996).

These failures of compensation have been interpreted by researchers and practitioners as evidence that expected-utility models provide inaccurate or incomplete descriptions of public responses to facilities. Unless a facility is perceived to be acceptably safe and there is some procedure for taking remedial action should future problems develop with the plant, then it is unlikely that a benefits package will convince a majority of the residents in a community to accept the facility. The telephone survey we undertook was designed to see what proportion of citizens would accept a facility in their backyard if a package of safety measures coupled with some types of compensation were provided to the host community. We hypothesized that compensation would be much more palatable if it were combined with measures that reassured citizens that the facility would be regularly inspected and that the facility would be shut down to correct any serious problems which emerged after the facility was online.

3   NATURE OF THE SURVEY

The telephone survey on facility siting was conducted by the University of New Mexico's Institute for Public Policy using their computer assisted telephone interviewing laboratory. Interviews were completed with 1234 continental U.S. residents in December 1992 through February 1993. The respondents were taken from a nationwide random-digit-dialing frame, using a sample list purchased from Survey Sampling Inc.

The survey design incorporated an experimental method of assigning respondents to subgroups at random for different 'treatments'. This method assures that statistically different responses are due to variations in the benefit/safety packages described and not an artifact of question wording. Using the American Association for Public Opinion Research (AAPOR, 1998) standard definitions,[2] the survey cooperation rate was 52.4 percent and the overall response rate was 45.7 percent. The survey refusal rate was 41.5 percent. The sample size results in an overall sampling error of plus of minus 3 percent, though the sampling error is larger for the analysis of subgroups.

We were particularly interested in using the survey questionnaire to determine whether there was a significant difference between public attitudes toward having four types of facilities in one's community. Past surveys of individuals and other studies of the siting process indicated that the more risky a facility is perceived to be the more it is shunned (Flynn et al., 1992; Jenkins-Smith and Bassett, 1994; Jenkins-Smith and Silva, 1998). Hence, we hypothesized that a medium security prison (PRISON)[3] would be viewed as the most acceptable of the group followed by a landfill for municipal waste (LANDFILL), an incinerator for hazardous waste (INCINERATOR) and a repository for disposal of high-level nuclear waste (REPOSITORY).

Questions were asked of each respondent as to how acceptable *one* of these facilities would be (ACCEPT) if it were located within a certain distance from their home. Thus, approximately 300 respondents were asked to evaluate each of the four facilities. For the prison, landfill and incinerator, half the individuals were given distances of 1 or 10 miles; for the repository the distances were either 10 or 50 miles.[4]

Given that we sought to measure attitudes, we employed Likert-type scales designed to measure variations in the degree of acceptance of these facilities (Likert, 1932; Converse and Presser, 1986). Measurement of attitudes using Likert-type scales in survey questionnaires has been successfully used in a wide array of empirical studies of attitude measurement (e.g., Maurer and Pierce, 1998), including recent studies of facility siting decisions (in particular see Frey and Oberholzer-Gee, 1996).[5]

When respondents were queried about the prospect of siting hazardous facilities near their homes, the question was asked outside of the context of a concrete public debate on the issue. Indeed, for many respondents, the survey interview may have constituted the first consideration they have given to such a question. Thus, the answers we obtained are akin to the *initial* reaction that would be obtained should a hazardous facility be proposed, on average, across communities in the U.S. The evolution of the policy debate and consideration of possible risks, equity implications and economic consequences may substantially change levels of public acceptance. The survey results thus highlight some of the important implications of efforts to craft mitigation and compensation packages for facility siting decisions.

4 INITIAL PUBLIC ACCEPTANCE OF FACILITIES

Table 4.1 shows the responses to the ACCCEPT question for each of the four facilities if it is located ten miles from the respondents' homes. The distribution of the responses provides evidence that initial levels of acceptance differ markedly across types of facilities. Approximately four in ten of the respondents perceive the prison to be at least somewhat acceptable, while less than one in ten would initially accept a nuclear waste repository. The distributions of responses for landfills and incinerators fall between these two extremes.[6]

Table 4.1   Perceived acceptabilty of different facilities in percent

(Based on 10-mile distance from residence)

	Prison	Landfill	Incinerator	Repository
Completely Acceptable	18	7	4	2
Mostly Acceptable	21	17	11	7
Neutral	23	17	11	7
Mostly Unacceptable	14	27	20	17
Completely Unacceptable	25	32	53	67
Sample Size (n)	160	169	166	136

Turning to the factors influencing the siting process, empirical studies have focused on the following three variables as primary factors in explaining the degree of acceptability of a facility: its perceived risk to the health and safety of those living nearby, how necessary it is that it be built and the degree of trust in public officials who will perform management and oversight of its operation.[7] Consistent with this line of research, our survey included the following measures: the perceived seriousness of the risk of each of the facilities (RISK), scaled from zero ('no risk') to ten ('extremely risky'), the perceived need for the facility 'in your state' (NEED) scaled from zero ('not at all necessary') to ten ('completely necessary') and trust for 'an independent agency hired by local government officials to perform regular inspections' of the facility (TRUST) scaled from zero ('no trust') to ten ('complete trust').

Figure 4.1 graphically depicts the mean value of each of these three factors for each facility. As shown in the figure, the prison had the highest perceived need, the lowest perceived seriousness of risk and engendered the greatest trust in the inspection process. As focus shifts from the prison to the landfill, incinerator and repository (in that order), the NEED and TRUST decline, while RISK increases.[8]

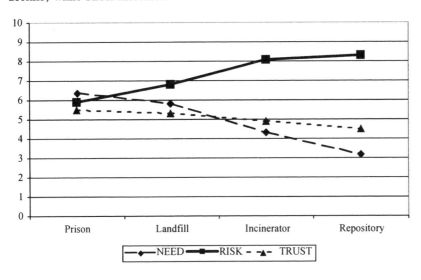

(Mean Values Shown)

Figure 4.1   Divergence of perceived seriousness of risk and need by type of facility

Table 4.2   Logit regression explaining acceptance of facility (ACCEPT) as a function of NEED, RISK and TRUST

(Coefficient p-values shown in parentheses)

	Prison	Landfill	Incinerator	Repository
Constant	2.04 (0.001)	0.03 (0.961)	1.33 (0.059)	0.09 (0.886)
NEED	0.08 (0.089)	0.15 (0.002)	0.11 (0.030)	0.16 (0.001)
RISK	-0.48	-0.33	-0.46	-0.36
	(<0.001)	(<0.001)	(<0.001)	(<0.001)
TRUST	0.09 (0.132)	0.11 (0.055)	0.07 (0.043)	0.14 (0.034)
Log-likelihood	-148.77	-157.74	-130.99	-112.67
Correctly Predicted	79.74%	75.59%	79.73%	82.76%
R2	0.30	0.20	0.25	0.21
Sample size	306	299	296	290

To determine the relative importance of each of these three factors for public acceptance of a facility, logistic regressions were run with ACCEPT as the dependant variable. ACCEPT was recoded into a dichotomous variable with values for 'completely' and 'mostly' acceptable set equal to one and all others set to zero. The coefficients associated with each of the three independent variables and the level of statistical significance for each of the four different regressions are shown in Table 4.2.[9] As expected, the most important factor, which determines the acceptability of a facility, is its perceived risk.

To illustrate how the perceived risk, need for facilities and trust in local officials influence the acceptability of a facility, the probability of acceptance calculated for two 'hypothetical respondents' was estimated based on the logit models shown in Table 4.2. The 'Supporter' is characterized by having a high perceived need for these facilities (8), high trust in local officials (8) and low risk perception (2). The 'Opponent' has a low perceived need (2), low trust in local officials (2) and high risk perception (8). The results are presented in Table 4.3.

As one would expect, there is a better than 80 percent chance that the 'Supporter' will find each of the facilities to be acceptable. On the other hand, there is less than a 20 percent chance that the 'Opponent' will perceive all of the facilities to be acceptable. It thus appears that for a majority of residents in a community to vote for a facility in a referendum, most individuals would have to feel that the facility is needed, have a relatively low perception of the risk and high levels of trust in the inspection process.

Table 4.3   Estimated probabilities of acceptance for supporters and opponents

	Prison	Landfill	Incinerator	Repository
Supporter	0.92	0.81	0.86	0.85
Opponent	0.19	0.11	0.12	0.10

5 ROLE OF SAFETY MEASURES AND ECONOMIC BENEFITS

After the respondents stated their degree of acceptance of one of the four facilities, they were given a series of questions to determine whether one or more of the following measures would cause them to change their stated opinion:

• An independent agency approved by the local government will perform

regular inspections to insure that the facility is meeting all federal and state regulations (INSPECT);
* The facility will not be built until local elected officials have approved the design (APPROVE);
* Local elected officials will have the authority to close down the facility if they detect any problems (SHUTDOWN); and
* Economic benefits were provided to residents living within 50 miles of the facility (BENEFITS).

The sample was randomly divided into two equal-sized groups. GROUP 1 respondents were given the measures, in an additive fashion, in the following order: INSPECT, APPROVE, SHUTDOWN and BENEFITS. GROUP 2 respondents began with BENEFITS, followed by INSPECT, APPROVE and SHUTDOWN in that order. The reason for the different orderings is to test whether the sequence of measures affects their acceptance of the facility.

6   HARD CORE SUPPORTERS AND OPPONENTS

We classified as HARD CORE SUPPORTERS those individuals who indicated that they initially viewed the facility as either completely or mostly acceptable and didn't budge from this position no matter what combination of these four measures were presented to them.[10] Those who initially viewed the facility as either mostly or completely unacceptable and retained this position for all four measures, were classified as HARD CORE OPPONENTS.[11] Those who did change their acceptance of the facility as the scenarios were presented to them were classified as MOVEABLES. Table 4.4 indicates the percentage of the sample that is in each of these groups for each of the four facilities.

Table 4.4   Classification of individuals for the four facilities (in percent)

	Prison	Landfill	Incinerator	Repository
Hard Core Supporters	19.74	13.09	6.98	3.38
Moveables	68.61	73.49	66.11	56.42
Hard Core Opponents	11.65	13.42	26.91	40.20

The large difference in the composition of these three groups between the four facilities is obvious. With respect to the prison and landfill there were relatively small percentages of hard core opponents and approximately the same (landfill) or larger (prison) percentage of hard core supporters. For the incinerator and the repository, there was a relatively large percentage of respondents who were hard core opponents and a very small group of hard core supporters. In fact, with respect to the repository, 40 percent of the sample were hard core opponents and less than 4 percent were hard core supporters – a ten-to-one ratio. Note that, for all facilities, a majority of the respondents fell into the 'moveable' category.

Consider only those individuals who are in either of the hard core groups. For each of the four facilities, logit regressions similar to the ones in Table 4.2 indicate that RISK and TRUST are the two factors that are most likely to predict the probability that an individual will be a hard core opponent or supporter of the facility.[12] These results have important policy implications because they suggest that mitigation and compensation will only be effective for those individuals who do not have extreme views on RISK and TRUST. For those individuals who feel a facility is not risky to their health and safety and also trust local officials to do a creditable job in inspecting the facility, there is no need to offer additional safety measures or a package of economic benefits. These people already view the facility as being acceptable. On the other hand, consider the group who feels the facility poses significant risks to their health and safety and does not trust the inspection process. Providing them with economic benefits is likely to be viewed as a bribe; the proposed set of safety measures is not viewed as making the facility safe *enough* to be acceptable. Among this group, the level of stigma may be such that acceptance is very difficult – if not impossible – to achieve (Flynn et al., 2001). This finding would appear to pose the greatest problem for siting nuclear waste disposal facilities, for which 40 percent of our respondents were hard core opponents. However, before declaring an *autodafe* for nuclear facility siting, one needs to recall that our data represent *initial impressions* about acceptance of the facility. These impressions and the accompanying level of acceptance may change as the policy debate concerning the facility siting matures.[13]

The Moveable Respondents

How important are the set of safety measures and the provision of economic benefits in changing the attitudes toward the acceptability of the facility? By combining the hard core groups and the 'moveables', insights can be provided as to what it will take to gain acceptance for the four facilities if some type of referendum were held. We assume that those who indicate the facility is either 'mostly or completely acceptable' would vote 'Yes' for it to be located in the vicinity of their residence and those who feel it to be 'mostly or completely unacceptable' would vote 'No'.

Tables 4.5a and 4.5b present the percentage of respondents who would support the facility for GROUP 1 and GROUP 2 under five different scenarios. The scenarios consist of the different combinations of mitigation and compensation packages that were given to the survey respondents. The tables also show whether the change in the percentage of respondents who accept the facility after each of the sequential steps in the mitigation scenarios was statistically significant.

Table 4.5a   Percentage completely or mostly accepting facilities based on combinations of safety and economic benefits measures (group 1 respondents: benefits offered last)

Sequence of Measures	Prison	Landfill	Incinerator	Repository
No Measures	30.5%	18.1%	14.5%	12.4%
INSPECT	54.9%***	53.7%***	42.1%***	31%***
APPROVE	51.8%	46.3%	36.8%	26.2%*
SHUTDOWN	59.8%	65.8%***	55.4%***	42.8%***
BENEFITS	62.8%	56.4%	42.8%***	31.7%

Notes:
Statistical significance of change from cell above: *** = <0.01; ** = <0.01; * = <0.05.

Table 4.5b   Percentage completely or mostly accepting facilities based on combinations of safety and economic benefits measures (group 2 respondents: benefits offered first)

Sequence of Measures	Prison	Landfill	Incinerator	Repository
No Measures	39%	25.2%	14.5%	10.2%
BENEFITS	52.1%***	49.0%***	30.3%***	13.4%
INSPECT	65.1%**	67.7%***	47.4%***	30.0%***
APPROVE	56.8%**	57.4%**	39.5%*	25.5%*
SHUTDOWN	56.2%	75.5%***	52.0%***	42.0%***

Notes:
Statistical significance of change from cell above: *** = <0.001; ** = <0.01; * = <0.05.

Recall that Group 1 was offered economic benefits last, while Group 2 was offered economic benefits first. The results indicate that it should be relatively easy to site prisons and landfills and much more difficult to find communities that will accept an incinerator. Even with a full package of safety measures and benefits, less than 43 percent of the respondents would accept a repository in their backyard. This suggests that, at the initial stages of the siting process, it may be difficult to find a host community that will accept a repository under a democratic voting procedure even if strong mitigation measures in the form of inspection and shutdown procedures are offered.[14]

Focusing on the specific measures, INSPECT and SHUTDOWN have strong positive effects on acceptance of the facility for both GROUPS 1 and 2. In other words, whether BENEFITS are offered first or last has no impact in the effects of these two measures. Tables 4.5a and 4.5b also reveal that the approval of design by local officials consistently has a *negative* impact on the percentage of respondents who support the siting of these four types of facilities.[15] This finding suggests that, from the perspective of the public, the oversight of independent inspectors and the power to shut down facilities should be left in the hands of local officials. On the other hand the technical issue of the approval of the facility design should not be delegated to state and local officials.[16]

Two explanations for this differentiation of public views of the roles of local officials have been offered. One, consistent with the findings of Jenkins-Smith and Stewart (1998), suggests that while local officials are trusted to express the residents' interests, they are not seen as sufficiently competent to directly oversee a complex hazardous materials management program. O'Connor et al. (1994, p. 192) offer an alternative suggestion; local officials may be seen as too susceptible to the influence of the facility operator and therefore cannot be trusted with decisions about facility design. Either way, program designs that seek public acceptance for hazardous facilities must account for the differentiation in public expectations of different kinds of public officials.

Turning to the BENEFIT measure, it makes a big difference whether it is offered first or last. For the landfill, incinerator and repository, the final percentage of supporters is at least 10 percent higher when economic benefits are offered first (Table 4.5b) rather than last (Table 4.5a). Apparently, when the facility is perceived to be risky, providing economic benefits *after* safety measures have been instituted has a negative influence on the percentage of individuals supporting the facility. This finding implies that when economic benefits are offered first, they are more likely to be perceived by the respondents as compensation for the increased risk from hosting a facility. When these benefits are offered *after* safety measures have been addressed, they are perceived by some as a bribe for taking the facility.

This finding is a puzzling one and requires further research. Indeed, it seems counter-intuitive in the light of Kasperson's (1999) argument that compensation is only ethically justifiable after safety measures have been addressed. Our findings suggest to us that, in the relatively untrusting times in which we live, the introduction of benefits after the safety issue has been addressed leads many of those affected to suspect that the facility is even more dangerous than they were initially led to believe. After all, if the facility is safe, why should those living nearby need to be plied with goodies? Hence, support for the facility is eroded by providing some forms of benefits as an apparent afterthought.

7 THE ROLE OF DIFFERENT TYPES OF COMPENSATION MEASURES

Another purpose of the survey was to examine the appropriateness of different compensation measures in judging the acceptability of a facility. The literature on the provision of benefits to either affected residents and/or the host community suggests that in-kind compensation is generally viewed as much more desirable than monetary payments (Portney, 1991; Gerrard, 1994; Kunreuther and Easterling, 1996). None of the empirical studies on siting to date have examined how attitudes toward specific compensation measures differ across facilities.

Table 4.6 *Types of benefits and compensation measures presented to survey respondents*

Measure	Variable Name
Large grants to local government	Public Grant
Free garbage pick-up	Garbage Pick-up
Tax rebates to residents	Tax Rebates
Compensation for property value losses	Property Value Guarantees
Reimbursement for new public services	Reimbursement
Paying medical costs for health effects from facility	Medical Costs
Trust fund for harm to future generations	Trust Fund
New special services to meet community needs	Special Services

Eight different types of compensation measures were presented to each of the respondents in relation to one of the four facilities. In all cases, the compensation would be provided by the developer of the facility. As shown in Table 4.6, these measures included direct monetary payments to individuals or the community as well as in-kind measures such as property value guarantees and new special services to meet community needs. The questionnaire was explicit in pointing out that the free garbage pick-up and tax rebates would only be provided to residents living within 10 miles of the facility. Special services were illustrated by explicitly mentioning additional police and fire protection or health clinics.

Before listing the specific measures, the respondents were told that the developer has agreed to implement the safety measures captured by the three variables INSPECT, APPROVE and SHUTDOWN. Table 4.7 presents the rank, mean values (ranging from a value of 1, meaning 'Completely Acceptable', to 5 meaning 'Completely Unacceptable') and standard errors for the appropriateness measures of each compensation option for the prison, landfill, incinerator and repository respectively.

Our data reinforce the findings from earlier empirical studies. Regardless of the type of facility, benefits provided directly to residents in the form of tax rebates or free garbage collection as well as monetary payments in the form of large grants to the local government are viewed as the least appropriate ones by respondents. The measures which were viewed as most attractive for all four facilities were either payments by the developer for community services or to those adversely affected by the facility either economically (Property Value Guarantees) or physically (Medical Costs).

Interesting differences are apparent across types of facility. For the incinerator and repository, which have the highest perceived risk, payment of medical costs for health effects from the facility (Medical Costs) get higher relative rankings. As is evident from inspection of the standard errors, for the incinerator the Medical Costs option is scored statistically significantly higher (i.e., it has a lower score) than any other option. The provision of free garbage pick-up, on the other hand, ranks highest for the landfill (sixth out of eight options). Garbage pick-up is seen as significantly more appropriate than either tax rebates or grants as compensation for hosting a landfill. These variations in the rankings of appropriateness of the compensation options suggest that linking the type of compensation to the characteristics of the facility may be important in efforts to gain acceptance.

Table 4.7 also shows that the attractiveness of all the compensation measures decreases as the facility is perceived to be more risky by respondents. In other words, any proposed types of compensation were viewed as less appropriate for the repository (overall mean 2.98) and incinerator (2.65) than for the prison (2.38) and landfill (2.21). A more detailed analysis of the data reveals that these differences are directly correlated with the proportion of respondents who were classified as Opponents, Supporters and Moveables when evaluating each facility. Hard core opponents at each of the facilities took a dim view of all of the proposed measures, with the mean values exceeding 3.5 for every type of proposed benefits package. Both the supporters and the moveables had a much more positive view of all the proposed compensation measures with the mean values for each of the measures generally below 2.0 for the supporters and below 2.6 for the moveables.

8 POLICY IMPLICATIONS AND FUTURE RESEARCH

This study has solidified our understanding of the factors influencing the siting process. In particular, we now have a much better understanding of the differences in attitudes by the public between siting facilities that are perceived to pose relatively low risks to health and safety and those that are viewed

Table 4.7 Perceived appropriateness of compensation measures for four facilities (1=completely acceptable, 5=completely unacceptable)

Type of Measure	Prison Rank Mean (Std Error)	Landfill Rank Mean (Std Error)	Incinerator Rank Mean (Std Error)	Repository Rank Mean (Std Error)
Reimbursement	1 2.05 (0.08)	1 2.07 (0.08)	2 2.51 (0.09)	1 2.77 (0.10)
Special Services	2 2.14 (0.08)	5 2.23 (0.08)	4 2.58 (0.09)	5 2.96 (0.09)
Property Value Guarantees	3 2.20 (0.08)	2 2.08 (0.08)	3 2.51 (0.09)	3 2.84 (0.10)
Medical Costs	4 2.32 (0.09)	4 2.09 (0.08)	1 2.39 (0.09)	2 2.81 (0.10)
Trust Fund	5 2.36 (0.08)	3 2.09 (0.08)	5 2.61 (0.09)	4 2.89 (0.10)
Public Grant	6 2.44 (0.08)	8 2.45 (0.08)	6 2.82 (0.09)	7 3.15 (0.09)
Tax Rebates	7 2.62 (0.08)	7 2.37 (0.08)	7 2.85 (0.09)	6 3.14 (0.09)
Garbage Collect	8 2.93 (0.09)	6 2.27 (0.08)	8 2.89 (0.09)	8 3.29 (0.09)
Overall Average Acceptance	2.38	2.21	2.65	2.98

as very dangerous. This section suggests policy implications of the findings and directions for future research.

Policy Implications

Gaining community approval for siting facilities that evoke perceptions of high risk coupled with low levels of trust will be extremely difficult. The developer is likely to be confronted by a large hard core group of opponents and hence will have fewer people who can be influenced by safety measures and a package of economic benefits. It is thus not surprising that we have had difficulty finding homes for incinerators (Davy, 1997) or an acceptable location for a high level nuclear waste repository (Flynn et al., 1995).

The type of safety and benefit measures and the order in which they are presented or framed will make a difference in how acceptable a given facility is likely to be. In particular, our results indicate that benefits should be presented first in the form of some type of non-monetary return to the community, so the compensation is not viewed as a bribe. Indeed, proffering benefits after mitigation measures have been taken may undermine the acceptability of the mitigation measures themselves. We speculate that such a strategy may lead the recipients of the benefits to believe that the economic incentives are offered *because* the safety measures are insufficient.

The economic benefits provided by the developer are also likely to be more successful if they satisfy residents, concerns about economic equity (property value guarantees and reimbursement for new public facilities necessitated by the facility) and health (medical costs). Other measures tend to be more attractive if they are related to the facility's use either in reducing risk (e.g. hospitals near an incinerator) or in providing for the needs of the community (e.g. free garbage in exchange for landfills) because they serve to make the proposed facility more acceptable.

With respect to the safety side, it is important for residents in the community to feel that their facility will have an acceptable risk today as well as in the future. Hence the concern by respondents that the facility be subject to oversight by independent inspectors hired by local officials and that local authorities will have the ability to close down the plant's operation if they detect any problems. These findings are consistent with those of Carnes et al. (1983), Sigmon (1987), Gerrard (1994), Davy (1997) and others that stress the importance of negotiating safety concerns and compensation agreements with local interests as an essential ingredient to a successful siting process.

More generally, giving a critical role to a public official may help achieve acceptance if the public trusts that official to carry out a particular task and perceives them to have the resources (e.g., expertise, funding and authority) necessary to carry out their assigned responsibilities. If not, what may appear to be a constructive safety measure (e.g., giving local officials more control) may actually decrease perceived safety and, therefore, acceptance.

If the public will be playing a key role in the siting of noxious facilities in the future, then it is important to understand more fully under what circumstances they are likely to support a particular facility. Frey et al. (1996) provides an example of their use in locating a radioactive waste repository in Switzerland. Kunreuther et al. (1993) describes the referenda process used by Browning Ferris in finding a home for a landfill in New York State.[17] At a broader policy level, the Swedish government held a nationwide referendum on the future of nuclear energy, coupled with the decision regarding the siting of nuclear waste disposal facilities (Jasper, 1990). It remains to be seen whether the use of referenda for siting potentially hazardous facilities will become more widespread over time.

The results of our survey suggest that community approval for facilities such as prisons and landfills can be obtained should a referendum be held and an appropriate set of safety and benefits measures incorporated in the siting package. Our data indicate that it will be considerably more difficult to use a referenda approach to find a home for a hazardous waste incinerator even with such a package and next to impossible to find a community that would vote for a high level radioactive waste repository in their backyard.

Future Research

Should different packages of safety measures and benefit-sharing approaches be recommended for different types of facilities? The current study suggests that some factors will transcend the facility (such as a trusted inspection process) while other elements may vary from one facility to another (such as specific compensation packages for a prison compared to an incinerator). Clearly, more research is needed to verify this finding and to assess whether it can be extended to other types of facilities.

One approach will be to focus on the *commensurability* of the measures and the proposed facility. Given the importance for public acceptance of the perceived riskiness of a proposed facility, it may be useful to design measures that make residents of the potential host community feel that the dimensions that create concerns about the risk are being directly addressed (i.e., that the measures and the risk are commensurable). For example, by creating a new research facility that is attached to a proposed nuclear waste repository and stipulating that the research facility will focus on reducing the future risks associated with radioactive materials, nearby residents may find the repository to be more acceptable (Bassett et al., 1995). This type of approach appears to have been successfully undertaken in France, where four deep geologic laboratories will study the storage and disposal of nuclear waste in different geologic settings (Bataille, 1994). Similarly, attaching a research mission focussed on reducing hazards of radioactive waste to a centralized nuclear waste repository in the U.S. may well reduce opposition to such a facility.

To return to the expected utility model discussed above in Section 2, our analysis suggests that the value of the benefits package, B, is not independent of the nature of the expected risk should the facility be built (p,L). To this extent, we believe the critics of the expected utility approaches to siting potentially hazardous facilities have been on the right track. It may not be a matter of providing *enough* benefits, but of providing *enough commensurable* benefits, given the nature of the expected risk. Systematic research on the implications of commensurable mitigation and compensation of measures for public acceptance of potentially hazardous facilities is needed.

ACKNOWLEDGEMENT

Special thanks to Richard Barke and Doug Easterling who helped us design the survey questions on which this analysis is based. Yu Li provided helpful research assistance in performing the statistical analysis. Hayden Lesbirel, Carol Silva and Sid Cullipher provided helpful comments on earlier drafts. Funding for the data collection was provided by a grant from the Waste Education/Research Consortium. The Wharton Risk Management and Decision Processes Center and the UNM Institute for Public Policy provided partial financial support for this project.

NOTES

1. In the three most affected villages, each of the 10,000 residents received NT$80,000. In addition, NT$670 million was distributed to 16 other villages in the area. NT$10,000 is worth approximately US$400.
2. We used the following formulae, as defined in AAPOR (1998): RR6, COOP4 and REF3.
3. Words in capital letters denote definitions of variables used in analyzing the data.
4. All experimental treatments (including both the identification of the hypothetical facility and the distance of the facility from the respondents' home) were based on random assignment.
5. In order to avoid, as much as possible, conflating attitude direction and intensity, we employed acceptance measures that indicated the 'completeness' rather than the 'strength' of the respondents' acceptance of the different facilities and policy measures. Thus, our interviewers asked whether the respondent found the facility to be 'completely acceptable, mostly acceptable, mostly unacceptable, or completely unacceptable' rather than the alternative of 'strong acceptance' to 'strong rejection' of the facility. For a discussion of the problem of conflating attitude direction with intensity (see Radin, 1960; Peabody, 1962; and Converse and Presser, 1986).
6. As expected, the level of acceptance was less if the facility was to be located nearer to the home. An examination of the mean responses for the ten-mile distance confirms that there is a statistically significant difference for ACCEPT ($p < 0.05$) across each of the facility types.

7. See Easterling and Kunreuther (1995) and Kunreuther, Fitzgerald and Aarts (1993) for a summary of these studies.
8. Using a difference of means test, the differences among the three facilities for each variable were statistically significant ($p < 0.01$). The one exception was that the difference in RISK between the incinerator and the repository was statistically insignificant.
9. There were no statistically significant interaction effects between these three variables when they were included in the equation.
10. As is shown below in Tables 4.5a and 4.5b, not all of the measures used were positively related to acceptance of the facility. For many respondents, acceptance was reduced when we added the requirements that local officials approve the facility design, or that a compensation package be provided to nearby residents.
11. An individual who changed their view from mostly acceptable to completely acceptable or from completely to mostly acceptable when one or more of these measures were proposed were still classified as HARD CORE SUPPORTERS. A similar classification system was used for those moving from mostly unacceptable to completely unacceptable or vice versa as different mitigation and compensation measures were offered them; these respondents were coded as HARD CORE OPPONENTS.
12. We have not shown the specific logit regression equations. The only difference from the ones in Table 4.2 is that the NEED variable was not statistically significant for any of the four facilities.
13. The New Mexico experience with acceptance of the Waste Isolation Pilot Plant (WIPP), a deep geologic repository for transuranic wastes, is illustrative of the possible changes. Statewide surveys had shown majorities to be opposed to opening WIPP through the mid-1990s (Cockerill et al., 1996). However, as legal disputes were resolved and the policy process closed in on an opening date, public acceptance began to rise. The most recent data show substantial public support for keeping WIPP open (Institute for Public Policy, 2000).
14. This finding has been born out by most of the attempts to site radioactive waste disposal facilities (Kunreuther and Easterling, 1996). However, it should be noted that a majority of those living in the communities near the Waste Isolation Pilot Plant (WIPP) in southern New Mexico support opening the WIPP. The WIPP is a deep geologic disposal facility for transuranic (heavier-than-uranium) wastes.
15. For GROUP 1 the APPROVE measure is only statistically significant for the repository. However, for GROUP 2 it is statistically significant (in reducing approval) for all four facilities.
16. More research is needed to determine who it is that people would trust to judge technical issues with respect to facility design. For recent work on this question, see Jenkins-Smith and Silva (1998).
17. In 1992, Browning Ferris Inc. (BFI) held a referendum for a landfill in Eagle, NY in which a majority of the residents decided that they would prefer not to have the facility in their town. True to their word BFI left town only to be called back six months later by community leaders saying that they wanted to hold another referendum. This one passed by a 70-30 majority. Interestingly enough when the permitting process was approved the town chose another company rather than BFI to construct the landfill.

REFERENCES

American Association for Public Opinion Research (1998), Standard Definitions: Final Dispositions of Case Codes and Outcome Rates for RDD Telephone Surveys and In-person Household Surveys, Ann Arbor, MI: AAPOR.
Bassett, Gilbert Jr., John Gastil, Hank Jenkins-Smith and Carol Silva (1995), 'High Level Nuclear Waste Management Strategies: Understanding Three Stakeholder Perspectives', Albuquerque, NM: University of New Mexico Institute for Public Policy Working Paper, Fall 1995.

Bataille, Christian (1994), 'The French Mediation Mission: Siting of Underground Research Laboratories', in High Level Radioactive Waste Management: Proceedings of the Fifth Annual International Conference (New York: American Society of Civil Engineers), 249–57.

Carnes, S.A., E.D. Copenhaver, J.H. Sorensen, E.J. Soderstrom, J.H. Reed, D.J Bjornstad and E. Peelle (1983), 'Incentives and Nuclear Waste Siting: Prospects and Constraints', *Energy Systems and Policy*, **7** (4), 324–51.

Cockerill, Kristin, Amy Fromer, John Gastil and Hank Jenkins-Smith (1996), 'Unfinished Business: New Mexican's Views on the Waste Isolation Pilot Plant, 1990–1996', Albuquerque, NM: University of New Mexico Institute for Public Policy.

Converse, Jean and Stanley Presser (1986), *Survey Questions*, Beverly Hills, CA: Sage.

Davy, Benjamin (1997), *Essential Injustice*, Berlin: Springer Verlag.

Dunlap, Riley E. and Rodney K. Baxter (1988), 'Public Reaction to Siting a High-level Nuclear Waste Repository at Hanford: A Survey of Local Area Residents', Report prepared by the Social and Economic Sciences Research Center, Washington State University, Pullman, WA for Impact Assessment, Inc.

Easterling, Doug and Howard Kunreuther (1995), *The Dilemma of Siting a High-Level Nuclear Waste Repository*, Boston: Kluwer Academic Publishers.

Elster, Jon (1992), *Local Justice: How Institutions Allocate Scarce Goods and Necessary Burdens*, New York: Russell Sage Foundation.

Flynn, James, James Chalmers, Doug Easterling, Roger Kasperson, Howard Kunreuther, C.K. Mertz, Alvin Mushkatel, K. David Pijawka and Paul Slovic with Lydia Dotto, Science Writer (1995), *One Hundred Centuries of Solitude: Redirecting America's High-Level Nuclear Waste Policy*, Boulder, CO: Westview Press.

Flynn, James, Paul Slovic and Howard Kunreuther (eds) (2001), *Risk, Media and Stigma*, London: Earthscan.

Flynn, James, William Burns, C.K. Mertz and Paul Paul Slovic (1992), 'Trust as a Determinant of Opposition to a High-Level Radioactive Waste Repository: Analysis of a Structural Model', *Risk Analysis*, **12**, 417–30.

Frey, Bruno and Felix Oberholzer-Gee (1996), 'Fair Siting Procedures: An Empirical Analysis of Their Importance and Characteristics', *Journal of Policy Analysis and Management*, **15**, 353–76.

Frey, Bruno, Felix Oberholzer-Gee and Reiner Eichenberger (1996), 'The Old Lady Visits Your Backyard: A Tale of Morals and Markets', *Journal of Political Economy*, **104**, 1297–313.

Gerrard, Michael (1994), *Whose Backyard, Whose Risk*, Cambridge, MA: MIT Press.

Gregory, Robin, Howard Kunreuther, Douglas Easterling and Ken Richards (1991), 'Incentives Policies to Site Hazardous Facilities', *Risk Analysis*, **11**, 667–75.

Herzik, Eric. (1993), 'Nevada Statewide Telephone Survey Data', report presented to Nevada State and Local Planning Group, University of Nevada, Reno, July 23.

Institute for Public Policy (2000), Public Opinion Profile of New Mexico Citizens, **12** (2), Spring/Summer.

Jasper, James (1990), *Nuclear Politics: Energy and the State in the United States, Sweden and France*, Princeton, NJ: Princeton University Press.

Jenkins-Smith, H. and C. Silva (1998), 'The Role of Risk Perception and Technical Information in Scientific Debates Over Nuclear Waste Storage', *Reliability Engineering and System Safety*, **59**, 107–22.

Jenkins-Smith, H. and G. Bassett (1994), 'Perceived Risk and Uncertainty of Nuclear Waste: Differences Among Science, Business and Environmental Group Members', *Risk Analysis*, **14** (5), 851–56.

Jenkins-Smith, Hank and Joseph Stewart (1998), 'Who Will Protect My Back Yard: Dimensions of Federalism in Political Trust', Institute for Public Policy Working Paper Series, University of New Mexico, Albuquerque, New Mexico.

Kasperson, Roger (1999), 'Process and Institutional Issues in Siting Facilities', Paper presented at International Workshop on Challenges and Issues in Facility Siting, Academia Sinica, Taipei, Taiwan, January 7–9.

Kunreuther, Howard and Douglas Easterling (1990), 'Are Risk-benefit Trade-offs Possible in Siting Hazardous Facilities?', *American Economic Review: Papers and Proceedings*, **80** (May), 252–56.

Kunreuther, Howard and Doug Easterling (1996), 'The Role of Compensation in Siting Hazardous Facilities', *Journal of Policy Analysis and Management*, **15**, 601–22.

Kunreuther, Howard, Kevin Fitzgerald and Thomas D. Aarts (1993), 'Siting Noxious Facilities: A Test of the Facility Siting Credo', *Risk Analysis*, **13**, 301–18.

Kunreuther, Howard, Joanne Linnerooth and Kevin Fitzgerald (1996), 'Siting Hazardous Facilities: Lessons from Europe and America', in P. Kleindorfer, H. Kunreuther and D. Hong (eds), *Energy, Environment and the Economy: Asian Perspectives*, Cheltenham, UK: Edward Elgar Publishing.

Likert, Rensis (1932), 'A Technique for the Measurement of Attitudes', *Archives of Psychology*, **140**, 44–53.

Maurer, Todd and Heather Pierce (1998), 'A Comparison of Likert Scale and Traditional Measures of Self-Efficacy', *Journal of Applied Psychology*, **83**, 324–9.

O'Connor, Robert, Richard Bord and Kerry Pflugh (1994), 'The Two Faces of Environmentalism: Environmental Protection and Development on Cape May', *Coastal Management*, **22**, 183–94.

Peabody, D. (1962), 'Two Components in Bipolar Scales: Direction and Intensity', *Psychological Review*, **69**, 65–73.

Portney, Kent (1991), *Siting Hazardous Waste Facilities: The NIMBY Syndrome*, New York, Auburn House.

Radin, David (1960), 'Strength Related Attitude Dimensions', *Social Psychology Quarterly*, **48**, 312–30.

Shaw, Daigee (1996), 'An Economic Framework for Analyzing Facility Siting Procedures in Taiwan and Japan', in P. Kleindorfer, H. Kunreuther and D. Hong (eds), *Energy, Environment and the Economy: Asian Perspectives*, Cheltenham, UK: Edward Elgar Publishing.

Sigmon, E. Brent (1987), 'Achieving a Negotiated Compensation Agreement in Siting: The MRS Case', *Journal of Policy Analysis and Management*, **6**, 170–79.

Williams, Brian, S. Brown and M. Greenberg (1999), 'Determinants of Trust Perceptions among Residents Surrounding the Savannah River Nuclear Weapons Site', *Environment and Behavior*, **31**, 354–71.

5. Social Pressure in Siting Conflicts: A Case Study of Siting a Radioactive Waste Repository in Pennsylvania

**Felix Oberholzer-Gee and
Howard Kunreuther**

1 INTRODUCTION

Public opposition to new major capital investments is often substantial. Consequently, it has become quite difficult to find locations for chemical plants, landfills, waste incinerators, and nuclear waste repositories. The fruitless search for new locations for such facilities is expensive. In the United States, the federal and state governments have spent several billion dollars to find locations for new hazardous and radioactive waste facilities.[1] So far, no new sites have been found. Paradoxically, the fear of new facilities, which is in part fueled by problems with old plants, makes it more difficult to clean up these old sites. The EPA reports that about 70 percent of all hazardous waste facilities fail current siting criteria for protecting the groundwater. It is estimated that up to 90 percent of these facilities release hazardous wastes into the water (Gerrard, 1994, p. 54). Without new sites, however, it is impossible to build safer waste facilities.

The economic solution for this Not-In-My-Backyard (NIMBY) problem is straightforward. As the net aggregate benefits of such projects are positive, the overall gains must be used to compensate prospective host communities.[2] If these financial incentives more than offset the negative externalities, communities will voluntarily host the project. Various compensation mechanisms have been proposed to guarantee an efficient allocation of NIMBY projects (for a survey, see Coursey and Kim, 1997).

Recent siting research shows that compensation policies are not always as effective as economic reasoning suggests. A theory of behavior in siting conflicts needs to be able to explain the following stylized facts that have emerged from the literature:

1. Compensation generally leads to successful siting if the facility in question does not pose a serious risk to the host community. Examples for such facilities include prisons and airports. However, for *riskier projects* such as waste incinerators and nuclear waste repositories, *increases in compensation are not effective* in eliciting the desired support (Kunreuther and Easterling, 1990).
2. More generous compensation packages for risky facilities sometimes have no effect at all. The support for these projects appears to be completely price inelastic (Carnes et al., 1983; Herzik, 1993; Jenkins-Smith and Kunreuther, 1998).
3. In a few cases, increases in compensation decreases the support for the facility if it is perceived to be risky (Dunlap and Baxter, 1988; Frey and Oberholzer-Gee, 1997).

This chapter offers a framework for the analysis of behavior in siting conflicts. We study how individuals interact with each other when they face a NIMBY problem. In our model, residents of prospective host communities are influenced by personal and by social concerns. They care not only about the characteristics of the facility but are also sensitive to public opinion in their community. In particular, individuals are reluctant to support the siting of a facility if they believe that a majority of the residents oppose the project. We show that these beliefs can be self-confirming. If everyone believes that there is strong opposition to the facility, few will speak out in favor of the project, and the project will be voted down. Social pressure to oppose the facility may be one reason why offers of more generous compensation packages do not increase stated public support. In fact, these packages may have the reverse effect by being perceived as a bribe to induce residents to take on additional risks. This may explain why an offer of compensation may decrease support for some facilities.

It seems quite natural to assume that social pressure plays an important role in siting conflicts. In fact, it is not difficult to find case studies that illustrate the bitter struggle between those who support and those who oppose NIMBY projects and the impact this has on the community (Rabe, 1994). In the Pennsylvania case that we will study empirically, a small business owner who was willing to study the possibility of hosting a nuclear waste repository was threatened with the boycott of his businesses. In the case of a Montana land use dispute, the bitter struggle over the construction of a new railway line has completely torn apart the small town of Birney in Montana's Tongue River Valley. Many of its citizens have stopped speaking to each other because they feel they cannot accept the position of the other group.[3] While nearly every community, which finds itself in a siting conflict, experiences such strains, previous research has neglected this dimension of the NIMBY problem. To our knowledge, this is the first paper that explicitly models behavior in siting conflicts as influenced by social interactions.

2 THE MODEL

We employ a model of social interaction where the benefits of one's decisions also depend on the decisions made by other individuals. Schelling (1978), Granovetter (1978) and Akerlof (1980) pioneered this class of threshold models. Their common characteristic is that the costs of undertaking an activity depend on the number of people who engage in it. In Schelling's example, it is less costly for members of a minority to move into a neighborhood if other members of the minority already live there. Granovetter uses riots to illustrate the same point: as the number of persons who riot increases, the costs of participating in the riot falls. In these models, small changes in the distribution of costs or preferences can generate large differences in the outcome. The models are capable of generating bandwagon or tipping effects. Kuran (1987) applied a threshold model to analyze collective conservatism. He shows that in a society where interest groups exert social pressure, changes in individual (private) preferences are not necessarily translated into changes in public policy.

Suppose the residents of a prospective host community face a choice of supporting or opposing a proposed NIMBY project. Each resident chooses $S_i \in \{0,1\}$, where $S_i = 0$ (1) means that he opposes (supports) the facility. An individual will choose $S_i = 1$ if expected net benefits x_i from the project being sited are positive. Otherwise, she will oppose it. For individual i, the expected net benefits of supporting the project if there is no social pressure are given by

$$x_i = p_i (B_i - C_i + E) \tag{5.1}$$

B_i denotes the benefits of the facility (e.g., jobs) and C_i represents the cost (e.g., health risks, possible decline in property values) as individual i perceives them and E is the compensation that the developer offers. We assume the amount of compensation offered is exogenous and of the same value for all citizens. p_i is the perceived probability of individual i that the project will be sited successfully. This probability depends on the support S_i of individual i, where $dp/dS_i > 0$.

For a typical individual living in the prospective host community, we view this probability p_i as being positive. In this respect, our analysis differs from the standard voting context where p_i is simply the probability that individual i

will cast the decisive vote. For our purposes, an exclusive focus on voting would be too narrow. Referenda on NIMBY projects do not fall from the sky. Someone first needs to initiate the public discussion. In the course of this discussion, citizens have the opportunity to evaluate arguments for and against the proposed facility. As the benefits and especially the costs (health risks, environmental impacts) of many proposed NIMBY projects are highly uncertain, citizens are likely to encounter very different opinions and they need to decide who they wish to believe. In other words, the pre-referendum process is one of persuasion where community leaders and well-connected citizens may well have the opportunity to swing the vote. The probability p_i thus differs from individual to individual. Moreover, this pre-referendum process may be more important than the voting mechanism itself. In the Pennsylvania siting case, which we study in the second part of this paper, not a single township actually voted on the facility. Where the possibility of siting the state's low- and mid-level radioactive waste repository was discussed at all, residents decided by other means not to pursue the project.

Now suppose that individuals take possible social pressure into account in their decision process. By supporting or opposing the facility, individuals become part of the respective group in their community. Both supporters and opponents reward membership in their own group and try to inflict cost on members of the other camp. Let $A(S_i)$ represent the approval function which we write as

$$A(S_i) = \begin{cases} f_0(a) & \text{if } S_i = 0 \\ f_1(1-a) & \text{if } S_i = 1 \end{cases} \qquad (5.2)$$

where a is the fraction of residents who oppose the facility and $(1-a)$ is the fraction of those who support it. The net benefits A of belonging to either group increases monotonically as the size of the group increases. Note that the supporting group and the opposition need not necessarily be equally efficient at producing social pressure. We assume, however, that the above approval function is the same for all individuals. Taking social pressure into account, the expected utility of supporting the project is now given as

$$U_i = p_i(B_i - C_i + E) + A(S_i) \qquad (5.3)$$

Now citizens no longer automatically support the project if it bestows expected net benefits on them. There are cases where the opposition may be sufficiently numerous or efficient at producing social pressure to win over individuals who, in the absence of approval, would have supported the project.

The residents of the host community play the following multi-period game. In time period 0, at the start of the public deliberation process, individuals expect a certain fraction of residents to oppose the facility. We denote these initial beliefs as $\hat{a}_0$. We assume that all residents share the same initial beliefs. Based upon the expected opposition, individuals choose $S_i \in \{0,1\}$. The resulting opposition a_0 need not be equal to $\hat{a}_0$. When expectations and actual opposition differ, some individuals will be unhappy with their previous choice and will wish to switch camps. In every period of the game, a_t becomes the belief $\hat{a}_{t+1}$ for stage $t+1$. Nash equilibrium in this game is reached in period t^* when the expected share of opposition induces exactly the expected number of individuals to actually oppose the facility, i.e., $a_{t^*-1} = \hat{a}_{t^*} = a_{t^*}$.

Figure 5.1 illustrates our analysis graphically. The vertical axis measures the expected benefits from the facility, which we denote as $x_i = p_i \times$

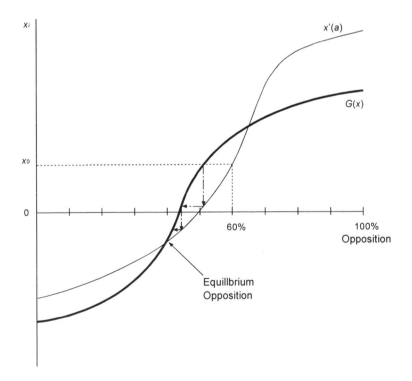

Figure 5.1 Equilibria with social pressure

$(B_i - C_i + E)$. The horizontal axis shows the percentage of residents who oppose the project. Let $G(x)$ represent the cumulative density function that defines, for every x, the fraction of residents for who $x_i < x$. (The function given in Figure 6.1 is for illustrative purposes only. There is no special reason to believe that the function actually takes on this shape.) We also define a social sensitivity function $x'(a)$, which is given by combinations of x_i and a that leave the individual indifferent between supporting and opposing the facility. Along this sensitivity function, the expected utility of supporting the project is always zero. If the function is very steep, this implies that a given increase in opposition must be compensated with a sizeable increase in net benefits x. In other words, residents are pretty sensitive to social pressure. If social pressure did not matter at all, the social sensitivity function would be flat and lie on the horizontal axis.

Proposition. Given our assumptions, there exists, for all distributions of x_i, at least one equilibrium that is characterized by beliefs satisfying $a = G[x'(\hat{a})]$.
Proof. See the Appendix A.

In Figure 5.1, all points of intersection of the sensitivity function (the light line) and the cumulative distribution function (the heavy line) represent equilibria. Some of these are locally stable, some of them are not robust to small decision-making errors. The importance of initial beliefs is evident. Assume that residents initially expect 60 percent to oppose the project. In this case, x_0 in net benefits is required to keep individuals indifferent between supporting and opposing the project. Citizens who believe that net benefits will fall short of x_0 will oppose the project. We read from the cumulative distribution function that about 52 percent actually have values of x that are lower than x_0. Thus, 52 percent becomes the expected opposition for the next stage and the individual now requires $x < x_0$ to support the project. This process will eventually lead us to the equilibrium opposition at 40 percent. However, had initial expectations been that $\hat{a}_0 > 64$ percent will oppose the project, the final outcome would have been unanimous opposition to the NIMBY facility (see Figure 5.1). Note that for all values of x on the social sensitivity function that are greater than the most optimistic estimate of expected net benefits, opposition is always 100 percent. Complete opposition results because there is no individual who sees the facility as sufficiently beneficial to be indifferent between opposing and supporting it. It is possible that the social sensitivity function lies above $G(x)$ for the entire range. In this case, any initial belief $\hat{a} < 100$ percent will result in a greater than expected opposition. In equilibrium, all residents will oppose the facility. Conversely, a sensitivity function that always lies below $G(x)$ yields 100 percent support as the only equilibrium.

3 COMPENSATION AS A POLICY TOOL

Now, let us consider how an increase in compensation affects the level of opposition. Such increases in E lead to increases in the expected utility of support. Thus, the cumulative density function shifts up as more generous compensation packages are offered. However, as Figure 5.2 illustrates, this shift does not necessarily lead to higher levels of support.

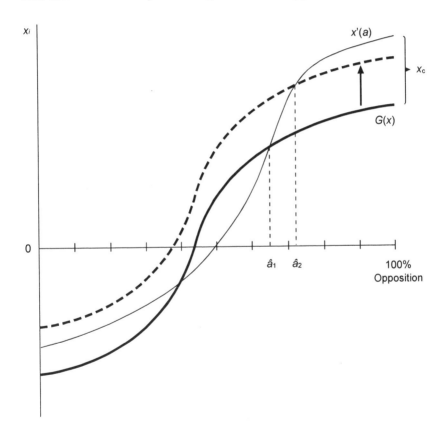

Figure 5.2   Increase in compensation

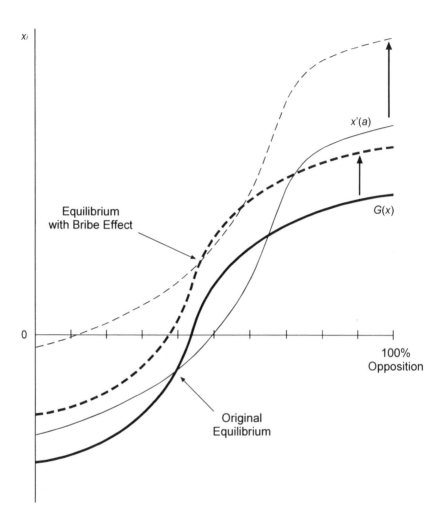

Figure 5.3   Bribe effect

Suppose that the initial equilibrium in Figure 5.2 is at 100 percent opposition. Note that any initial belief $\hat{a} < \hat{a}_1$ would have led us to the equilibrium
where 40 percent of the residents oppose the project. An increase in compensation shifts the locally instable equilibrium to $\hat{a}_2$. However, unless this
increase in compensation leads to beliefs $\hat{a} < \hat{a}_2$, the outcome will be unchanged and everybody will continue to oppose this facility. While the outcome remains unchanged, the corner equilibrium has become less robust due
to the increase in compensation. Before this increase, any belief $\hat{a} < \hat{a}_1$ would
have led to the equilibrium where a majority favor the facility. Now, beliefs

need only be more optimistic than $\hat{a}_2$ to have the same effect. In general, the increase in compensation must be at least as large as Δx_c in Figure 5.2 to move us out of the corner equilibrium. Similarly, in the case where $G(x)$ lies below the sensitivity function, increases in compensation will not lead to higher levels of support if $G(x)$ does not intersect the sensitivity function at least once.

Our framework also allows us to analyze the use of different compensation mechanisms. In the siting literature, it is often argued that cash compensation is ineffective because people regard this type of compensation as bribes (O'Hare et al., 1983; Zeiss, 1996). Frey et al. (1996) report that more than 80 percent of the residents living in a prospective host community in Switzerland declined a compensation offer stating that their support could not be bought. In cases where compensation is regarded as a bribe, the opposition will become more efficient at producing social pressure. If people feel guilty for accepting bribes, the benefits of belonging to the supporting camp are lowered. In both cases, the sensitivity function will shift up because individuals demand higher net benefits for a given level of opposition. Figure 5.3 shows a case where the simultaneous shift of the cumulative density function and the sensitivity function lower the level of support for the facility. Such a simultaneous shift reproduces the 'anomaly' found in a few siting studies that higher levels of compensation may decrease the level support for the facility.

4 EMPIRICAL TEST

In this section, we test some of the assumptions underlying our model of behavior in siting conflicts. The theoretical models suggests the following hypotheses:

1. Individuals are more likely to support a NIMBY facility if other residents support it as well.
2. Failure to take social pressure into account is likely to lead to biased estimates of the effectiveness of compensation measures.
3. Social pressure influences individual decisions more strongly if morally objectionable forms of compensation are used.

Hypothesis (1) corresponds to the key assumption made in our model. Hypothesis (2) is related to research that uses surveys to study the effectiveness of different compensation mechanisms. Our model suggests that respondents take into account what other residents do when they indicate that they would support a NIMBY facility in exchange for a particular compensation package. If social pressure is omitted from the analysis, the resulting estimates may be biased. Hypothesis (3) follows from the assumption that morally objectionable forms of compensation make the opposition relatively more efficient. If this is the case, an individual needs, for every given increase in the size of the opposition group, a more optimistic estimate of x_i to remain indifferent between opposing and rejecting a facility. In other words, unethical forms of compensation increase the slope of the sensitivity function. Thus, individuals should become more sensitive to the size of the opposition.

We test our hypotheses using Pennsylvania's search for a site for a low-level radioactive waste repository as our example. In July 1995, the State of Pennsylvania abandoned its previous approach of using technical criteria to find a suitable community and then force that community to accept the facility. Instead, the Department of Environmental Protection Secretary James M. Seif announced a voluntary siting approach (Chem-Nuclear Systems, 1996). Three elements characterized the 'Community Partnering Plan' that was developed by the State, the developer Chem-Nuclear Systems Inc., and interested local officials and citizens. First, the process would be entirely voluntary. No community could be forced to accept the facility.[4] Second, an interested municipality would have to demonstrate that its residents agreed to host the facility. This would be accomplished through 'an open, public approval process'. Third, the host community would receive compensation. The 'Community Partnering Plan' promised 70 permanent jobs (preference would be given to local hiring); a cash payment of $600,000 per year to the host community, for the next 30 years; the payment of all township and school property taxes for primary residences within two miles of the facility, for the next 30 years; and a two-year guarantee of home sale prices within two miles of the facility (Chem-Nuclear Systems, 1996). The plan also mentioned that Chem-Nuclear Systems Inc. would negotiate 'other benefits' with the host community.

The Pennsylvania State Association of Township Supervisors played an important role in the siting process. By cooperating with the Association, the developer hoped to make contact with township supervisors who might be interested in hosting the facility. For example, the entire September 1996 issue of the Pennsylvania Township News was devoted to the search for a volunteer municipality.

In December 1997, the Association mailed out a survey to all township supervisors in the state that was developed by us in cooperation with the Association and the developer. To guarantee anonymity, supervisors mailed back their survey to the Association.

We chose the township supervisors as our group of respondents for several reasons. As mentioned above, these local officials were supposed to play an important role in the siting process. For example, the Association recommended that townships should only enter the voluntary process after the

Board of Supervisors had determined that public opinion would support holding expert panel discussions in the township. Thus, supervisors represented important gatekeepers in the process and it was interesting to study their behavior. In addition, we expected supervisors to be much better informed about the process than a randomly selected group of citizens. Both the Association and the developer had spent considerable resources on educating the supervisors. Finally, cooperating with the Association allowed us to have respondents send back their surveys to an organization they were familiar with and trusted. Five hundred and nine out of 1402 respondents answered our questionnaire.

5   EMPIRICAL SPECIFICATION

To test our hypotheses, we estimate a standard probit model of the form

$$\Pr(S=1) = \Phi \ (\beta_1 + \beta_2 B_i + \beta_3 C_i + \beta_4 E + \beta_5 A + \beta_6 F + \beta_7 \mathbf{X} \qquad (5.4)$$

where Φ is the cumulative normal distribution. The dependent variable is the respondents' willingness to vote for the siting of the proposed low-level radioactive waste repository in their township (see appendix B for wording of the questions used in this appendix).[5] Respondents indicated their expected economic benefits from the facility (B_i) on a scale ranging from –3 ('would personally be much worse off') to +3 ('would personally be much better off'). We used the expected health risk as a measure of cost (C_i). For this variable, the supervisors indicated their expectations on a six-point scale ranging from 'personal health risk not at all serious' to 'very serious'. We anticipated $\beta_2 > 0$ and $\beta_3 < 0$.

We used the compensation package described in the Community Partnering Plan as our first measure of compensation E. In subsequent questions, we varied the compensation package by offering $1.8 million cash (instead of $600,000). Next, we offered 210 jobs (instead of 70). Finally, we offered $600,000 in cash compensation that would exclusively be used to 'sustain and improve the quality of life' in the host community. This last question is an attempt to test if compensation becomes more effective if it is presented in more positive terms. Economic theory suggests $\beta_4 > 0$. Previous siting research has identified at least two reasons to be cautious in making this prediction. Several studies find that individuals interpret the size of the compensation as a signal for the magnitude of the risks involved. As a consequence, compensation may be viewed as a bribe to take on additional risk and may decrease the support for the facility. In addition, Frey and Oberholzer-Gee (1997) show that compensation may undermine feelings of civic duty. In *crowding theory*, financial benefits serve as a signal that individuals ought to evaluate the proposed facility solely in terms of pecuniary gains. This signal may undermine a citizen's willingness to contribute to public goods such as the siting of a socially beneficial facility (for a more general discussion, see Frey (1997)). Given the different theories, at this point it is an empirical question if increases in compensation increase or decrease the willingness to accept a risky facility.

For each of these compensation packages, we also asked the township supervisors to estimate the fraction of residents who would vote for or against this proposal. We will use the share of supporters $(1-a)$ as a proxy for social pressure A. In accordance with hypothesis (i), we expect township supervisors to be more likely to support the facility if A increases, $\beta_5 > 0$. Note that we view township supervisors like other residents with respect to the importance of social pressure for individual decision-making. In contrast, one could argue that supervisors see themselves as local leaders and that they have more expertise in making difficult public decisions than the average resident. Consequently, one would expect that supervisors are less impressionable than other residents. However, it is also possible to argue just the opposite. Supervisors are elected local officials and they thus need to pay considerable attention to the political views of their voters. Hence, we would expect them to be more responsive to social pressure. Ultimately, these are empirical questions. In this chapter, we assume that supervisors are neither more nor less responsive to social pressure than other citizens.

Previous siting research has shown that the willingness to accept a facility is also determined by characteristics of the siting process (Frey and Oberholzer-Gee, 1996). We include a variable F which measures the perceived fairness of the process where larger values of F imply that the siting process is perceived as fairer (see first question in appendix B).

Finally, $\mathbf{X}$ is a matrix of variables that control for township characteristics. For example, to be a candidate for a facility a township must have 500 acres of qualified land. Based on a detailed technical study, the developer disqualified 78 percent of the state land as unsuitable for siting the proposed facility. The Community Partnering Plan contains maps, which show these areas. While very few townships have no suitable land at all, we wanted to make sure that this information did not bias the results of our study. We thus include a dummy variable which takes on a value of one if the respondents believes that his township has at least 500 acres of land that is not disqualified.

We also asked respondents to indicate whether they believed that their township was poorer or richer than the PA average. The public debate surrounding environmental justice suggests that many citizens regard it as unfair if noxious facilities are located in poorer communities (Been, 1994). If this factor is important in the siting process, then a township supervisor who believed his township was poorer than others would be less likely to support the facility in his/her backyard, other things being equal.

When offered the Community Partnering Plan compensation package, 29 percent of all township supervisors stated that they would vote for the facility. They expected the residents of their township to be much more skeptic, indicating that only 15 percent would support the facility. Table 5.1 presents the estimates of our probit analysis for two models: Model I does not include the variable which reflects the township supervisor's perception of residents' support for the facility while Model II incorporates this factor into the analysis.

The results of both models conform to our expectations. Most importantly, social pressure appears to have the hypothesized effect. Township supervisors are more likely to support the facility if more residents favor the project. With every one percentage point increase in popular support, supervisors are 1 percent more likely to endorse the facility. On the basis of these results, it is not possible to reject hypothesis (i). There is an interesting difference of the effects of

Table 5.1   Probability of voting for LLRW facility (results of probit analysis)

Model	(I)		(II)	
Independent Variables	Est. Coefficient (Std. Error)	Δ Prob 'Yes' (asymptotic z-value)	Est. Coefficient (Std. Error)	Δ Prob 'Yes' (asymptotic z-value)
Benefits	0.37 (0.05)	11 percent** (6.81)	0.29 (0.06)	8 percent** (5.05)
Health risks	-0.38 (0.05)	-11 percent** (-7.04)	-0.40 (0.06)	-10 percent** (-6.32)
Percent residents supporting project			0.05 (0.01)	1 percent** (5.87)
Land available	0.74 (0.20)	25 percent** (3.62)	0.73 (0.22)	23 percent** (3.29)
Township richer	-0.150 (0.05)	-4 percent** (-2.86)	-0.18 (0.06)	-5 percent** (-3.06)
Fairness	-0.14 (0.06)	-4 percent** (-2.61)	-.09 (0.06)	-2 percent (-1.46)
Constant	-0.63 (0.25)		-1.30 (0.31)	

Notes:
** significant at the 99 percent level.
Model I: N=415, Log Likelihood = -161.73498, chi2(5) = 124.76, Pseudo R2 = 0.3787.
Model II: N=402, Log Likelihood = -127.07412, chi2(6) = 122.81, Pseudo R2 = 0.4932.

fairness between model 1 and 2. In both specifications, respondents are more likely to support the facility if they perceive the process as fair. However, the effect is only half as big and insignificant in the second model where we control for popular support. One interpretation of this finding is that the perceived fairness of a process serves as a proxy for the general support of residents.

Contrary to our expectations, we find that supervisors from poorer townships are more likely to accept the waste repository. This is consistent with hedonic price studies of the value of life. These studies generally find that the income elasticity of the demand for risk reductions is quite sizeable (Viscusi, 1993). Our result suggests that the unequal distribution of environmental risks with which the environmental justice movement is concerned may partially be due to differences in the demand for such risks.

Figure 5.4 depicts the cumulative density function (solid line) which shows, for different points of the benefit scale used in the questionnaire, what fraction of respondents had indicated that they anticipated benefits lower than these points. For example, 65 percent of the supervisors expected less than 4 benefit points on the six-point scale. Using the estimates of Model II and keeping all other covariates at their mean values, we calculate that, for 65 percent opposition, supervisors have a 50 percent probability of supporting the project when they expect benefits to be 2.8 points. Points like these lie on the sensitivity function which is shown as a dashed line in Figure 5.4. Evidently, the slope of the sensitivity function is greater than the slope of the cumulative density function. At the time of the survey, respondents expected that 84 percent of the residents would oppose the proposed nuclear waste repository when the standard compensation package was offered. This expectation clearly lies to the right of the point of intersection between the two functions. Based on the results of our model, we would thus predict that the opposition in the average PA Township would grow over time. This appears to be consistent with the actual development in Pennsylvania. While about one quarter of all townships discussed the possibility of siting the proposed repository, none of these townships entered formal negotiations with the developer. In the third year of the program, it became increasingly clear that it would be extremely difficult to find a volunteer community. Finally, as of the end of 1998, the State of Pennsylvania gave up and discontinued financing this unsuccessful siting effort.

We next turn to the analysis of compensation effects. Recall that we offered an increase in cash compensation from $600,000 to $1.8 million. In a separate question, we increased the number of jobs from 70 to 210. Township supervisors were more likely to accept the facility when we offered more

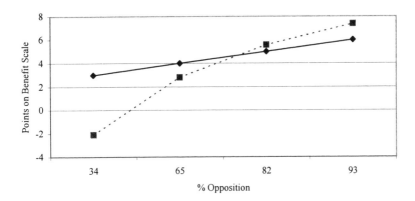

Figure 5.4   Cumulative density and threshold functions estimated from model II

generous compensation packages. With $1.8 million cash being offered, support increased from 29 percent to 38 percent. In the case of jobs, support increased from 29 percent to 31 percent. Table 5.2 analyzes the determinants of support with increased compensation packages.

The first two columns in Table 5.2 analyze the effectiveness of an increase in cash compensation. Not controlling for popular support, the analyst would have concluded that increases in cash compensation make township supervisors 13.4 percentage points more likely to support the project. This is not true (Model IV). This increase in compensation makes respondents 10 percent less likely to support the facility. In equilibrium, their support only increases because they believe that other residents are more likely to support the facility when more compensation is offered. Recall that supervisors believed that 15 percent of the residents would support the facility when the standard compensation package with $600,000 was offered. With $1.8 million, they now think that 38 percent of all residents would endorse the project. It is this swing in popular opinion, and not the increase in compensation per se, that results in an overall increase in the supervisors' support for the facility.

Similar conclusions hold for the increase in jobs. Model V that does not control for popular support shows a much smaller, but statistically significant, increase in support due to the increase in compensation. As can be seen in Model VI, this estimate is biased as well. The true effect of increases in compensation is negative. The positive equilibrium response is due to the supervisors' belief that 24 percent of all residents would favor the facility if it created 210 jobs.

Given these results, it seems natural to ask why the supervisors' reaction

Table 5.2 Probability of voting for LLRW facility with increased compensation (results of probit analysis)

Independent Variables	(III) Est.Coef. (Std. Error)	(III) Δ Prob 'Yes' (z-value)	(IV) Est.Coef. (Std. Error)	(IV) Δ Prob 'Yes' (z-value)	(V) Est.Coef. (Std. Error)	(V) Δ Prob 'Yes' (z-value)	(VI) Est.Coef. (Std. Error)	(VI) Δ Prob 'Yes' (z-value)
Benefits	0.36 (0.05)	12 percent (7.57)	0.26 (0.06)	8 percent (4.48)	0.35 (0.05)	11 percent (6.96)	0.31 (0.06)	8 percent (5.45)
Health Risks	-0.36 (0.05)	-12 percent (-7.50)	-0.41 (0.06)	-13 percent (-6.81)	-0.35 (0.05)	-11 percent (-6.97)	-0.37 (0.06)	-10 percent (-6.30)
Triple Cash	0.40 (0.06)	13 percent (6.17)	-0.33 (0.12)	-10 percent (-2.86)	—	—	—	—
Triple Jobs	—	—	—	—	0.09 (0.05)	3 percent (1.94)	-0.23 (0.08)	-6 percent (-3.00)
Percent Residents Supporting	—	—	0.04 (0.00)	1 percent (9.14)	—	—	0.04 (0.00)	1 percent (8.03)
Land Available	0.66 (0.18)	24 percent (3.60)	0.58 (0.21)	20 percent (2.84)	0.68 (0.19)	24 percent (3.59)	0.59 (0.20)	19 percent (2.89)
Twsp Richer	-0.11 (0.05)	-4 percent (-2.38)	-0.10 (0.1)	-3 percent (-1.93)	-0.14 (0.05)	-4 percent (-2.87)	-0.14 (0.05)	-4 percent (-2.68)
Fairness	-0.14 (0.05)	-5 percent (-2.84)	-0.10 (0.06)	-3 percent (-1.69)	-0.13 (0.05)	-4 percent (-2.65)	-0.08 (0.06)	-2 percent (-1.46)
Constant	-0.63 (0.23)		-1.05 (0.30)		-0.63 (0.24)		-1.21 (0.29)	

Notes:
Model III: N = 815, Log Likelihood = -341.596, chi2(6) = 173.94, Pseudo R2 = 0.3623.
Model IV: N = 783, Log Likelihood = -245.68951, chi2(7) = 183.71, Pseudo R2 = 0.5230.
Model V: N = 822, Log Likelihood = -336.14478, chi2(6) = 135.88, Pseudo R2 = 0.3541.
Model VI: N = 797, Log Likelihood = -266.45508, chi2(7) = 148.80, Pseudo R2 = 0.4706.

to compensation is so different from those of the other residents. Why does compensation decrease the supervisors' support while it seems to increase everyone else's? Crowding theory would probably argue that public officials have particularly strong feelings of civic duty. If compensation crowds out these feelings, supervisors will reduce their support for the facility. Similarly, one might argue that supervisors know more about the developer that offers the compensation. If their view was that these businesses generally do not behave like philanthropic organizations, supervisors might be more likely to interpret the increase in compensation as a signal that the facility is more risky than they originally thought it to be.

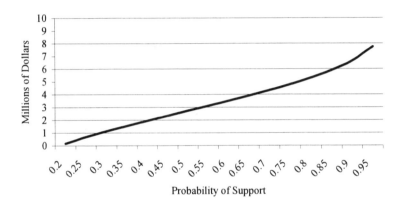

Figure 5.5   *Probability of support by supervisors when compensation increases*

While it is possible to entertain such conjectures, we wish to emphasize that there need not be any differences between supervisors and residents to produce the patterns of support that we observe. As discussed in the theory section, beliefs tend to be self-confirming. Supervisors will publicly declare that they are more willing to accept the facility because they believe that this would be the typical reaction of other residents. If these residents behave in the same manner as the supervisors, they too would state that increases in compensation lower their reluctance to support the facility, thereby confirming the supervisors' initial expectations. In our theoretical framework, it is entirely possible that everybody finds the facility less appealing when more compensation is offered, and yet equilibrium support will increase. Note that the underlying beliefs are not irrational. They are consistent with the *observed* behavior of other residents living in the host community. Figure 5.5

Table 5.3   Influence of other residents on own probability to support the facility (results of probit analysis)

	$1.8 million Cash	210 Jobs	Quality of Life
Est. Coefficient for per-cent residents supporting (Std. Error)	0.04 (0.00)	0.04 (0.00)	0.05 (0.01)
Δ Prob 'Yes' (asymptotic z-value)	1 percent (9.14)	1 percent (8.03)	1 percent (9.09)

presents a simulation of the probability that supervisors will support the facility when compensation increases.[6] Given the publicly observable reaction function in Figure 5.5, it seems perfectly reasonable if residents conclude that their supervisors find increases in compensation attractive.

We now turn our attention to the effectiveness of different compensation measures. Our working hypothesis is that morally questionable forms of compensation would make the opposition relatively more efficient at exerting social pressure. In other words, adding another 10 percent of the residents to the opposing camp should lead to a larger decrease in overall support if the form of compensation is perceived as improper. To test this hypothesis, we varied the basic compensation package by indicating to the supervisors in a separate question that the $600,000 cash compensation would exclusively be used to 'sustain and improve the quality of life' in the host community. This enabled us to contrast responses with the question on cash compensation that did not say how the money would be used. Table 5.3 compares the estimated coefficients for the variable that measures the expected support of residents. The estimated model is identical to the one presented in Table 5.2. In the interest of brevity, we omit all other variables.

We reject the hypothesis that the influence of other residents decreases when morally acceptable forms of compensation are used. As can be read from the coefficients in Table 5.3, a one percentage point increase in the number of residents who support the project always results in supervisors being slightly more than 1 percent more likely to support the facility. Thus, merely changing the form of compensation does not appear to significantly influence the efficiency with which the groups exert social pressure.

6 VEIL OF SILENCE

Our empirical analysis has shown that the support for the proposed nuclear waste facility in Pennsylvania crucially depends on expectations about the level of support by other residents. Given the average expected costs and benefits, our model predicts a corner equilibrium where everyone opposes the facility. This seems to be roughly consistent with the actual developments in Pennsylvania. Despite the generous compensation package and the ability to negotiate even higher benefits, the developer was not able to identify a voluntary host community. As of the end of 1998, the State of Pennsylvania has discontinued this unsuccessful siting effort. In our survey, 78 percent of all township supervisors report that they did not even discuss the siting proposal with residents in their township. Of those who have discussed the siting plans, almost no one expected to continue the discussions in the following year.

In the absence of social pressure, it would be difficult to rationalize this lack of discussion.[7] It would be sufficient to have a single resident who saw the siting plan as a winning proposition. This person could then start a public debate. However, when social pressure is important, the minority who is interested in receiving the compensation is reluctant to bring up the issue. To merely mention the possibility of siting the facility in one's township will surely be interpreted as endorsing the project. What other reason could there be to start a public debate? Thus, the minority of supporters will choose to remain silent if the opposition is expected to be numerous or efficient at producing social pressure. Social pressure thus hides private preferences behind a veil of silence. As Kuran (1995) emphasizes, this silence may permanently distort the information available to society in the long run. If no one articulates the advantages of a policy, society may be lulled into the belief that no such advantages exist. This bias in the available information may then facilitate the emergence of preferences that favor the status quo.

7 PRIVATE AND PUBLIC DECISIONS

We have modeled decision-making in siting conflicts as publicly observable behavior. Thus, there appears to be an easy way out of the dilemma that we described above. If siting decisions were taken privately, for example in a secret poll, individuals need not pay attention to social pressure. They then could reveal their private evaluations of the siting proposal. We feel that this view is misleading for two reasons.

First, as we had emphasized above, political decisions do not fall from the sky. In fact, all decision-making starts with a decision (or a suggestion) to make a decision. Even if a secret ballot is used for the final round of decision-making, someone first needs to come forward and suggest that we should vote on a particular issue. The veil of silence, where it exists, appears to be particularly important in explaining which issues are explicitly on the political agenda and which ones remain hidden.

Second, it is at least an open question if voting processes in fact reveal the citizens' private evaluations. Imagine an intensive political campaign in which individuals publicly either support or oppose a proposed facility. They learn all the arguments that support their publicly stated view. They occasionally reward members of their own group and may even punish individuals belonging to the opposing camp. How likely is it that these individuals, come Election Day, simply forget about their public stance? At this point, we are not able to offer a definite answer to this question. However, our survey appears to indicate that social pressure may matter even in the voting booth. Note that we asked the township supervisors how they would *vote*. In the empirical section, we showed that public opinion matters for these voting intentions. Thus, it seems to be a serious possibility that publicly stated preferences at least influence private voting decisions.

8 CONCLUSIONS

Behavior in siting conflicts is considerably influenced by social pressure. Social pressure is particularly important for very risky projects that impose sizeable negative externalities on the residents of the host community. Once public opinion is formed, increases in compensation do not necessarily lead to an increase in popular support, even if the residents of the prospective host community find the project more attractive. If individuals expect very little support for the proposed facility, a veil of silence may prevent them from even discussing the benefits and costs that are associated with the facility. Outcomes in these processes are sensitive to initial expectations. Given an identical distribution of expected net benefits, different expectations regarding popular support may lead to very different equilibria.

ACKNOWLEDGEMENTS

We would like to thank John Burk, B. Kenneth Greider and James Wheeler for helpful comments. We are indebted to the Pennsylvania State Association of Township Supervisors for their generous help in administering the survey and to the Risk Management and Decision Processes Center of the Wharton School, University of Pennsylvania, for financial support.

NOTES

1. Private waste management companies regularly spend millions of dollars in abortive efforts to site new facilities (Gerrard, 1994, p. 227).
2. We define NIMBY projects as all undertakings that increase overall welfare, but impose net costs on the individuals living in the host community. At the time when the problem became visible, O'Hare (1977) was among the first to suggest the use of compensation to win local support for otherwise unwanted projects.
3. New York Times, 13 December: Section 1:36.
4. 'The Commonwealth of Pennsylvania indicated that it would not use eminent domain to acquire a site in the Community Partnering process unless the host municipality asked it to do so' (Chem-Nuclear Systems, 1996).
5. After mentioning all the benefits and costs associated with the facility, we asked the township supervisors: 'Suppose your township holds a referendum on hosting the facility tomorrow. Would you personally vote for or against the facility in such a referendum?'.
6. The simulation is based on Model II in Table 6.2. All covariates are kept at their mean values. The compensation needed to reach a value V of the mean normal index that is associated with the desired probability of support is given by

$$E = \frac{V - \beta_1 - \beta_2 B_i - \beta_3 C_i - \beta_5 A - \beta_6 F - \beta_7 \mathbf{X} - \beta_5 \alpha_1}{\beta_4 + \beta_5 \alpha_2}$$

where the parameters α_1 and α_2 come out of a supplementary regression $A = \alpha_1 + \alpha_2 E$ which describes how supervisors expect residents to change their support when compensation increases.
7. Our view is that – in the absence of social pressure - it would be virtually costless for an individual to start discussing the project with her neighbors. Thus, the standard economic rationale that individuals do not contribute to public goods does not apply here.

APPENDIX A

Proof of Proposition

There are four cases to consider. In case 1, the individual sensitivity function lies above the cumulative distribution function. This implies that for any initial belief $\hat{a}_{t1} < 1$, the actual opposition will be greater than expected and individuals will update their beliefs accordingly, $\hat{a}_{t1} < \hat{a}_{t2}$. At $\hat{a} = 1$, the expected opposition equals the realized opposition. Given this self-confirming belief, everyone opposing the facility is a Nash equilibrium because not even the individual expecting the highest net benefit is willing to support the project, i.e., in case 1 $x'(1) > G(x_h)$. The same logic applies to case 2, where the individual sensitivity function lies below the cumulative distribution function. Here, actual opposition turns out to be always smaller than expected opposition for any initial belief $\hat{a}_{t1} > 0$. In equilibrium, everyone supports the facility.

In case 3, $x'(0) > G(x) > x'(1)$. Given that both functions are continuous, they intersect at least once. At the point of intersection, expected opposition equals actual opposition, $a = G[x'(a)]$. Now, no individual has an incentive to deviate from his policy position. This self-confirming belief is locally stable. In case 4, $G(x) > x'(0)$, $G(x) < x'(1)$. The same reasoning as in case 3 applies here. However, the self-confirming beliefs at the point of intersection are not locally stable.

APPENDIX B

Survey Questions

(Listed in the order in which they appear in the questionnaire; possible answers are given in parentheses.)

- The current process is fair.
  (rated on a six-point scale from 'do not agree at all' to 'fully agree')
- How serious do you believe your personal health risk would be from the facility if it is built in your township?
  (rated on a six-point scale from 'not at all serious' to 'very serious')
- Pennsylvania and Chem-Nuclear Systems, the developer of the Pennsylvania waste disposal facility, offer benefits to a municipality if it is willing to host the LLRW disposal facility. Suppose the offer was to provide 70 permanent jobs (preference would be given to local hiring); a cash payment of $600,000 per year, for the next 30 years; payment of all township and school property taxes for primary residences within two miles of the facility, for the next 30 years; and a two-year guarantee of home sale prices within two miles of the facility.
  How much better off or worse off would you personally be if your municipality hosted the nuclear waste facility and received the above benefit package?
  (rated on a seven-point scale from 'much worse off' to 'much better off')
- Given the benefits package mentioned above, what percentage of residents do you think would vote for and against the facility?
  (percent vote for, percent vote against, percent not vote)
- How would you vote in such a referendum?
  (vote for the facility, vote against the facility, and not vote)
- Suppose the nuclear waste project created 210 jobs instead of 70. Half of these jobs paid more than $30,000, the other half less. Preference would be given to local hiring. The rest of the benefits package remains the same.
  What percentage of residents do you think would vote for and against the facility?
- Given the higher number of jobs, how would you vote in such a referendum?

- Suppose the voters in your township knew that the cash payment of $600,000 per year would be used exclusively to sustain and improve the quality of their lives (for example, by preserving the rural character of your township and keeping farming attractive).
  What percentage of residents do you think would vote for and against the facility?
- Given this use of the cash payment, how would you vote in such a referendum?
- Suppose the developer tripled the cash payment to the municipality from $600,000 per year to $1.8 million while keeping the rest of the benefits package the same.
- What percentage of residents do you think would vote for and against the facility?
- Given this higher cash payment, how would you vote in such a referendum?
- Have you discussed the possibility of hosting the LLRW disposal facility with the residents in your township?
  (yes, no)
- If no, how likely do you feel that there will be discussion in the next year? (rated on a six-point scale from 'very unlikely' to 'very likely')
- In your opinion, is your township richer or poorer than the PA average? (rated on a seven-point scale from 'much poorer' to 'much richer')
- Does your township have at least 500 acres of land that has not been disqualified as a potential site for the disposal facility?
  (yes, no, don't know)

REFERENCES

Akerlof, George A. (1980), 'A Theory of Social Custom, of Which Unemployment May Be One Consequence', *Quarterly Journal of Economics*, June, **94** (4), 749–75.

Been, Vicki (1994), 'Locally Undesirable Land Uses in Minority Neighborhoods: Disproportionate Siting or Market Dynamics?', *The Yale Law Journal*, April, **103** (6), 1383–422.

Carnes, S.A. (1983), 'Incentives and Nuclear Waste Siting', *Energy Systems and Policy*, June, **7** (4), 324–51.

Chem-Nuclear Systems, Inc. (1996), *Community Partnering Plan: Pennsylvania Low-level Radioactive Waste Disposal Facility*, Harrisburg: CNSI.

Coursey, Don and Sangheon Kim (1997), 'An Examination of Compensation Mechanisms to Solve the NIMBY Problem', The Irving B. Harris Graduate School of Public Policy Studies, The University of Chicago.

Dunlap, Riley E. and Rodney K. Baxter (1988), 'Public Reaction to Siting a High- level Nuclear Waste Repository at Hanford: A Survey of Local Area Residents', Report prepared by the Social and Economic Sciences Research Center, Washington State

University.

Frey, Bruno S. (1997), *Not Just for the Money: An Economic Theory of Personal Motivation*, Cheltenham: Edward Elgar.

Frey, Bruno S. and Felix Oberholzer-Gee (1996), 'Fair Siting Procedures: An Empirical Analysis of Their Importance and Characteristics', *Journal of Policy Analysis and Management*, Summer, **15** (3), 353–76.

Frey, Bruno S. and Felix Oberholzer-Gee (1997), 'The Cost of Price Incentives: An Empirical Analysis of Motivation Crowding-Out', *American Economic Review*, September, **87** (4), 746–55.

Frey, Bruno S., Felix Oberholzer-Gee and Reiner Eichenberger (1996), 'The Old Lady Visits Your Backyard: A Tale of Morals and Markets', *Journal of Political Economy*, December, **104** (6), 193–209.

Gerrard, Michael B. (1994), *Whose Backyard, Whose Risk: Fear And Fairness in Toxic and Nuclear Waste Siting*, Cambridge, Mass: MIT Press.

Granovetter, Marc (1978), 'Threshold Models of Collective Behavior', *American Journal of Sociology*, March, **83** (1), 1420–43.

Herzik, Eric (1993), 'Nevada Statewide Telephone Poll Survey Data', Report presented to Nevada State and Local Government Planning Group, University of Nevada, Reno.

Kunreuther, Howard and Douglas Easterling (1990), 'Are Risk-Benefit Tradeoffs Possible in Siting Hazardous Facilities?' *American Economic Review*, May, **80** (2), 252–56.

Kuran, Timur (1987), 'Preference Falsification, Policy Continuity and Collective Conservatism', *Economic Journal*, September, **97** (387), 642–65.

Kuran, Timur (1995), *Private Truths, Public Lies: The Social Consequences of Preference Falsification*, Cambridge: Harvard University Press.

O'Hare, Michael (1977), 'Not on My Block You Don't – Facility Siting and the Strategic Importance of Compensation', *Public Policy*, June, **25** (3), 407-58.

O'Hare, Michael, Lawrence Bacow and Debra Sanderson (1983), *Facility Siting and Public Opposition*, New York: Van Nostrand Reinhold.

Pennsylvania State Association of Township Supervisors (1996), 'Any Volunteers?', *Pennsylvania Township News* September.

Rabe, Barry G. (1994), *Beyond NIMBY: Hazardous Waste Siting in Canada and the United States*, Washington, DC: Brookings Institution.

Schelling, Thomas C. (1978), *Micromotives and Macrobehavior*, New York: Norton.

Jenkins-Smith, Hank and Howard Kunreuther (1998), 'Mitigation and Compensation As Policy Tools for Siting: Evidence from Field Survey Data', Mimeo, The Wharton School, University of Pennsylvania.

Viscusi, W. Kip (1993), 'The Value of Risks to Life and Health', *Journal of Economic Literature*, December, **31** (4), 1912–46.

Zeiss, Christopher (1996), 'Directions for Engineering Contributions to Successfully Siting Hazardous Waste Facilities', in Don Munton (ed.), *Hazardous Waste Siting and Democratic Choice*, Washington, DC: Georgetown University Press.

6. The Limits of Flexible and Adaptive Institutions: The Japanese Government's Role in Nuclear Power Plant Siting over the Post War Period*

Daniel P. Aldrich

This chapter systematically examines the Japanese government's deliberate creation of institutions and strategies designed to alter citizen preferences and reduce resistance to often controversial facilities. I show that the Japanese state has not only created such strategies in an attempt to smooth the siting of nuclear power plants and other large scale facilities, but has continually upgraded and refined these tools as it has learned from its experiences. My results support previous work which found that bureaucratic and political leaders in democracies are not swayed by public opinion; instead, they attempt to sway it. This study demonstrates that the Japanese government simultaneously delegates authority for bargaining to private utility companies while intensively utilizing a variety of policy tools to structure citizen preferences before any actual citizen-utility bargaining over specific sites. Finally, despite the innovation and flexibility shown by the Japanese state in pursuing its siting goals through flexible, adaptive institutions (see Kasperson, Chapter 2; Barthe and Mayes, Chapter 8), Japanese citizens have stalled or ended many siting projects in the past decade.

1 HOW HAS JAPAN BEEN SO SUCCESSFUL AT SITING CONTROVERSIAL FACILITIES?

Observers have been struck by a seeming incongruity: Japan, the only nation in the world against which atomic weaponry has been used, has been able to develop one of the most advanced civilian nuclear energy programs in the world, complete with plans for fast breeder reactors, nuclear fuel recycling and new plants, while other advanced industrial democracies have done the opposite (Pickett, 2002). Germany recently set up a moratorium on nuclear reactors, America ceased ordering new plants in the mid 1970s, and even

France has cancelled its ambitious plans for a fast breeder reactor. Furthermore, despite protests which began against the very first attempt at siting reactors (Asahi Shinbun, 3 September 1957) and continued against almost every consecutive attempt (Hangenpatsu Undō Zenkoku Renraku kai, 1997; Nikkei Shinbun, 6 August 1988), and repeated talk amongst Japanese scholars of a *kaku arerugi* (nuclear allergy), Japanese communities continue to volunteer to host such facilities, and some have even offered to host interim radioactive waste storage facilities (Interviews with Diet members, Winter 2002).

In terms of other large scale public works facilities, such as dams and airports, the Japanese state has also pushed ahead of other advanced democracies. Japan's ministries continue to pursue a myriad of costly construction projects despite protests from local communities and data showing that initial estimates of long term demand which triggered project planning were often inflated (McCormack, 1997; Kerr, 2001). Japan has more than 3,000 dams, eight international airports, and 52 nuclear reactors – and the government plans to build more of each. How has the Japanese state been so successful in its siting of nuclear power plants, dams, and airports? Cultural and procedural explanations provide two often-heard answers to this question.

Many researchers have argued that cultural factors have been the primary issues in citizen-state relations. Doi (1974), Lebra (1976), Nakane (1978), and Pye (1985), among others, have argued that Japan's political culture involves vertical hierarchy, tradition, social consensus, repression of the self for the sake of the group, and compromise. These culturalist theories share the belief that citizens will often refrain from speaking or acting out against a policy due to peer pressure and socialization. Comparative studies of Japan's political culture have labeled it as one of low political efficacy, that is, a society in which citizens do not believe that their input makes a difference in the outcome of political processes (Nakamura, 1975). These scholars argue that due to social peer group pressure against resistance, and stress placed on obedience to higher level political figures, Japanese citizens have often been unable to effectively organize and alter central government plans. More importantly, they argue, Japanese citizens' lack of belief in their efficacy itself acts as a barrier to participation – believing their involvement to be a waste of time, many opt for exit, not voice (Hirschman, 1970; see LeBlanc (1999) for an analysis of how women in Japan often remove themselves from the world of 'mainstream' politics).

Others have posited that procedural and constitutional structures, not cultural factors, deeply effect state-citizen interactions. Cohen, McCubbins, and Rosenbluth have argued that the lack of access points to the civilian nuclear program has prevented citizens and NGOs from slowing down or stopping the process of constructing new plants as was done in America (Cohen et al.,

1995). Similarly, Pekkanen has argued that political factors, more specifi-
cally the regulations and procedures relating to formal recognition as a
nonprofit group in Japan, have created a situation with many often ineffective local citizen groups and lack of powerful national ones (Pekkanen,
2000a; 2000b). Vosse has similarly shown how nonprofit status has been an
elusive goal for the majority of NGOs which have remained unrecognized by
the central government and hence unable to incorporate, without access to
resources like cheaper mail rates, the benefits of tax deductible contributions,
and the ability to sign contracts (Vosse, 2000; see also Nakamura, 2002).
Groups which sought nonprofit status could only do so with the sponsorship
of a government ministry or agency, which would place a retired bureaucrat
on its board of directors (Broadbent, 2002, p. 22). Although the number of
NGOs has surged after alterations to the NGO Law, as one author put it,
'[i]n terms of actual policy outcome, their influence has been largely limited'
(Kamimura, 2001, p. 13). These analysts have focused upon the passive
ways in which procedures discourage citizens from mobilizing around political and social issues.

2   AN ACTIVE AND INNOVATIVE CENTRAL GOVERNMENT

No doubt both Japan's political culture and existing procedures and regulations have dampened citizen resistance to government policies. But this
chapter elucidates the extent to which the Post-War Japanese state has created and then improved institutions designed to penetrate society in order to
alter citizen preferences and suppress resistance. Earlier studies of Japan's
nuclear power field focused on the reciprocal consent between states and
power utilities, arguing that the state maintains jurisdiction over nuclear
power but delegates negotiation for specific plants to energy companies
(Samuels, 1987). Similarly, Lesbirel understood that the state had delegated
negotiations to the private sector and investigated bargaining power between
local communities and private utilities (Lesbirel, 1998).

This study builds on earlier works to illuminate how the state simultaneously delegates the task of siting nuclear power plants to private companies
but nevertheless seeks to penetrate civil society through a wide variety of
policy tools and strategies. I join with other scholars like Garon (1997) and
Nakamura (2002) in emphasizing the active and creative responses of the
state in handling, avoiding, and co-opting citizen resistance. McAvoy (1999)
and Jacobs and Shapiro (2000) have begun to underscore the importance of
the ways in which public opinion does not sway bureaucratic and political
leaders; rather, they attempt to sway it.

This chapter will focus on the ways in which the central state has attempted to further its national energy, infrastructure, and transportation goals often over the objections of local citizens movements. In order to construct the airports, dams, nuclear power plants, and waste dumps so necessary for advanced industrial societies as a whole but so unwanted by their neighbors, the Japanese state has developed a range of methods and strategies, from coercive to voluntary, to further what state authorities see as the national interest over what critics have branded 'local egoism' (*chiiki ego* in Japanese). This chapter will center on the siting of nuclear power facilities as that struggle has led the government to develop the broadest range of strategies from the earliest days of the technology. Although private utility companies in Japan carry out the siting of nuclear power plants much like private firms in America, the government here plays a fundamental role in the process. Like other democracies which have promoted energy plans involving nuclear power, Japan has faced increasing resistance to atomic reactors over time (Rosa and Dunlap, 1994). The Japanese state has identified the possible obstacles to its energy plans, primarily fishing cooperatives, local government leaders, youth, and women, and has targeted them with a variety of programs designed to make them more receptive to nuclear power and hence more likely to host a nuclear reactor in their community or refrain from opposing one elsewhere. Although these strategies may not have always been successful in recent years, their presence has until now been understudied and the Japanese government's role in siting them undertheorized.[1]

3 CLASSIFYING STATE TOOLS

This chapter builds on the work of Schneider and Ingram (1990) by classifying state tools in five main categories: authority, incentive, capacity, symbolic/hortatory, and learning. Authority tools 'grant permission, prohibit, or require action under designated circumstances' (Schneider and Ingram, 1990, p. 514) and include land expropriation measures. Incentive tools rely on 'tangible payoffs, positive or negative, to induce compliance or encourage utilization' (Schneider and Ingram, 1990, p. 515), and among other mechanisms, involve redistribution to host communities. Capacity tools 'provide information, training, education, and resources to enable individuals, groups or agencies to make decisions or carry out activities' (Schneider and Ingram, 1990, p. 517). This chapter focuses on programs which provide pro-nuclear energy education and information to citizens who seek to know more about it. Symbolic and hortatory tools 'bring into decision situations cultural notions of right, wrong, justice, individualism, equality, obligations, and so forth' (Schneider and Ingram, 1990, p. 519). Yearly awards ceremonies to 'helpful' local politicians, personal visits by bureaucrats to targeted communities, the creation of Nuclear Power Day to celebrate atomic energy, and targeted public relations campaigns on television and in the media comprise some of the hortatory tools that the Ministry of International Trade and Industry (MITI, now METI) has developed. Learning tools are those used by the state to learn from past experience and draw lessons through evaluation. I will argue that MITI has constantly monitored citizen responses in order to better update its tactics and strategy, and has created, among other learning tools, environmental assessment and public hearings to learn what issues concern citizens as well as a new ministerial council to coordinate analysis of siting problems.

Table 6.1   *Tools for siting nuclear power plants (from Schneider and Ingram 1990)*

Type of Tool	Goal	Paradigm Example	Specific Application	Frequency
Authority	Prohibit or require action	Land Expropriation	Maki-machi	Infrequent
Incentive	Induce compliance	Dengen Sanpō	Aid money to host communities	Constant
Capacity	Provide information and education	Educational programs	Pro-nuclear energy syllabi	Constant
Symbolic	Appeals to tangible symbols	MITI 'coming to the people'	Pep talks and awards ceremonies	Less frequent
Learning	State seeks to draw lessons	New analytical institutions	Inter ministerial Council	Infrequent

As I have mentioned above, the government has not allowed the tactics to stagnate, but has constantly improved its strategies by, among other methods, enlarging and improving its redistribution mechanisms and delegating responsibility for public relations to professional, 'independent' organizations.

Authority Tools: Eminent Domain

Japan's protection of individual property rights has a long history, but the post War Constitution provided a mechanism for the government to override citizens in certain cases. Called the *Tochi shūyō hō* in Japanese, Japan's law of eminent domain allows government officials at the prefectural and central levels to approve the forced removal of land from citizens for *kōkyō jigyō* (public industries and facilities), projects which provide not just private goods but semi-public and public ones as well. Railroad tracks, subway stations, power transmission lines, dams, airports, and power generation stations fall under this designation. Even though private companies often carry out the planning and construction of these facilities, project planners, if a prefectural level committee approves, can expropriate land as necessary (Adachi, 1991).

In an interesting twist, government and private authorities actually need to use the full force of the law. If citizens refuse to sell initially, and project planners seek permission to force the individuals to sell their land, planners who carry the expropriation process through to the end have no obligation to provide 'market price' for that property. In many cases, if prefectural councils approve their request for use of eminent domain, authorities can merely use the threat of buying the land in question for less than market value to encourage citizens to engage in *wakai*, or compromise, with authorities (Interview with Japanese government officials, 2002).

Land expropriation has been used most infamously by the central government during the construction of the New International Airport at Narita in Chiba prefecture in the mid 1960s and early 1970s. At that time, activist farmers of the Sanrizuka movement refused to sell, and the government, upon receiving permission to expropriate the land, sent in thousands of police troops to forcibly evict the tenants. In the resulting battles, which resembled a medieval combat zone – with student radicals and farmers dug into towers and trenches raining metal missiles, Molotov cocktails, and rocks on riot police equipped with shields and staves – four police officers carrying out and two citizens resisting the expropriation were killed (Bowen, 1975; Apter and Sawa, 1984).

The Ministry of Construction regularly uses the Land Expropriation Law to force an end to struggles with local land owners over the construction of dams which would destroy their villages and flood their homes (Interviews with officials from the Ministry of Land, Infrastructure, and Transport, February 2003). For example, several hundred citizens had to be relocated because a reservoir created by a recently completed dam in Kanagawa Prefecture would soon submerge their houses (Interview with dam authorities, February 2003). Even with the understanding that their resistance could mean receiving less than market value for their property, some refused to sell willingly; hence the Ministry of Construction used the Expropriation Law to complete the forced move. The expropriations of land from unwilling citizens in the Shimouke and Matsubara Dam cases in Oita Prefecture and the Ainu minority group in the Nibutani Dam case in Hokkaido provided anti-dam opponents with more ammunition against 'coercive' dam siting methods. In several cases, authorities have used eminent domain to appropriate the necessary land for thermal power plants, such as the Matsushima coal-fired reactor and the Ohsaki liquefied petroleum gas plant. One Diet member, a former high ranking official in a power utility, believed that his former company had used the expropriation law in at least 20 cases involving thermal plant or electricity transmission line location.

Interestingly, Japanese authorities have, at various times, discussed using the expropriation law in the field of nuclear power plant siting, but have never done so. The desire to use expropriation was especially strong during the Maki-machi wrangle, when many years after the siting process of a nuclear power plant had begun local citizens successfully brought about a referendum (*jūmin tōhyō*) which prevented the sale of land to the utility. Internal memos from MITI bureaucrats to their colleagues indicate that they all agreed that the plant would fit under the definition of 'public enterprise' but that the possible negative reaction combined with the difficulties in convincing the legal authorities that the plant could not have been located in another spot prevented them from using the powers available to them. In interviews METI officials stated that they felt if they had used land expropriation in the Maki case, future mayors who had the possibility of being more pro-facility would respond negatively (Interviews with METI officials, Fall 2002).

Officials who had worked with the Narita case and government bureaucrats currently working on siting issues agreed that after the negative publicity and causalities of the Narita Airport case, the government began to think more seriously about citizen reaction before expropriating land. As a result, authorities argue that they have become more careful about applying eminent domain due to the negative image of such coercive strategies (Interviews with bureaucrats in dam siting, nuclear power siting, airport siting, 2002–2003).

Hortatory Tools

MITI officials decided that their presence, often absent in the affairs of communities far from Tokyo, would make the siting process of often unwanted projects a more legitimate one, so they began to visit targeted localities to explain the energy needs of the nation and warn about the coming shortages if nuclear power plants were not constructed (OECD, 1984). For example, in the case of Kaminoseki, as negotiations between land owners, fishermen, and the utility dragged on in the 1980s, MITI officials visited the local citizens and gave a series of talks about the need for the plants in the scheme of the overall energy plans (Interviews with utility officials, 5 November 2002). MITI and STA also began establishing branch offices and 'atomic energy centers' in 1972 in possible host localities to show the seriousness of government intent and provide the bureaucrats more direct access to their 'constituents'. These centers allowed citizens to speak directly with representatives from the local government, a rare event for many of them.

When anti-nuclear groups protested against the Kashiwazaki Kariwa complex in Niigata prefecture, the STA sent in the former Science and Technology minister to give a 'pep talk' [*happa wo kake*] to the people emphasizing the importance for the national energy crisis of building such plants quickly (Kamata, 1991, p. 239). MITI officials from local branch offices, such as those in Hiroshima, often travel to or invite bureaucrats and citizens from towns targeted for nuclear power plants to discuss implementing the planned project. Beginning in 2001, MITI officials began traveling to the prefectures of Fukui, Fukushima, and Niigata – prefectures with the highest concentration of nuclear power plants – to carry out PR activities on a permanent basis in three to four person teams (Interviews with MITI officials, 28 August 2002).

Along with 'coming to the people' to encourage them to invite in nuclear power plants, MITI officials decided to create a series of yearly awards ceremonies to praise officials who assisted in the siting process and 'bring the people to them'. Beginning in the early 1980s, MITI and the Prime Minister's office began a program which would celebrate and reward those local government officials who had contributed to the success of nuclear power plant and other energy facility siting. This program, called the *Dengen ricchi sokushin kōrōsha hyōshō*, or Citation Ceremony for Electric Power Sources Siting Promoters occurs yearly, usually in July (METI, 2001). At the ceremony the winners come to Tokyo to meet with the Prime Minister at his residence and receive their rewards directly from him in front of national media outlets (Asahi Shinbun, 28 July 2000; 27 July 1989; 28 July 1988; 28 July 1987; 31 July 1986). MITI created this hortatory program to encourage mayors from towns targeted for reactors to do all that they could to assist the nation in its push for indigenous power supplies (Denki Shinbun, 28 July 2000).

Along with awards ceremonies, central government bureaucrats established yearly safety and promotion days to help keep the issue of nuclear power positive and salient in the minds of Japanese citizens. Until 1964 the Science and Technology Agency held various commemoration events throughout the country under the sponsorship of the government during the week from 18 April, which had been designated 'invention day', with another day in the week selected as 'Atomic Energy Day'. In 1964 the Japanese government decided to promote its plans for nuclear power development by establishing a Nuclear Power Day to be celebrated yearly on 26 October (Asahi Shinbun, 31 July 1964).[2] On Nuclear Power day the government sponsors children's essay contests on the necessity and safety of nuclear power, provides free concerts and pavilions focusing on energy use, and runs commercials in both print and television media to emphasize the need for atomic power. Additionally, the government began from the earliest days of Nuclear Power Day to open museums for free to the public, hand out pamphlets in subways and put up posters there, and allow the public access to nuclear facilities themselves (Japan Atomic Industrial Forum (JAIF), 1969, 13 (11), p. 30).

Government planners, responding to years of opinion polls which showed that young women and mothers had the greatest antipathy to nuclear facilities, began to focus their efforts on that demographic subset of the population. Newspaper articles have stressed that women have been at the heart of anti-nuclear power plant campaigns (Asahi Shinbun, 5 July 1988). In interviews, METI officials confirmed that women were 'important opinion holders' and that they believed swaying their opinion was important (Interviews with METI officials, 21 January 2003). The ads on Nuclear Power Day soon shifted to become images of women, often with children, accompanied by messages of safety, security, and energy need. Public relations activities carried out by MITI were not limited to Nuclear Power day. Spending more than 900,000 yen a year through the early 1970s, MITI sponsored the distribution of materials to communities already having or targeted for nuclear power plants to spread 'understanding about the safety of nuclear power' (JAIF, 1970, 14 (10), p. 26).

Along with shifting its persuasive messages to focus upon women, Japanese government officials early on recognized the power held by local fishermen's cooperatives, *gyogyō rōdō kumiai*. Because Japanese utility companies decided to utilize water drawn in from the ocean for cooling down their nuclear reactors, the cooperation of fishing cooperatives became vital to the successful planning of Japan's nuclear power industry. Japanese law requires companies which impinge upon the fishing areas of cooperatives to purchase the rights to those areas, with the fishing cooperative needing a two-thirds majority to approve compensation plans for selling those fishing rights (*gyogyō hoshōryo*). Without the approval of the local cooperatives, siting cannot continue. Cooperatives have a number of reasons to resist siting, and primary among them are concerns about the loss of livelihood from the fishing that must be suspended indefinitely once they transfer their rights to the utility. Beyond that, however, cooperatives have feared the higher temperatures of water discharged by the plants will negatively affect aquatic life and its habitats. Further, utilities used to discharge radioactive liquids along with the water back into the ocean, creating additional worries for fishermen (JAIF, 1966, 10 (2)).

Reluctant fishing cooperatives who have not been willing to deal with authorities have been the cause of a number of abandoned projects and lengthy delays. In Kaminoseki, the fishing cooperative at Iwaishima continues to refuse to deal with government and business negotiators, a factor involved in the ever lengthening 'lead time' necessary for the plant's construction (Interview with local activist, Kaminoseki, 4 November 2002). In Ashihama, Maki, and elsewhere, activist fishermen derailed plans for nuclear power plants (see Lesbirel, 1998). Utilities interested in purchasing the fishing rights from these cooperatives have had to continually increase the amount of money they have offered, in some recent cases reaching more than 15 billion yen.

The prime Minister's office ordered a number of studies to be done to reassure fishermen that the effects of both temperature increases and possible radioactivity would be negligible. Over time, the government developed more sophisticated approaches to ensuring the cooperation of fishermen. The government sponsored fish farms which would be heated by the discharge itself, along with studies and lectures to be published and discussed in media read and watched by fishermen reassuring them that there would be no danger to their livelihood. These studies, published in regular columns in journals read by fishermen like *Suisankai* [Fishing World] assure readers that they should not be concerned about radioactivity and that presence of nuclear power plants will not damage or reduce fishing catches (Suisankai, 2000; 2002). In many cases, the MITI contracted the project to organizations like the Japan Fishery Resources Conservation Association, with budgets ranging from 40 million yen for each fish farm project. The Siting Center, a METI spin-off which produces public relations materials on nuclear power, co-publishes studies of waste water discharge with the Association for the Development of Warm Water Fish Farming. By providing aid in the creation of effluent water-using fish farms and greenhouses and publishing studies which downplay the dangers of waste water, MITI helped to ensure the cooperation of fishing cooperatives, which not only gained assurances about safety, but also jobs in these fish farming projects.

Incentive Tools

MITI has created several systems of rewarding communities which host electricity producing facilities, whether hydroelectric, thermal, or nuclear. In the language of political economy, the central government provides side payments to host communities through a redistributive system. For example, as a bonus to communities willing to accept nuclear power plants, MITI, whose responsibility includes setting electricity rates, provided them with major discounts on their electricity bills. The central government created the most well known compensation system called *Dengen Sanpō* in the early 1970s by institutionalizing previously *ad hoc* compensation to host communities.

Dengen Sanpō began as series of local incentive measures for communities which hosted nuclear power plants. Initially called the Atomic Energy Zoning Plan for Tokaimura district, the first area to receive a nuclear reactor in Japan, the plans sponsored by the Atomic Energy Commission provided funds for roads, ports, and bridge construction to assist the construction efforts in the area in the late 1960s.[3] Until 1971, Tokai was the only area to receive such funding. In 1973, after years of urgent pleas from localities which believed that they should be receiving some sort of 'compensation' for the presence of these facilities in their towns, MITI proposed a Diet bill which would 'facilitate the development of local areas near power plants through roads, ports, industrial infrastructure, and radiation monitoring' (JAIF, 1978, 17 (2), p. 30). The bill had the central government bear a certain percentage of the costs of infrastructure development in towns with nuclear, fossil fueled, and hydroelectric power facilities. According to the bill, if local governments which hosted such power plants wanted a new school, road system, or similar infrastructure project, the government would help pay for a large percentage of it (Asahi Shinbun, 1 July 1974).

The final version of the bill brought with it three laws, eventually gaining the name *Dengen Sanpō* in Japanese, an abbreviation for the Three Power Source Development Laws. The Power Sources Development Taxation Law levied a tax on the power sold by utilities at the rate of 85 yen per 1000 kilowatt hour. The Power Resources Development Special Account Law set up the particulars of the ways in which the money would be collected and distributed, while the third law, known as the Law on Adjustment of Areas Surrounding Generating Plants, laid out the subsidy system of grants in aid. When first established, the Dengen Sanpō had with it ceilings on the amount of money that the central government would provide to infrastructure projects and a five-year time limit (the shorter of the following two: the period from start to finish of the plant construction work or five years after the beginning of the construction work) (see Yoshioka, 1999, pp. 144–5; also JAIF, 1974, 19(9), p. 19). While the money was available to host communities with hydroelectric, fossil, and nuclear plants, the amount available to nuclear power plant hosting communities was the largest (Lesbirel, 1998, p. 36). For example, by 2002, out of the 20 subcategories of grants and subsidies available to communities hosting power plants, all 20 were available only to nuclear power plant hosting communities, while only 10 were connected to thermal plants and 11 to hydroelectric plants (METI, 2002, p. 7).

Officially, Japanese officials deny that Diet politicians become directly involved in the siting of nuclear power plants and other facilities (Interviews with bureaucrats and Diet members, Fall and Winter 2002). However, Dengen Sanpō fits overall with Japan's pork barrel system, in which the Liberal Democratic Party, Japan's long ruling conservative party, distributes money to construction and other firms in conservative rural areas who have traditionally supported the LDP (see Johnson, 1982; Woodall, 1996). One scholar argued that '*Jiminto seiji de wa okane wa kaiketsu*' [For the LDP, money provides the solution] (Interview, 5 July 2002). A newspaper reporter told me that 'Construction firms are huge fans of nuclear power plants, and support mayors who in turn push for additional subsidies and funds that can be used in construction' (Interview with Asahi Shinbun staff writer, 28 August 2002). A number of critical scholars have argued that they see evidence of the hands of LDP politicians in the process, whether in the siting of a number of power plants in the Niigata constituency of former PM Tanaka Kakuei or in the initial siting of the first nuclear plant in Tokaimura. Descriptions of the siting processes of the Narita airport, for example, have underscored the role played by LDP politicians eager to have their friends profit from selling previously unwanted property suddenly needed by the state (Kamata, 1991). Additionally, a number of Diet members sit or officiate as members or directors of pro-nuclear siting organizations, such as the Council for Nuclear Fuel Cycle (accessible at http://www.cnfc.or.jp).

Capacity Tools: Tours and Trips for Citizens

Beginning in the 1970s, MITI came to the realization that many citizens had at least two distinct fears about nuclear power facilities. The first involved a generalized concern about health and lifestyle over the possibility of an accident or the leakage of radiation. The second concern focused on livelihood, especially for farmers and occasionally fishermen, who believed that if their community were to host a nuclear power plant, customers, fearful of radiation in their product, would cease to buy their goods. MITI responded with a program in which citizens in areas being targeted for nuclear power plants would be taken via bus or airplane to other localities to view working power plants and speak with neighbors of the plants. (A program to assist the producers of goods in reactor-hosting communities was developed later, as will be shown below.)

By being exposed to a situation in which the power plant was already accepted, citizens were taught the normalcy of life near plants and shown success stories of how farmers, fishermen, and women coexisted peacefully with these facilities (Asahi Shinbun Yamaguchi Shikyoku, 2001). One activist told me that the government had been involved in flying local residents from their small coastal village in a coastal prefecture at the southern tip of Japan, all the way up to Rokkasho in Aomori prefecture in the north, to see nuclear facilities there (Interview with local activist, Winter 2002). Utility company employees supported this story and added that the government had also funded trips to Shimane and Genkai, closer sites of nuclear plants, so that a 'consensus' could be built among local citizens (Interview with electric utility officials, 5 November 2002).

Educational activities have taken up much of the time of government officials concerned with nuclear energy. As early as 1958 governmental authorities in Japan began to realize that local communities were wary, if not opposed, to the idea of atomic power, and authorities believed that providing additional information about atomic energy would reduce those fears. The government began to set up educational structures which would provide information to local communities. Through lectures by central government affiliated scientists, slide shows, and movies, nuclear power was promoted to students across the nation.

JAERO (Japan Atomic Energy Relations Organization) began offering 300 or so free classes and seminars a year in the early 1970s to local communities and schools which can vouch for the presence of five or more people at the meeting. Given three weeks notice, JAERO will send its trained cadre of teachers to schools, houses, hospitals, and public facilities to provide one- to two-hour seminars on the safety and necessity of nuclear power (JAERO brochure, 2002). Additionally, MITI, both directly and through JAERO, provides a number of programs for middle and high school students, ranging from educational materials for syllabi on nuclear energy and atoms to field trips for students who visit functioning nuclear power plants. To teach children, JAERO provides primers which use events from the history of Japan's development of its nuclear program along with weekly comics often reprinted or serialized in national newspapers and thick comic books (*manga*). Along with teaching students about the benefits of nuclear power, JAERO provides seminars to local government officials (Communication with JAERO officials, 8 August 2002). JAERO records of activities in 2001 show that educators provided classes and seminars to more than 4,500 people across Japan, ranging from Hokkaido in the north to Yamaguchi prefecture in the south (JAERO, 2002).

More recently, governmental authorities have extended nuclear related educational programs to include nuclear expert team lectures, which began in October 1988 and involve sending out teams of scientists to lecture around the country, and on line information sources. These teams also are sent out after accidents or leakages to explain to the press and the community exactly what happened and why citizens should not be concerned about any health consequences. In the late 1980s, as dial up modems became prevalent among computer users, the Science and Technology Agency developed the so-called 'STA Village', an online database accessible to citizens containing information about nuclear power (see *Financial Times*, 25 April 1991).

Along with focusing upon the citizens who would be living near the nuclear power plant, MITI began programs which would educate and train local government leaders to be able to convince their citizens of the importance of their role in the larger energy program. In the 1980s, the central government began to invite in local government officials from areas suitable for nuclear power plants. In these three-day seminars, organizations like JAERO provide information to local politicians and town council members who decide upon inviting in a nuclear power plant. Along with detailing the funding that will be made available to the local community if citizens accept the plant, JAERO also lays out arguments for the plant and ways to handle negative reactions from concerned citizens. MITI set up a 'Junior Leaders Conference' where information on nuclear power plants can be passed along to town politicians and bureaucrats, along with bringing in leaders from 'failed' siting attempts who can explain what went wrong and how to avoid it (Interview with city hall bureaucrats, town targeted for nuclear reactors, Winter 2002).

Learning Tools

Over time, as citizen resistance increased, the government decided that a more coordinated approach to siting, involving not only the prime actor of MITI but also agencies like the Ministry of Construction which issues relevant permits, the Ministry of Finance which vets the budget, and the Environment Agency, which could theoretically suspend siting on environmental grounds, would further assist the siting process. In December 1976, the government established the Ministerial Council for Promoting a Comprehensive Energy Policy (*Sōgō Enerugi Taisaku Suishin Kakuryō Kaigi*) under the chairmanship of the Prime Minister. This council brought with it two new strategies for furthering siting: (i) setting up a liaison meeting for the construction of the power plants, and (ii) designation by the council of a power plant as an Important Electric Power Resource Requiring Special Measures (*Yō Taisaku Juyō Dengen*). Being designated as an important electric power resource meant that localities could receive extra levels of subsidies, up to double the normally allowed level. The liaison meeting involved representatives from the closest Regional Bureau of MITI, along with bringing in the officials from the local ministerial offices, the local prefectural governor, and the mayor of the relevant local towns.

4   ALTERATION OVER TIME

MITI has not stood idly by, allowing the various strategies it developed to smooth the siting process to sit unchanged. Rather, it has constantly responded by increasing the ways in which it receives information about changing citizen interests and concerns and altering its strategies accordingly. While the Dengen Sanpō incentives were institutionalized in 1974, within two years METI began to alter them to meet the new demands of communities (Asahi Shinbun, 6 July 1976). The public hearing and environmental assessment procedures were added in this vein, and METI also responded to its increasing responsibilities for handling citizen unrest and resistance to nuclear power plant siting by creating 'independent' new institutes and centers for public relations.

MITI and the STA developed additional learning tools which would enable them to gauge citizen reactions and to better handle citizen resistance. In 1973, after many complaints about the secrecy of the nuclear power planning system, and despite the passage of a bill in 1959 in the Diet which called for the holding of public hearings on nuclear plants, the Science and Technology agency outlined a plan which would allow for 'public hearings' which would be held when officials in the Atomic Energy Commission felt necessary. At public hearings, pre-selected citizens with pre-screened questions receive a short period of time to present their concerns before moderators cut them off. In many cases, anti-nuclear groups have simply boycotted them on the grounds that they exist merely as *pro forma* procedures and in fact have no bearing on the actual outcome of the process (see Hangenpatsu Shinbun, 1978–98).

The late 1970s also brought calls for more attention to the environment, and MITI responded by introducing environmental assessment procedures into the nuclear power plant siting system. In the assessment procedure the opinions of local citizens must be collected by the surveying bureaucrats and included in reports to higher ups. These two procedural changes reflected MITI's desire to be seen as responsive to citizen concerns about democratic and environmental processes. However, there has not been a case in which the results of these two procedures have ended a siting process. Further, METI and other central government ministries have never denied a license nor withheld approval for any nuclear power plant (Interviews with electric utility personnel, Fall 2002).

By 1970, increasing responsibilities for handling citizen concerns about siting caused MITI to discharge its public relations activities upon the governmental organization called Japan Atomic Energy Relations Organization (JAERO), which maintains a close relationship with MITI and gets all of its funding from it (Interviews with central government bureaucrats, Fall 2002). JAERO to this day handles publicity and public relations campaigns for nuclear power, sending out teams of teachers, providing curricula to schools, holding essay contests, and other activities at the national level.

To handle the enormous amount of material directed at encouraging specific localities to take on nuclear power plants, and to cut down on their already overburdened schedules, MITI bureaucrats spun off a another government organization called the Japan Industrial Location Center in 1978, which itself later spun off the Center for the Development of Power Supply Regions in 1990.[4] The Industrial Location Center handled not only nuclear power plant siting but also often unwanted facilities like petroleum storage facilities along with overall public acceptance issues until 1990. The Japan Industrial Location Center tightened its focus to assisting the siting of petroleum refineries, large scale factories, *kombinato*, and the like.

At that point, the Center for the Development of Power Supply Regions became the sole organization handling the public relations campaigns for nuclear, thermal, oil, and other electric plants. The Center for the Development of Power Supply Regions handles the execution of the Dengen Sanpō by assisting with industrial promotion activities and acting as a clearing house for information on the benefits of hosting nuclear plants. Among other activities, the Center publishes monthly bulletins on changes in programs which can assist host communities and manages and hosts an annual symposium on the development of regions which have power plants (Center for Development of Power Supply Regions, 1997). The development of the central government's institutions for altering citizen preferences regarding nuclear power plant siting can be represented graphically as I have done in Figure 6.1.

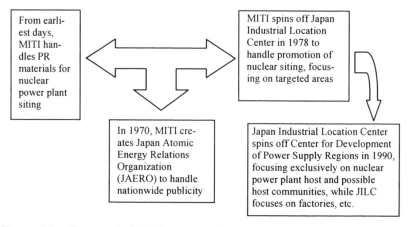

Figure 6.1   Changes in MITI institutional structure between 1950s and 2002

The Center for the Development of Power Supply Regions has also been responsible for the popular annual 'Electricity Home Town Fair' which features products from local areas with power plants held at the Makuhari Messe Convention Center outside Tokyo in Chiba. In a clever reversal of earlier fears that the presence of a nuclear plant would drive away customers, this fair has heightened the awareness of local brands from these communities and increased their profits (Interview with Center personnel, 20 November 2002). The Center, like the other bodies spun off by MITI, receives its funding from Dengen Sanpō and other governmental sources and concentrates upon convincing targeted communities of the safety and merits of accepting nuclear power plants.

Along with increasing its capacity to deal with citizen resistance by establishing 'independent' public relations organizations targeted at both potential host communities and the country as a whole, MITI regularly altered its incentive tools such as the Dengen Sanpō laws so that as rural, coastal villages (the most common site for nuclear power plants) became richer, the incentives would increase accordingly. As mentioned above, within two years of the creation of the Three Electricity Laws, bureaucrats began to alter them. Over time, MITI has regularly improved upon Dengen Sanpō and other subsidies to host communities by enlarging: (i) the amount of money available to communities, (ii) the type of projects which could be targeted with the money, and (iii) the period of time over which the money would be available.

5   AMOUNT OF MONEY

Although initially the amount of subsidies which could be brought in from the government to localities with nuclear power plants was severely limited, over time METI increased its magnitude. By 1979, for example, the government allowed localities to use provided subsidies to handle up to 70 percent of the cost of the facilities. The tax rate base for providing subsidies increased from the initial 85 yen per 1,000 kWh in the 1970s to 445 yen per 1,000 kWh of electricity sold by 2000, with approximately one third of that money going to the special account for redistribution to areas with power plants, and the remaining going into the account for the diversification of power resources (Ohkawara and Baba, 1998, p. 7). METI advertises that a community accepting a 1.35 million kW reactor could receive as much as 450 billion yen from the government (METI, 2002). Figure 6.2 illuminates the increasing budget for siting measures between 1974 and 2002.

6   TARGETS FOR MONEY

At the beginning of the Dengen Sanpō MITI allowed the money to be used only for subsidies for 'hard' infrastructural projects like roads, bridges, and ports, but over time they allowed localities and prefectures to spend the money on parking places, industry and commerce halls (JAIF, 1978, 22 (1), p. 20). Citizens soon wearied of the *hakamono*, or empty box, approach to compensation, where local governments with small, older communities would build beautiful but unused structures like cultural halls, concert halls, gyms, and the like (Interview with Japanese scholar, Summer 2002). Because of such feedback from citizens, MITI altered the mix included in Dengen Sanpō even further. Since the 1980s the subsidies have spread out to encompass completely 'soft' items like job training, publicity and invitations for companies

MITI Spending on NPP Siting, in Yen

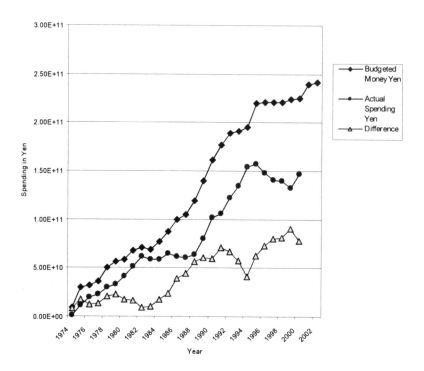

Figure 6.2   Changes in MITI budget for nuclear power plant siting

to re-settle in the host community, and so on. More than 25 categories and subcategories of funds available to communities hosting power plants have been introduced since 1974 (MITI, 2000). For example, in 1978 the government allowed industrial development promotional facilities, such as vocational training facilities and commerce pavilions, to be included. Then, in 1983, industrial lands, waterworks, and testing fields were added to the acceptable projects, then financing expenses for promoting development in these regions, and in 1992 interest payments for industrial land development (Ohkawara and Baba, 1998, p. 8). As time has progressed, subsidies moved from road paving monies to become vehicles for inviting in and training new industries and developing job skills.

7 TIME PERIOD FOR MONEY

Initially, subsidies were available only for five years. By 2002, the time period available for subsidies and grants such as Dengen Sanpō and other systems from the central government had been increased four-fold to more than 20 years (METI, 2002). Furthermore, communities began to receive funds even for merely considering, but not necessarily constructing, a nuclear power plant by allowing surveys of their locale. METI further responded to ever critical citizens by allowing Dengen Sanpō funds to be spent not only by localities that were receiving a plant, but also those that were merely considering them (Interviews with nuclear plant researchers, 8 August 2002). Thus what began as a subsidy for infrastructure once plant construction was underway became an incentive to consider construction.

Figure 6.3 summarizes the overall changes to the Dengen Sanpō siting institution.

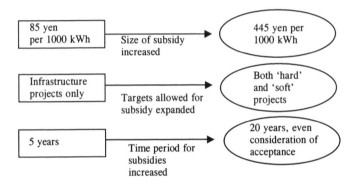

Figure 6.3   Changes in Dengen Sanpō institutions between 1974 and 2002

8 A COMPLEX WEB OF TOOLS

Although I have organized into separate categories descriptions of the strategies and tools created by the central government to further nuclear power facilities, citizens experience them as an interactive whole. For example, long before utility companies approach fishermen, local government officials, women, or other veto-holding groups, these citizens have been exposed to educational curricula in middle and high school stressing the safety and need for nuclear power, public relations materials extolling the operating record of Japanese plants, study groups run by scientists on the minimal amount of radiation given off by reactors, and publications in industry journals assuring fishermen and others that waste water from nuclear plants will not affect their fish catch. MITI and other central government representatives may have visited them to give pep talks and express the nation's need for an indigenous energy cycle and the urgency of siting new plants.

Local citizens in localities targeted for reactors receive brochures and lectures about the wide ranging financial benefits their community can acquire, ranging from new facilities, roads, schools, and medical centers to grants to draw in new firms to the area and jobs for their unemployed. Bureaucrats and mayors from those communities fly to Tokyo to gain knowledge of how to 'sell' the reactor to their citizens and, if successful, be rewarded by the Prime Minister for doing so. Government-funded organizations help to fill Tokyo exhibition halls with goods from reactor-hosting communities, reassuring citizens that their foodstuffs are still valuable despite their hosting of nuclear reactors. Overall, the Japanese government has created a comprehensive set of tools which have developed and refined over time.

9 CHANGE OVER TIME: TOWARD A LESS THAN ROSY FUTURE

It is important to stress that in the initial days of nuclear power, many of the approaches detailed here did not yet exist. When discussing the siting of nuclear power plants in Fukushima in the 1960s, for example, utility employees remarked how lucky they had been to be able to site facilities before strong anti-nuclear sentiment grew (Interviews, Fall 2002). In many of the initial siting cases in the 1960s and early 1970s, no comprehensive redistributive tools existed to provide local citizens with roads, schools, or other facilities. Governmental educational programs on nuclear energy were in their nascent stage, and MITI bureaucrats had no need to give 'pep talks' to local people. Anti-nuclear sentiment along with national level anti-reactor groups able to coordinate collective action developed slowly, and the government reacted to those shifts in consciousness and political strategies by creating new tools and upgrading older ones. Since the accidents at Three Mile Island and Chernobyl, however, anti-nuclear fears and protests have expanded dramatically, and the government has not been able to keep up.

Anti-facility citizens groups have in the last decade or so developed countermeasures against which the central government seems all but helpless. Despite the pronouncement of one local bureaucrat who informed me that 'Direct democracy is not appropriate' in siting cases (*chokusetsu minshushugi tekitō de wa nai yo*), Maki-machi in Niigata prefecture passed a citizen referendum (*jūmin tōhyō*) on 4 August 1996 blocking nuclear plant construction and other communities have followed suit (Nanto and Kisei cho in Mie Prefecture among them). These referenda bring with them no legal or administrative consequences and do not legally bind executives to a certain course, but local mayors have been loathe to ignore clear mandates from their citizens. Several communities targeted for controversial facilities, such as Kubokawa, have begun to use the strategy of electoral recall to punish mayors who go against their preferences and support hosting nuclear power plants (see Nikkei Shinbun, 17 March 1981). Faced with opponents who no longer find monetary, hortatory, and educational strategies effective or appealing, the central government has been at a loss.

A series of accidents in Japan, especially the deaths of two workers in Tokaimura in late September 1999 and a series of cover-ups in August 2002 by TEPCO and other utilities of cracks in reactor pipes have further shaken public confidence. As a result of increasingly aggressive opposition groups, the time necessary for planning, siting, and constructing nuclear power plants have increased, in some cases three-fold, from the 1960s and 1970s (Lesbirel, 1998). Citizens have regularly opposed attempts to find solutions to long-term radioactive waste storage and disposal (Yagi, 1995) and the government has given a new institution called NUMO [Nuclear Waste Management Organization of Japan, in Japanese *Genshiryoku Hatsuden Kankyō Seibi Kikō*] 30 years to find an appropriate site for it.

The actual number of reactors in Japan, 52, has fallen far short of initial OECD projections from the late 1970s of at least 100 plants by the year 2000. In short, Japan's nuclear power plant siting program has begun to slow down, and many bureaucrats lack optimism about the possibility of the government reaching its energy production goals. Despite this recent slowdown, however, important lessons emerge from more than forty years of government programs designed to alter public opinion.

10 CONCLUSIONS

This chapter has revealed the active and innovative role that the central government of Japan has played in the process of siting controversial facilities. Lesbirel's work on nuclear power plant siting in Japan, focusing primarily on private sector bargaining (Lesbirel, 1998), looked only indirectly at the role of the state while Samuels' book on Japanese energy markets focused on the reciprocal relations between private utility companies and the central government (Samuels, 1987). As a result, many analysts have categorized Japan's nuclear power plant siting environment as a purely 'voluntary market' one with only occasional reference to the role of the central government. Focusing directly on the activities of the state, this chapter has revealed the deep and wide ranging efforts of the central government across a variety of policy fields to actively alter the preferences of citizens and smooth the siting of such controversial facilities.

The Japanese government has employed a variety of institutions to manage the transaction costs of siting facilities, building an environment in which negotiations proceed far more smoothly than in the absence of such incentives and programs. Institutionalized compensation systems developed by the Japanese central government reduce the uncertainties of bargaining and create focal points for negotiators. For example, compensation laws guarantee fishermen who sell their fishing rights or farmers who sell private property to private utilities certain income streams often above market value. But by altering the preferences of citizens and politicians, the central government has departed from typical descriptions of 'democratic' siting processes and gone beyond merely reducing transactions costs.

Political theorists often utilize normative models of democratic governance in which the goals and values of citizens drive politicians and hence bureaucrats to create new programs and advance the society toward a shared future. In Japan's facility siting environment, it is reversed: non-elected bureaucrats, working in conjunction with LDP members and electric power companies, seek to alter citizen preferences so that Japan's movement toward the state's goals of energy independence will not be impeded. While citizens initially requested the 'compensation' provided by redistributive programs like Dengen Sanpō, the vast majority of authority, incentive, capacity, symbolic and learning tools used by the state were not created at the request of the Japanese people.

As a result, citizens do not enter the negotiating rooms as blank slates ready to bargain compensation for acceptance, or seek mitigation in return for cooperation; they have long been the target of complex, multi-vectored public relations efforts funded by their own taxes. The state has sought to penetrate civil society using flexible and adaptive institutions which move citizens away from positions of resistance due to concerns about risk and inequity toward conciliation and negotiation as a result of side payments, focused public relations, and constant messages of reassurance. While Japanese political culture and in-place procedures may have reduced resistance among some citizens, MITI's creation and then improvement of educational, compensatory, and persuasive policy tools no doubt have, at least in the past, further increased barriers to collective action against the state.

Interestingly, despite years of such programs and hundreds of millions of dollars of expenditure on incentive, capacity, and symbolic policy instruments, citizens have become increasingly immune to such techniques. Progressively more active and organized citizens movements have utilized citizen referenda, mayoral and town council recalls, and information dissemination to combat central government and utility efforts at resistance-free siting. Many citizens no longer accept explanations from central government bureaucrats at face value, and have pushed the state to enact more open and citizen-centered siting procedures. These actions from citizens, combined with fatal management errors and recent cover-ups of poor reactor mainte-nance by private utilities have created a situation in which green-fields siting of new reactors in the future seems all but impossible and lead times continue to grow.

MITI and other government ministries worked to improve their strategies, increasing the amounts of compensation available, broadening their targets, and stretching out the time period of availability for which the side payments along with creating learning tools to provide more accurate feedback on the interests and demands of citizens. Nonetheless, these upgrades have not improved recent siting rates. Perhaps the most important lesson from this study has been that despite the use of flexible and adaptive institutions in the siting processes, even the best designed and improved techniques cannot promise continued siting success in an era of increasingly active and con-cerned citizenry.

NOTES

* This chapter is a subsection of my doctoral dissertation, a cross-national, over-time investigation of state-citizen interaction through the lens of controversial facility siting. I wish to thank Kaneko Kumao sensei of Tōkai University and Mr. Masumoto Teruaki of TEPCO for their invaluable assistance in procuring inter-views. The Reischauer Institute at Harvard University and the National Science Foundation provided the funding for initial fieldwork and the A50 Group of the IIE Fulbright program provided funding during extended fieldwork in Japan. I am also grateful to the staff of the JUSEC Fulbright office in Tokyo, especially Ms. Iwata Mizuho, the librarians at the Institute of Social Science at the University of Tokyo (Shaken), and the staff at the Nihon Genshiryoku Sangyō Kaigi (Japan Atomic Industrial Forum) library who were all immensely helpful. My thanks as well to Yael Aldrich for her self-sacrifice and support and Dr. Howard Aldrich and Prof. S. Hayden Lesbirel for their excellent suggestions.

1. I do not believe that the Japanese state is a unitary actor, as many studies of strug-gles between ministries have made clear. Rather, this chapter will focus upon the efforts of the Ministry of International Trade and Industry (reorganized and rena-med the Ministry of Economy, Trade, and Industry, METI as of January 2001) which contains the Agency of Natural Resources and Energy (ANRE) and various nuclear power subsections, the organizations at the core of efforts to deal with citizen resistance. Occasionally I will refer to the activities of the Science and Technology Agency (STA) and of the Ministry of Education (formerly Monbus-ho), two organizations which have been merged into the Ministry of Education, Culture, Sports, Science, and Technology (MEXT). Because of the historical con-text of this chapter, I will continue to use the older names for these organizations when appropriate.

2. The date was chosen with two events in mind. It represented both the date of Japan's entry into the International Atomic Energy Agency in 1956 and the first day on which the Japan Power Demonstration Reactor (JPDR) reactor built by Japan

Atomic Energy Research Institute generated electricity.

3. This description of the creation of Dengen Sanpō as the institutionalization of a previously existing *ad hoc* measure is at odds with those, like some of my informants, who have described it as the personal work of former Prime Minister Tanaka Kakuei (Interview with high ranking TEPCO official, 5 August 2002; see also Samuels, 1987, p. 246).

4. The core differences between JAERO and the Center for the Development of Power Supply Regions are that JAERO focuses upon national level public relations efforts while the Center concentrates its efforts upon targeted communities. Neither organization is independent in either the formal or informal sense; both receive funding and their mandate from MITI. In interviews, leaders of both centers agreed that they 'merely carry out the plans formulated by the bureaucrats at MITI' (Interviews, Winter 2002).

REFERENCES

Adachi, Tadao (1991), *Tochi shūyō Seido no Mondaiten* [Some problems with the Land Expropriation System], Tokyo: Nihon Hyoron Sha.

Apter, David and Nagayo Sawa (1984), *Against the State: Politics and Social Protest in Japan*, Cambridge, MA: Harvard University Press.

Asahi Shinbun Yamaguchi Shikyoku (2001), *Kokusaku no Yukue: Kaminoseki Genpatsu Keikaku no Nijū nen* [The Direction of National Policy: 20 Years of Planning for a Nuclear Power Station at Kaminoseki], Kagoshima: Nanbo Shinsha.

Barthe, Yannick and Claire Mays (2005), 'Communication and Information: Unanticipated Consequences in France's Underground Laboratory Siting Process', Chapter 8 in Hayden Lesbirel and Daigee Shaw (eds), *Managing Conflict in Facility Siting*, Cheltenham, UK: Edward Elgar.

Bowen, Roger (1975), 'The Narita Conflict', *Asian Survey*, **15** (7), 598–615.

Broadbent, Jeffrey (2002), 'Japan's Environmental Regime: The Political Dynamics of Change', draft manuscript, in Uday Desai (ed.) *Environmental Politics and Policy in the Industrialized Countries,* MIT Press.

Center for Development of Power Supply Regions (1997), Outline of Operations Booklet.

Cohen, Linda, Mathew McCubbins and Frances Rosenbluth (1995), 'The Politics of Nuclear Power in Japan and the United States', in Peter Cowhey and Mathew McCubbins (eds), *Structure and Policy in Japan and the United States,* Cambridge University Press, 177–202.

Doi, Takeo (1974), *Amae no Kōzō* [The structure of dependence], Tokyo: Kobundo.

Financial Times (1991), 'Electricity Industry (3): Energy Policy Divided', 25 April, p. 37.

Garon, Shelden (1997), *Molding Japanese Minds*, Princeton NJ: Princeton University Press.

Hangenpatsu Shinbun [Anti-Nuclear Newspaper] (1978–1998), Issues 1–240, Tokyo: Hangenpatsu Undō Zenkoku Renraku kai.

Hangenpatsu Undō Zenkoku Renraku kai (1997), *Han Gennpatsu Undō Mappu* [An Outline of the Anti Nuclear Movements], Tokyo: Ryokuhu Shuppan.

Hirschman, Albert (1970), *Exit, Voice, Loyalty*, Cambridge MA: Harvard University Press.

Jacobs, Lawrence and Robert Shapiro (2000), *Politicians Don't Pander*, Chicago: University of Chicago.

Japan Atomic Energy Relations Organization (JAERO) [*Zaidan Hōjin Nihon Genshiryoku*] (2002), Activities Report.

Japan Atomic Industrial Forum (JAIF) (Various years), 'Atoms in Japan', Industry Notes.

Johnson, Chalmers (1982), *MITI and the Japanese Miracle*, Stanford: Stanford University Press.

Kamata, Satoshi (1991), *Kamata Satoshi no Kiroku 3: Shōsūha no Koe* [The Third Diary of Kamata Satoshi: The Voices of Small Groups], Tokyo: Iwanami Shoten.

Kamimura, Naoki (2001), 'Japanese Civil Society, Local Government, and U.S.–Japan Security Relations in the 1990s: A Preliminary Survey', *Japan Center for Area Studies*, Occasional Paper 11.

Kasperson, Roger E. (2005), 'Siting Hazardous Facilities: Searching for Effective Institutions and Processes', Chapter 2 in Hayden Lesbirel and Daigee Shaw (eds), *Managing Conflict in Facility Siting*, Cheltenham, UK: Edward Elgar.

Kerr, Alex (2001), *Dogs and Demons*, London: Penguin Books.

LeBlanc, Robin (1999), *Bicycle Citizens*, Berkeley: University of California Press.

Lebra, Takie (1976), *Japanese Patterns of Behavior*, Honolulu HI: University of Hawaii Press.

Lesbirel, S. Hayden (1998), *NIMBY Politics in Japan: Energy Siting and the Management of Environmental Conflict*, Ithaca: Cornell University Press.

McAvoy, Gregory (1999), *Controlling Technocracy: Citizen Rationality and the NIMBY syndrome*, Washington, DC: Georgetown University Press.

McCormack, Gavan (1997), 'Village vs. State', *The Ecologist*, Nov/Dec.

METI (2002), *Dengen ricchi no Gaiyō* [A Summary of Power Supply Siting].

Ministry of Economy Trade and Industry [*Keizaisangyōshō shigen enerugi chō*, METI, Agency for Natural Resources and Energy, ANRE] (2001), *Heisei 13 nendo Dengen ricchi sokushin kōrōsha hyōshō ni Tuite* [About the 2001 Citation Ceremony for Electric Power Sources Siting Promoters].

Ministry of International Trade and Industry [*Tsūshosangyōshō Shigen enerugi chō*, MITI, ANRE] (2000), *Dengen Sanpō katsuyō jireishū* [Listing of Actual Uses of the Three Laws Relating to Electricity Production], MITI Booklet.

Nakamura, Karen (2002), 'Resistance and Co-optation: the Japanese Federation of the Deaf and Its Relations with State Power', *Social Science Japan Journal*, **5** (1), 17–35.

Nakamura, Kikuo (ed.) (1975), *Gendai Nihon no Seiji Bunka* [Contemporary Japanese Political Culture], Kyoto: Mineruba.

Nakane, Chie (1978), *Tateshakai no rikigaku* [The workings of vertical society], Tokyo: Kodansha.

OECD (1984), *Nuclear Power and Public Opinion*, Paris: OECD.

Ohkawara, Toru and Kenshi Baba (1998), 'Nuclear Power Plant Siting Issues in Japan: Relationships between Utilities and Host Communities', Central Research Institute of the Electric Power Industry (CRIEPI), Report Number EY97003.

Pekkanen, Robert (2000a), 'Japan's New Politics? The Case of the NPO Law', *Journal of Japanese Studies*, **26** (1) (Winter).

Pekkanen, Robert (2000b), '*Hō, kokka, shimin shakai* [Law, the State, and Civil Society]', *Leviathan*, **27** (Fall).

Pickett, Susan (2002), 'Japan's Nuclear Energy Policy', *Energy Policy*, **30**, 1337-55.

Pye, Lucian (1985), *Asian Power and Politics*, Cambridge, MA: Harvard University Press.

Rosa, Eugence and Riley Dunlap (1994), 'Poll Trends: Nuclear power: Three decades of opinions', *Public Opinion Quarterly,* **58**, 295–324.

Samuels, Richard (1987), *The Business of the Japanese State*, Ithaca: Cornell University Press.

Schneider, Anne and Helen Ingram (1990), 'Behavioral Assumptions of Policy Tools', *The Journal of Politics*, **52** (May), 510–29.

Suisankai [Fishing World] (2000), '*Genhatsu to Gyogyō no Kyōsan wa Kanō ka* [Can Fishing Cooperatives and Nuclear Plants Live Together?]', **2**, 64–7.

Suisankai [Fishing World] (2002), '*Genhatsu to Gyogyō no Kyōsan wa Kanō ka* [Can Fishing Cooperatives and Nuclear Plants Live Together?]', **2**, 62– 5.

Vosse, Wilhelm (2000), 'The Domestic Environmental Movement in Contemporary Japan', Unpublished Ph.D. Dissertation, University of Hannover, Germany.

Woodall, Brian (1996), *Japan Under Construction*, Berkeley: University of California Press.

Yagi, Kenzo (1995), *Kita no Shizen wo Mamoru* [Defending the Nature up North], Sapporo: Hokkaido University Press.

Yoshioka, Hitoshi (1999), *Genshiryoku no Shakaishi* [The Social History of Nuclear Power], Tokyo: Asahi Shinbun sha.

7. Implementing Structured Participation for Regional Level Waste Management Planning

Elke Schneider, Bettina Oppermann and Ortwin Renn

1 INTRODUCTION

The issue of waste management not only involves complicated technical issues but also touches upon the main concepts of fairness and equity. The unwanted effects of waste treatment are concentrated in a small area, while the benefits are spread throughout a whole county or even throughout the whole region. There are controversies about the health impacts, long-term consequences, institutional trust, and economic disadvantages associated with waste treatment sites. Risk perception and perception of fairness are hence the driving agents of the debate.

Informing the public may help to clarify the issues involved, but cannot resolve the existing conflicts, which are not caused by ignorance or misreading the relevant information, but by different value commitments and diverging interests between proposers, regulators, stakeholders, and the affected public. Resolving these conflicts necessitates a process in which stakeholders and affected citizens are given the opportunity to take part in the decision. This is hardly disputed among risk managers (Fiorino, 1990; Renn et al., 1993).

There is, however, a controversial debate over the desirable structure and process of participation and the role and authority of the public to take part in the decision making process (Dienel, 1978; Barber, 1983; Lynn, 1986; Kasperson, 1986; Carpenter and Kennedey, 1988; Chen and Mathes, 1989; Fiorino, 1989; Renn et al., 1991).

2   WASTE MANAGEMENT IN GERMANY

Dealing with waste management always means dealing with a difficult problem where no 'easy' solutions can be found. The NIMBY-Syndrome is only one obstacle especially important in the siting process, but other problematic aspects like uncertainties in waste prognoses, a range of complex technologies with multi-dimensional consequences for the surrounding area and changes in the legal framework have to be dealt with.

In Germany, special administrative entities named 'Gebietskoerperschaften' (a county or a city) are responsible for the question of waste collection, treatment and disposal. But in a densly poulated country like Germany it becomes more and more difficult to assign new sites for waste disposal. Together with increased efforts for recycling and waste reduction, a law has been established, defining specific standards for any material to be legally disposable after the year 2005. To comply with these legal requirements, all counties or cities have to upgrade their waste treatment system until the year 2005 in a way that the product can meet these standards and therefore can be disposed. While the legal setting does not explicitly call for a certain technical option of waste treatment, in practice a priority for incineration is set, because at the moment the only treatment technology to produce a material meeting the official criteria for disposal is incineration. But neither the scientific validity of the criteria nor the stability of the law itself are undoubted, and both topics are discussed widely amongst experts and politicians.

3   THEORETICAL BACKGROUND

Trying to resolve conflicts in Risk debates – and the most important questions in waste management planning are risk related – there is a need for a structure or organizational model that acknowledges the conditions of the respective risk arena and addresses all three levels of risk conflicts. Most authors agree that such a debate should be organized according to the rules of a rational discourse (cf. McCarthy, 1975; Habermas, 1984; Kemp, 1985; Bacow and Wheeler, 1984, pp. 190–94; Burns and Überhorst, 1988; Fiorino, 1990; Renn, 1992). A rational discourse is defined as a communication process in which all affected parties resolve a conflict or engage in joint problem solving by a specific set of rules. These rules are summarized in Table 7.1. The success or failure of a rational discourse depends on many factors. Among the most influential are:

- **Time:** A discourse cannot be organized in a week or a month. Sufficient time for a discourse has to be allocated before the decision has to be made (Kasperson, 1986).

Table 7.1   Rules of a rational discourse

Rule setting	Reaching a consensus on the procedure the participants want to employ in order to derive the final decision or compromise, such as majority vote or the involvement of a mediator. (Majone, 1979)
Evidence	Basing factual claims on the 'state of the art' of scientific knowledge and other forms of legitimate knowledge; in the case of scientific dissent all relevant camps should be represented. (Rushefsy, 1984)
Argumenta-tion	Interpreting factual evidence in accordance with the laws of formal logic and argumentative reasoning. (Habermas, 1971)
Disclosure of values	Disclosing the values and preferences of each party, thus avoiding hidden agendas and strategic game playing. (Renn, 2004)
Fair bargain-ing	Attempting to find a fair solution whenever conflicting values or preferences occur, including compensation or other forms of benefit sharing. (Bacow and Wheeler, 1984, pp. 42 ff)

- **Openness of result:** A discourse will never accomplish its goal if the decision has been made (officially or secretly) and the purpose of the communication effort is to 'sell' this decision to the other parties (Fiorino, 1989).
- **Equal position of all parties:** The internal rules have to guarantee for every participant the same status and the same rights to speak, make proposals, or evaluate options (Kemp, 1985). This requires a consensual decision about procedure and agenda.
- **Willingness to learn:** All parties have to be ready to learn from each other, not necessarily implying that participants have to change their preferences or attitudes. Learning in this sense entails the recognition of different forms of rationality in decision making and of different forms of knowledge, be it systematic, anecdotal, personal, or cultural (Perrow, 1984; Habermas, 1971; 1984) as well as the willingness to subject oneself to the rules of argumentative disputes.
- **Resolution of allegedly irrational responses:** Discourses with public interest groups or individuals frequently demonstrate a conflict between two contrasting modes of evidence: the public refers to anecdotal and personal evidence mixed with emotional reactions, whereas the professionals play out their systematic and generalized evidence based on abstract knowledge (Lynn, 1986; Keeney and von Winterfeldt, 1986; Dietz et al., 1989). This conflict can only be resolved if both parties are willing to accept the rationale of the

other party's position and to maybe even empathize with the other's party
view (Bacow and Wheeler, 1984, p. 191; Zeiss, 1989–90).

• **De-moralization of positions and parties:** As soon as parties start to
moralize positions, they cannot make tradeoffs between their allegedly
moral position and the other parties' immoral position without losing face.
Moralizing also violates the equality principle stated above. Nobody can
assign equal status to a party, which is allegedly morally inferior to the other
parties involved. Finally, if somebody has only weak arguments to support
his/her position, assigning blame to other actors and making it a moral issue
can help to win points in the public arena. The absence of moralizing does
not mean refraining from using ethical arguments, which are essential for
resolving environmental disputes.

4   THE MODEL OF COOPERATIVE DISCOURSE

Many models for public participation have been suggested in the literature that
promise to meet these reqirements and to facilitate a rational discourse
(Crosby et al., 1986; Kraft, 1988; Burns and Überhorst, 1988; Chen and
Mathes, 1989; see reviews in: Nelkin and Pollak, 1979; Fiorino, 1990). One
of these suggestions is a hybrid model of citizen participation, termed 'Cooperative Discourse', which has been applied with several modifications to
studies on energy policies and waste disposal issues in West Germany, for
waste-disposal facilities in Switzerland and to sludge-disposal strategies in the
United States (Renn et al., 1985; 1989; 1991; 1993). Figure 7.1 illustrates the
functions and procedures of the model. The model entails the following three
consecutive steps, also known as the 'Three-Step-Participation-Model':

1   **Identification and selection of concerns and evaluative criteria:** The
identification of concerns and objectives is best accomplished by asking
all relevant interest groups (i.e., socially organized groups that are or
perceive themselves as being affected by the decision) to reveal their
values and criteria for judging different options. It is crucial that all
relevant value groups be represented and that the value clusters be
comprehensive and include economic, political, social, cultural, and re-
ligious values. To elicit the values and criteria for such a list the technique of value-tree analysis has proven appropriate (Keeney et al., 1987;
von Winterfeldt and Edwards, 1986; von Winterfeldt, 1987). The resulting output of such a value-tree process is a list of hierarchically
structured values that represent the concerns of all affected parties, as
illustrated in an example in Figure 7.2 (see page 141).

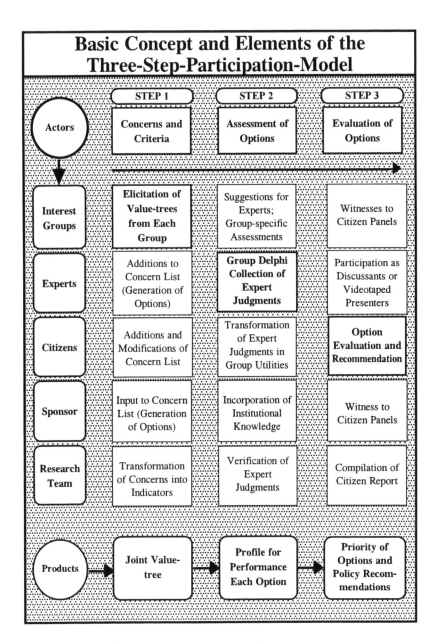

Figure 7.1   The three-step-participation-model

2   **Identification and measurement of impacts and consequences related
     to different policy options:** The evaluative criteria derived from the
     value-tree are operationalized and transformed into indicators by the
     research team or an external expert group. These operational definitions
     and indicators are reviewed by the participating stakeholder groups. Once
     approved by all parties, these indicators serve as measurement rules
     forevaluating the performance of each policy option on all value dimen-
     sions. Experts from varying academic disciplines and with diverse per-
     spectives on the topic of the discourse are asked to judge the performance
     of each option on each indicator. For this purpose, a modification of the
     Delphi method has been developed and applied (Renn and Kotte, 1984;
     Webler et al., 1991). This method is similar to the original Delphi format
     (Linstone and Turoff, 1975; Turoff, 1970), but based on group inter-
     actions instead of written responses. The objective is to reconcile conflicts
     about factual evidence and reach an expert consensus via direct con-
     frontation among a heterogeneous sample of experts. The desired out-
     come is a specification of the range of scientifically legitimate and de-
     fensible expert judgments and a distribution of these opinions among the
     expert community with verbal justifications for opinions that deviate from
     the median viewpoint.

3   **Conducting a rational discourse with randomly selected citizens as
     jurors and representation of interest groups as witnesses:** The last step
     is the evaluation of potential solutions by one group or several groups of
     randomly selected citizens (Dienel, 1978; Dienel, 1989). These panels are
     given the opportunity to evaluate and design policy options based on the
     knowledge of the likely consequences and their own values and prefer-
     ences. The participants are informed about the options, the evaluative
     criteria, and the consequence profiles. The representatives of interest
     groups and the experts take part in the process as witnesses; they provide
     their arguments and evidence to the panels who ultimately decide on the
     various options. This deliberation process takes time: citizen panels are
     conducted as seminars over three to five consecutive days. All partici-
     pants are exposed to a standardized program of information, including
     hearings, lectures, panel discussions, videotapes, and field tours. The
     process is similar to a jury trial with experts and stakeholders as witnesses
     and advisers on procedure as 'professional' judges.

Several procedures lend themselves to application during such a discursive
process. They have to be chosen according to the specific requirements of the
case in question and, due to the nature of any dialogue with the uncertainties

of a constantly changing system of actors, the procedures have to be checked during the process and adjusted to emerging new situations as well.

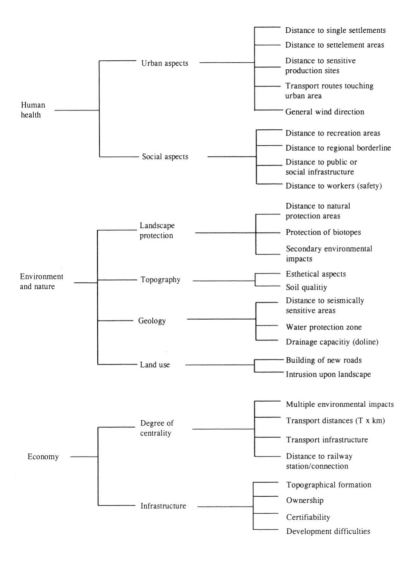

Figure 7.2   Value-tree of one citizen panel for ranking of potential sites for waste treatment plants

5   SPECIFIC APPLICATION OF THE MODEL

The official process of waste management planning in the Northern Black Forest Region was influenced by the above mentioned legal situation in Germany, but had an even more complicated political nature than the usual waste management planning process.

After a history of seperate planning efforts and different systems implemented in this field, in 1993 the three counties and the City of Pforzheim formed a cooperation to seek a common solution on the regional level for their waste problems. For this task a special planning organization (called 'P.A.N.') was established and supported by the counties and the City. An engineering consultant was hired to provide the decision making committees with the necessary technical information. When P.A.N. representatives learned about Professor Renn and his experiences with conducting public participation, they decided to incorporate such a program in the upcoming planning process and started a cooperation with the Center of Technology Assessment in Baden-Wuerttemberg. To meet the specific requirements in the region, elements of the model of cooperative discourse were modified as follows.

In the official process of decision making the task of developing the waste management concept was divided into three consecutive decision phases, each of them setting the necessary framework for the following phase. The first step consisted of a waste prognosis for the planning horizon of the year 2005, setting the minimum and maximum benchmarks of the treatment capacity needed for the regional concept. Based on this result, in the second phase the appropriate treatment techniques had to be selected in order to define the technique specific selection criteria for the third step of siting the facilities. The results of the participation program had to be available according to this time frame and the discussions had to proceed parallel to the topics of the official phases. Hence, three seperate phases of participation were planned, each with a specific task and the actors especially legitimized to decide on this problem. Figure 7.3 illustrates the modified scheme that was developed for the case, based on the conflict analysis prior to the start of the participation program.

Also the participation methodologies changed according to the conditions in the three phases. In the phases II and III we applied the method of value-tree analysis (Keeney et al., 1987) for structuring the decision process, as the   nature of these tasks allowed for such a procedure in providing the basic requirement of different options to choose from (different treatment techniques in phase II, siting alternatives in phase III). The first phase (waste prognosis) did not call for such a procedure, as forecasting is an evolutionary procedure.

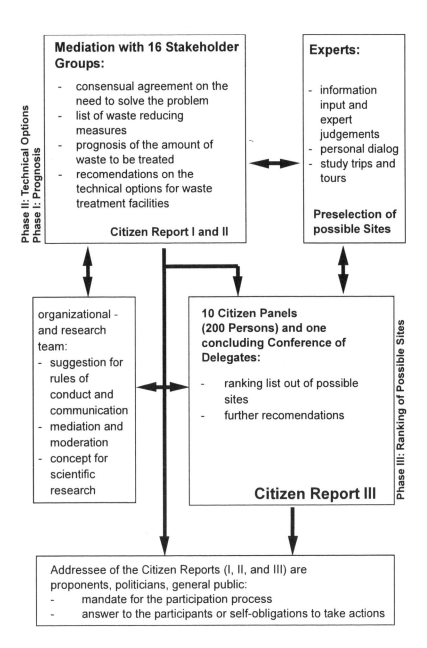

Figure 7.3 Applied model in the project: macrostructure

In terms of participatory methodologies, in the phases I and II, the team followed the mediation concept. Stakeholder groups came together in a series of consensus conferences, first developing a waste prognosis and then ranking possible technical options for waste treatment. After these tasks were completed and the political decision for a combination concept for the region was made, the third phase of site selection could be started. One central incinerator and two biomechanical treatment plants should be located in the region. Sixteen communities had been identified in a preliminary suitability study by the consultant as potential sites for treatment plants, some of them being suitable for both basic methods.

In this phase a modified version of the concept of planning cells (Dienel, 1978;1989) was applied instead of the mediation concept. The team worked in a deductive way, basically following the Multi Attribute Decision Theory with the following stages:

- building of a value-tree in introductory brainstorming and following discussion sessions, so all members of the group could agree on the values and on their hierarchical structure;
- construction of a catalogue of criteria which could be filled with information;
- weighting of the criteria;
- judging and ranking of the options relatively to each other according to their performance profiles with regard to the different criteria;
- discussing the results and compiling a final document.

A random selection of around 200 inhabitants from the potential sites for waste treatment facilities in the region formed ten parallel working citizen panels, each consisting of the same number of representatives from each potential site community. The panels were given the mandate to find the most suitable sites among these 16. Four of the panels focussed on the siting of the incinerator and six groups developed criteria for siting the biomechanical treatment plants. They developed site selection criteria and a resulting ranking list of the sites, considering social, political, ecological, and economic impacts as well as equity issues including benefit sharing packages. Each of the ten panels reached a unanimous conclusion with respect to the ranking list. Fairness issues played a major role in assessing relative burden to the communities and in balancing economic and social concerns. In the end, every group elected three delegates, who met in a specific conference with the objective of composing one common suggestion for a combination concept incorporating both treatment techniques in the best way. Finally each panel was given the opportunity to comment on the result of the conference of delegates and all suggestions were included into the citizen report. Figure 7.4 shows the applied set of methodologies in each of the three project-phases:

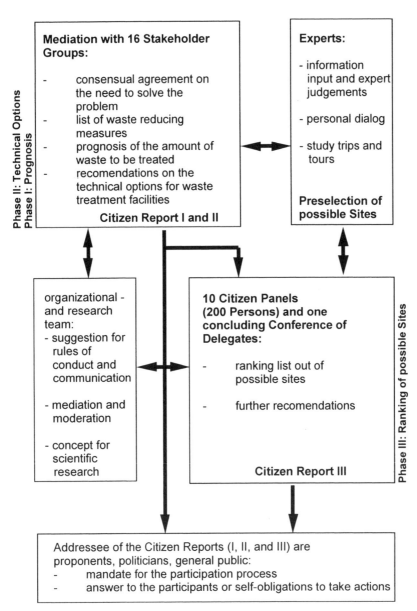

*Figure 7.4   Applied methodologies in the phases of the project: micro-
structure*

One critical aspect we had to cope with was the information management during an open planning process. Prior to the decision making by weighting and ranking of the options in question we had to select and transmit all relevant information the participants wanted to obtain. This was an especially difficult task in the third phase of the project as we were dealing with very complex problems in the field of waste management, which is at the moment character-ized by a range of technical innovations and legal changes. Furthermore we were not too well experienced with respect to the comprehensional capabilities of lay people and, in addition to these difficulties we were obliged to maintain our neutral position. Finally, we simply had to deal with the logistical problems of providing almost 200 people during a short period of meetings following closely on one another with a lot of information from different fields of expertise, often receiving this information at very short notice.

The consulting engineers of the proponent worked parallel to the citizen panels with a different method (pairwise comparison of options) on their site recommendations. We did not adopt this method because we did not want to create a situation in the citizen panels where the individual inhabitants of the potentional sites would discuss the site selection as opponents against each other. Our objective in using multiattributive utility techniqes was to help the participants recognize that there was no 'ideal' option to be found and that all options had their specific advantages or disadvantages in regard to certain criteria. In Germany it is very unusual to discuss compensative measures using this scheme, so the resulting recommendations of the citizens consisted of a list of preferred sites based upon special basic conditions or scenarios.

6 PRACTICAL EXPERIENCES AND IMPLICATIONS

Although the participatory process was completed in 1997, the implications of the process have not been fully disclosed at the time of publication. Not even the final political decision concerning the siting of the facilities has been made by the local parliaments until now (2004). As the quantity of waste decreased considerably in the late 1990s, the politicians opted to delay the final decision until the time when new waste facilities would be urgently needed. In addition, with the reunification of Eastern and Western Germany more waste disposal capacity was available so that large fractions of the waste stream could be exported. Evaluative studies surrounding our project, touching on various aspects of the process were conducted in the time be-tween 1997 and 1999 (Roch, 1997; Vorwerk and Kämper, 1999). They confirmed that the process was regarded as fair, competent, and innovative by most of the actors involved. In particular, the participants felt very comfortable with their role in the process and liked the outcome. Yet it is still to early to call closure as the real test of acceptance is still pending due to the decision not to decide until there is absolute necessity for building more facilities. In spite of the missing test for the viability of the process for siting unwanted facilities, some preliminary insights can be drawn here that could serve as hints for future research and further development of the participatory model:

- The development of a regional waste management as an extremely complex task combined with the challenging political context made it necessary to split up the task into several steps. While this helped to structure the phases, to generate the relevant technical information and to select the participants for each phase according to legitimization and special competence, the topics could not be completely separated during the discussions, thus influencing each step of the process. A consecutive structure like the one applied in this case with each phase depending on the results of the prior one gives room to problems if the tasks of any period are not fulfilled completely.
- The applied structure in this case study combined the basic model with a phased process, each phase dealing with a specific subject to decide on. For logistical and economic reasons as well as for better motivation of the participants the concept gave up the strict division of work between the different parties involved (see Figure 7.1: 'actors' like interest groups, citizens, experts, research team). Instead of repeating the whole set of the model three times, local interest groups as well as citizens were invited to become main actors in one specific project phase, according to their special competence. The interest groups did not only elicitate value-trees and pass them on to the citizens. Both actors, organized groups as well as possibly affected citizens, elicitated their value-trees *and* ran the complete process of ranking and weighting on a range of options in one specific field. Interest groups brought in their knowledge concerning waste management and treatment. Citizens living near the possible host communities contributed their anecdotal and local knowledge on the different sites to the process and were especially legitimized to participate in the siting decision. A challenging task in a structure like this is to define the links between the phases very well. The change between the main actors implied additional meeting time for knowledge transfer and the willingness of the parties to accept their changing importance.
- The first and second phases were conducted by mediation with all its chances and difficulties. For example, the voluntary participation turned out to influence the composition of the consensus conference, as not all groups participated regularly. This question should be touched upon in the rules of conduct defined at the beginning of each project, but there will be inherent limits of control.

- The research team in the basic model became an organizing team with a whole range of practical functions as mediator or moderator. The third phase with its large scale of running ten parallel groups turned out to be extremely demanding in regard to management capabilities and cannot become a regular standard for similar projects.
- Composing a final recommendation was left in the hands of three delegates from each group, who met at a late state of the siting phase. The allotted time for this important element of the process turned out to be not sufficient and more than one feedback loop should be integrated for this task in the future.
- The role of the sponsor in the model changed drastically. Political conflicts were raised in the region and it was necessary to support the participation process by press releases and public relations efforts. As the project was very innovative in complexity and scale for the state of Baden-Wuerttemberg, the Center of Technology Assessment held an intrinsic research interest and sponsored part of the costs. Without this funding, a similarly large scale project is not very likely to be implemented in Germany. Hence, research efforts should be allocated in developing smaller layouts for specific planning questions.
- The P.A.N. as the project proponent, who functions in the basic model as the sponsor, paid also for the participation process, but the P.A.N. representatives had to work hard at gaining the trust of the participants throughout the three years of the project.
- The model's feature of a group Delphi was not applied, because of a lack of time during the siting discussion. But expert input was invited by a range of other methods. Site visits, expert presentations, video interviews and supplementary information material gave the participants sufficient possibilities to draw their own conclusions and find a balanced opinion. Looking back, the best appreciated information tools were study trips and face-to-face-discussions with technical experts.
- Not only a variety of information methods has to be employed in projects like this, but also different types of information are necessary. The participants want to know to whom they will address their recommendations, how the political decision making process works in detail, etc. Any participation procedure is contingent on having an addressee to whom the recommendations are directed. In this case the transboundary cooperation between the administrative entities forming the P.A.N. made it difficult. During the 'working' phases of the process the P.A.N. representatives were responsible adressees, while the decisions at the end of each phase had to be left to the legal political parliaments in the different counties and in the City of Pforzheim.
- Expert input cannot be limited to technical issues in a case like this, and the wide range of fields of expertise within the planning context, e.g. knowledge of legal, political, planning preconditions, do not always lend themselves to

a specific type of input. Also the different interpretations of information cannot be resolved by a common method applicable to all kinds of expert disputes.

7 DISCUSSION OF SPECIFIC FEATURES OF THE 'CO-OPERATIVE DISCOURSE'

In the light of the more general question of a model's applicability and feasibility in other cases of environmental planning, characteristic features of the 'Cooperative Discourse' should be mentioned in order to point out the specific strengths of this model in the fields of improved analysis and practice.

The Cooperative Discourse tries to fulfil two main requirements of a fair and legitimized participation process, i.e. providing a *transparent and rationality-centred method of decision making* for the participants themselves as well as for the external, 'general' public outside of the project meetings on one hand and *incorporating local knowledge* into the broader decision making issues on the other hand. To meet these objectives, a step-by-step process provides clear, easy and 'close-to-everyday-life' methods of identifying, analyzing and ranking of options. The Multi Attribute Decision Making Theory is a helpful 'tool', as it offers step-by-step procedures easily comprehensible by lay people. Criteria-based decision making is familiar to almost anybody in their important decisions in life (consciously or not) and the methodology can be easily illustrated using examples from evaluations of cars, TV movies and cosmetics in a range of magazines. This does not mean an undue simplification of complex technical problems and moral dilemmas, but the 'corset' of a fixed and logical procedure contributes to a rationalized discussion style. The value-tree as a form of a detailed criteria catalogue supports the participants in the difficult task of managing the available and often contradictory information during the discussions. The catalogue can be filled in systematically with information from all available sources, and 'blank spots' without valid information can be identified. The discussion can be focused on difficult questions of dissenting opinions whilst bringing other parts of the criteria catalogue to a quick close, if a consensus can be reached easily or information is strikingly clear on a specific point.

The structure of a criteria catalogue also supports the incorporation of local knowledge into the discussion, as it lends a valid 'grid' to *all* information input in the process. This applies to technical expertise as well as to any anecdotal information given by the participants. The usual unbalanced situation of 'valid, neutral, scientific information' as opposed to 'emotionally biased, unvalid information' is dissolved by relating all information to *one* common criteria grid the group has developed and discussing contradicting information in regard to these criteria.

In our experience this approach proved to be an important and very well accepted decision supporting method for interest groups as well as for lay people. But a method like the one employed in our project cannot be used in a project geared toward involvement of a great number of individuals or the 'general' public. The Three-Step-Model does not account for this objective implicitly. The method is focused on improving the decision quality by incorporating public values into the official planning process. The described procedure is elaborate and needs willingness to participate on a long term basis and to discuss the relevant issues. But this can only be achieved with a limited number of individuals to choose from. This limitation does not mean that the results of such a procedure would not lend themselves to being incorporated in public information campaigns with a broad focus. But these activities have to accompany the discussion process and the issue of providing the participants for a certain time with a 'protected' arena for their meetings should be counterbalanced with the call for early and complete information for the external public.

Following the focus on resolving difficult decisions amongst a limited number of participants and taking into account the need for voluntariness and motivation to take part in the process, another challenge has to be mastered. In our case study, a substantial amount of time was needed for the preparation of the invitation phase. Planning experts were involved in defining the 'affected area', statistical mimimum chances for being invited had to be taken into account and all these objectives had to be counterweighted with the quest for a 'transparent' invitation process, which could not be too complicated and confusing. Response rates differed in the communities and an additional invitation campaign had to be launched in some areas to guarantee the balanced composition of the ten groups. In further research the difficulty of developing smaller scale procedures to increase cost efficiency and at the same time prevent too strict a limitation of the number of possible participants should be touched upon. And – coming to a very 'down to earth' problem – all invitation procedures in future projects will likely have the same strict time limits and late specification of important details to cope with.

To conclude the discussion, one should mention one important feature of the model, which also relates to the German political and planning system. The model follows the directive of assigning roles and functions to specific actors in the different stages. This seperation of tasks holds strongly for the link between the official political decision making and the participation procedure. Laid down in the basic model and defined as one of the main conditions for assigning the participation mandate was a strict separation of these two procedures. No politicians were allowed to participate in the groups and the citizens had to accept that their results had the status of a recommendation to the politicians. This did not demotivate the participants throughout the process, but caused problems in the end of the decision making process.

The final decision made in the political arena did not satisfy the participation process as well as the technical consultant. But from the point of view of environmental planning in a field of turbulent technical, political and economic changes, the result was not so astonishing. Near the end of the three year process, a new technical solution was brought forward, changing the technical feasibility of the concept. In addition, the waste prognosis at the end of the process had to be corrected down to 50 percent of the original estimate made at the beginning. The economic landscape of price policies throughout Germany had gone through major and unforeseen shifts, which made it impossible for waste management experts to give a reasonably sound cost estimate for long periods of time during the discussions. These factors lead to the final decision being delayed for over one year, as the conditions were so difficult. After this time the result was not to follow a regional solution for the four original partners in the P.A.N., but to seek individual cooperations with other communities adjacent to the region, as these proved to be economically more promising.

The delay and the unsatisfying outcome caused disappointment with the participants, but in the evaluative studies, which accompanied the project, the majority of participants still gave a positive feedback to the participation process itself and stressed the importance of a personal learning experience in making the difficulties of such a decision more transparent to them.

8 CONCLUDING REMARKS

Involving citizens in the decision making process requires careful planning, thoughtful preparation, and flexibility to change procedures on the demand of the affected constituencies. A cooperative discourse aims at getting public input prior to the final decision. It is meant to address public concerns, to collect local knowledge, and to exchange arguments among the various stakeholder groups. Such a pre-decisional discourse can only succeed if the following requirements are met:

- **A clear mandate for the discourse participants:** What are topics of discussions? What is the product that they are asked to deliver?
- **A clear understanding of the options and permissible outcomes of such a process:** If, for example, the site for a risk producing facility is already chosen, the discourse can only focus on issues such as choice of technology, emission control, and compensation.
- **A predefined timetable:** It is necessary to allocate sufficient time for all the deliberations, but a clear schedule including deadlines is required to

make the discourse effective and product-oriented.
* **A mutual understanding of how the results of the discourse will be integrated in the decision making process of the regulatory agency:** As a pre-decisional tool the recommendations cannot serve as binding requests. But they should be regarded as consultancy reports similar to the scientific consultants who articulate technical recommendations to the legitimate public authorities.

The transfer of the cooperative discourse model to a planning situation as it existed in the Northern Black Forest Region has not been easy and implied a range of problems.Not all of them could be discussed in this paper, nor could all of them be solved during the process. But the experiences from our project, together with other case studies in this field, clearly show that it is a difficult task to develop a case specific structure that can meet the two-fold requirements of science and reality at the same time – on one hand being methodologically sound by applying a transparent and logical procedure and at the same time serving the practical interests of the involved parties by facilitating the process of finding a well-balanced solution for their problem.

However, it is not so much the structure of the process that determines the success or failure of a cooperative planning approach incorporating risk and equity issues, as the willingness of all participants to meet the conditions of adequate time allocation, openness of the process, willingness to learn, acceptance of different rationalities, and the agreement to refrain from moralizing about the positions of other participants. One might be tempted to ask: if citizen involvement is so difficult and painful, why should any agency or project proponent bother to promote participation or go beyond the mandated public hearing to elicit citizens concerns?

The first response to this question is that social acceptance of any policy is closely linked with the perception of a fair procedure in making the decision (Rayner and Cantor, 1987). The best 'technical' solution cannot be implemented if the process of decision making is perceived as unfair or biased. In addition to this argument our experiences from the implementation of the cooperative discourse model in this case study indicate clearly that the public has something to contribute to the planning process. The rationality of public input depends, however, on the procedure of involvement. Provided citizens are given a conducive and supportive structure for discourse, they are capable of understanding and processing risk-related information and of articulating well-balanced recommendations. The discourse models are an attempt to design a procedure that allows citizens to take advantage of their full potential and includes the professional knowledge and expertise necessary to make prudent decisions.

REFERENCES

Bacow, L.S. and Wheeler, M. (1984), *Environmental Dispute Resolution*, Plenum: New York.

Barber, B. (1983), *The Logic and Limits of Trust*, Rutgers University Press: New Brunswick.

Burns, T.R. and R. Überhorst (1988), *Creative Democracy: Systematic Conflict Resultion and Policymaking in a World of High Science and Technology*, Praeger: New York.

Carpenter, Susan L. and W.J.D. Kennedey (1988), *Managing Public Disputes*, Jossey-Bass.

Chen, K. and J.C. Mathes (1989), 'Value Oriented Social Decision Analysis: A Communication Tool for Public Decision Making on Technological Projects', in C. Vlek and G. Cvetkovich (eds), *Social Decision Methodology for Technological Projects*, Kluwer: Dordrecht.

Crosby, N., J.M. Kelly and P. Schaefer (1986), 'Citizen Panels: A New Approach to Citizen Participation', *Public Administration Review, 46*, 170-8.

Dienel, P.C. (1978), *Die Planungszelle*, Westdeutscher Verlag: Opladen.

Dienel, P.C. (1989), 'Contributing to Social Decision Methodology: Citizen Reports on Technological Projects', in C. Vlek and G. Cvetkovich (eds), *Social Decision Methodology for Technologial Projects*, Kluwer Academic Press: Dordrecht, 133-50.

Dietz, T., P.C. Stern and R.W. Rycroft (1989), 'Definitions of Conflict and the Legitimation of Resources: The Case of Environmental Risk', *Sociological Forum, 4* (1), 47-70.

Fiorino, D.J. (1989), 'Technical and Democratic Values in Risk Analysis', *Risk Analysis, 9* (3), 293-9.

Fiorino, D.J. (1990), 'Citizen Participation and Environmental Risk: A Survey of Institutional Mechanisms', *Science, Technology, and Human Values, 15* (2), 226-43.

Habermas, J. (1971), *Knowledge and Human Interests*, Boston: Beacon Press.

Habermas, J. (1984), *Theory of Communicative Action. Vol. 1: Reason and the Rationalization of Society*, Boston: Beacon Press.

Kasperson, R.E. (1986), 'Six Propositions for Public Participation and Their Relevance for Risk Communication', *Risk Analysis, 6* (3), 275-81.

Keeney, R. and D. von Winterfeldt (1986), 'Improving Risk Communication', *Risk Analysis, 6* (4), 417-24.

Keeney, R.L., O. Renn and D. von Winterfeldt (1987), 'Structuring West Germany's Energy Objectives', *Energy Policy, 15* (4), 352-62.

Kemp, R. (1985), 'Planning, Political Hearings, and the Politics of Discourse', in J. Forester (ed.), *Critical Theory and Public Life*, Cambridge, MA: MIT Press.

Kraft, M. (1988), 'Evaluating Technology Through Public Participation: The Nuclear Waste Disposal Controversy', in M.E. Kraft and N.J. Vig (eds), *Technology and Politics*, Duke University Press: Durham, N.C., 253-77.

Linstone, H.A. and M. Turoff (eds) (1975), *The Delphi Method: Techniques and Applications*, Reading, MA: Addison-Wesley.

Lynn, F.M. (1986), 'The Interplay of Science and Values in Assessing and Regulating Environmental Risks', *Science, Technology and Human Values, 11* (2), 40-50.

Majone, G. (1979), 'Process and Outcome in Regulatory Decision-Making', *American Behavioral Scientist, 22* (5), 561-83.

McCarthy, T. (1975), 'Translator's Introduction', in J. Habermas (ed.), *Legitimation Crisis*, Boston: Beacon Press.

Nelkin, D. and M. Pollak (1979), 'Public Participation in Technological Decisions: Reality or Grand Illusion', *Technology Review*, **9**, 55–64.

Perrow, Charlees (1984), *Normal Accidents: Living with High-risk-technologies*, New-York, Basic Books.

Rayner, S. and R. Cantor (1987), 'How Fair is Safe Enough? The Cultural Approach to Societal Technology Choice', *Risk Analysis*, **7**, 3–13.

Renn, O. (1992), 'Risk Communication: Towards a Rational Dialogue with the Public', *Journal of Hazardous Materialss*, **29** (3), 465–519.

Renn, O. (2004), 'The Challenge of Integrating Deliberation and Expertise: Participation and Discourse in Risk Management', in T. McDaniels and M.J. Small (eds), *Risk Analysis and Society: An Interdisciplinary Characterization of the Field*, Cambridge, MA: Cambridge University Press, 289–366.

Renn, O. and U. Kotte (1984), 'Umfassende Bewertung der vier Pfade der Enquete – Kommission auf der Basis eines Indikatorkatalogs', in G. Albrecht and H.U. Stegelmann (eds), *Energie im Brennpunkt*, HTV Edition, 'Technik und Sozialer Wandel', 190–232.

Renn, O., T. Webler and B. Johnson (1991), 'Citizen Participation for Hazard Management', *Risk – Issues in Health and Safety*, **3**, 12–22.

Renn, O., G. Albrecht, U. Kotte, H.P. Peters and H.U. Stegelmann (1985), *Sozialverträgliche Energiepolitik. Ein Gutachten für die Bundesregierung*, HTV Editon, 'Technik und sozialer Wandel': Munich.

Renn, O., R. Goble, D. Levine, H. Rakel and T. Webler (1989), *Citizen Participation for Sludge Management,* Final Report to the New Jersey Department of Environmental Protection, CENTED, Clark University: Worcester.

Renn, O., T. Webler, H. Rakel, P.C. Dienel and B. Johnson (1993), 'Public Participation in Decision Making: A Three-Step-Procedure', *Policy Sciences*, **26**, 189–214.

Roch, I. (1997), *Evaluation der 3. Phase des Bürgerbeteiligungsverfahrens in der Region Nordschwarzwald*, Research Report No. 71, Akademie für Technikfolgenabschätzung: Stuttgart.

Rushefsky, M. (1984), 'Institutional Mechanisms for Resolving Risk Controversies', in S.G. Hadden (ed.), *Risk Analysis, Institutions, and Public Policy*, Washington, NY: Associated Faculty Press, 133–48.

Turoff, M. (1970), 'The Design of a Policy Delphi', *Technological Forecasting and Social Change*, **2** (2), 84–98.

Vorwerk, V. and E. Kämper (1999), *Evaluation der 3. Phase des Bürgerbeteiligungsverfahrens in der Region Nordschwarzwald*, Research Report No. 77, Akademie für Technikfolgenabschätzung: Stuttgart.

Webler, T., D. Levine, H. Rakel and O. Renn (1991), 'The Group Delphi: A Novel Attempt at Reducing Uncertainty', *Technological Forecasting and Social Change*, **39** (3), 253–63.

Winterfeldt von, D. (1987), 'Value Tree Analysis: An Introduction and an Application to Offshore Oil Drilling', in P.R. Kleindorfer and H.C. Kunreuther (eds), *Insuring and Managing Hazardous Risks: From Seveso to Bhopal and Beyond*, Springer: Berlin, 439–477.

Winterfeldt von, D. and W. Edwards (1986), *Decision Analysis and Behavioral Research*, Cambridge, MA: Cambridge University Press.

Zeiss, C. (1989–1990), 'Impact Management Priorities at Waste Facilities: Differences between Host Community Residents' and Technical Decision Makers' Values', *Journal of Environmental Systems*, **19** (1), 1–23.

8. Communication and Information: Unanticipated Consequences in France's Underground Laboratory Siting Process[1]

Yannick Barthe and Claire Mays

The Waste Act of 30 December 1991, relating to research on the management of high level radioactive waste, is considered by many observers to be a radical turning point and even a totally unprecedented event in the history of nuclear affairs in France (Barrère, 1991). The procedure set up by this law stands out as the sign of a fundamental change in approach by the public authorities. No definitive management solution is dictated; the Act attempts rather to conjugate the technical and political aspects of radwaste management. Among the innovations of the Act is the definition of three research avenues, progress in which is evaluated annually by an independent expert commission.[2] Based on research outcomes in the three defined directions, France's Parliament in 2006 should decide which technical solutions (or combination thereof) to retain for the management of high level[3] nuclear waste. Research is to be carried out on separation and transmutation of long-lived elements, and, on waste processing and packaging; the third avenue explores retrievable and non-retrievable disposal methods. At least two underground laboratories are to be constructed in this latter research goal. They will serve to evaluate the feasibility of a permanent deep storage facility. The present study, performed in 1996–97, bears on communication processes in the context of geological feasibility studies at a set of three laboratory candidate sites.

The language of the Act makes explicit a shift from an authoritarian, 'technocratic' decision style: secrecy and dependence on the all-powerful expert give way to 'dialogue' and 'concerted action' (see Mays, 1999). Throughout the parliamentary debates leading up to the Act's vote, particular attention was given to the problem of acceptance by future neighbors of a possible underground storage facility. Article 14 of the Act addresses this concern by creating on each actual laboratory site a *local information and monitoring commission*[4] (LIC) grouping scientists, local elected officials, and other stakeholder representatives.

Subsequent to the passing of the law, the French government designated a Mediator;[5] he traveled around the country to meet and listen to stakeholders at potential volunteer candidate sites. On his suggestion, LICs would be instituted *earlier*, from the very start in 1993 of the geological site investigations carried out on three candidate laboratory sites by Andra, France's national radwaste management agency. This initiative highlights the evolving understanding that public information, and some form of dialogue, are not to be treated as a luxury add-on to a technological project after it has reached a certain point of development, but rather, to be effective, must accompany the project in all its stages. Moreover, this initiative reveals the strategic importance given to information procedures in view of obtaining local acceptance of radwaste management policy implementation.

The importance given to the problem of public information and to consultation of local stakeholder spokespersons may be explained by the failure of the prior period in radwaste management research. In the mid and late 1980s, laboratory site search had been performed on purely technical grounds with little or insufficient consultation with the public (OPECST, 1990).[6] The intensity of local opposition – to the point of violent confrontation with armed riot police – had led the Prime Minister in 1990 to interrupt that search with a moratorium. These conflicts led to the reformulation of the problem posed by the existence of nuclear waste: decisions could no longer be evaluated on their sole technical merits. Their social acceptability emerged as a criterion of equal importance.

This was not the first time in France's nuclear history that the authorities would identify information, communication, discussion and negotiation as central to achieving their mission. From the beginning of the Messmer Plan in 1973, when France made the deliberate choice to move toward electronuclear power as a dominant energy source, one of the singularities of management policy was the place given to public information (Garraud, 1980). The multiplication of conflicts around nuclear plant sitings demonstrated to the authorities that communication must evolve from a matter of little concern into a high priority. An offensive strategy was developed and public information no longer was seen primarily as a constraint. On the contrary, it became a resource, reducing the taint of secrecy and defusing opposition. From that point in time onward, communication practices in the nuclear domain must be analyzed as a strategic tool, taking on their sense in the context in which they are applied, in the light of given objectives (Garraud, 1980, p. 130).

In his tour around France after the vote of the 1991 Waste Act, the Mediator identified three volunteer sites for feasibility studies in view of the construction of underground laboratories (one in the East, one in the South East, and one in the West). Andra subsequently began geological site investigations in these three localities. The beginning of this technical research phase thus marked the beginning too of information exchanges with local publics, and of local information commission deliberations. According to the original calendar, the government in early 1998 was to validate the effective construction sites, on the basis not only of scientific criteria but also local reaction. The Act requires that two laboratories at least be constructed. Based on the findings of experiments to be conducted in the underground laboratories, and on the advice of the independent expert commission, Parliament at term (in 2007 at the earliest) will then decide upon whether to construct a final repository on the site of one of the laboratories.

This study will examine the concrete form given to the Act's information requirements, and the communication practices as they took shape in the context of the candidate sites. Our empirical and sociological approach will distance itself from two stereotypical discourses on risk communication. The first involves reference to idealized 'communication models', whose distance from reality has been analyzed (Turner and Wynne, 1992). That discourse is based often on prescriptive texts, seeking to establish norms for communication with the public, with the central hypothesis that the expert 'knows' and the public must 'learn'. When distortion occurs in the transmission of the message, this may be attributed to the interference of e.g. the media.[7] The opposite discourse consists of treating institutional communication practices as exercises in manipulation, targeting the gaps between official statements and realities in the field. On the one hand, information and communication programs are virtuous pedagogical tools, and on the other, they are devices of illusion. Neither perspective lends much attention to the concrete and unanticipated effects of a given information practice in a specific local context.

This case study seeks to describe such contextual effects, on the basis of field observations carried out in two candidate localities for laboratory feasibility studies: in the *départements* of the Vienne (in the West, visited in December 1996) and Gard (in the South East, visited in April 1997). The first author observed the local information commissions in session and performed interviews with the majority of their members, as well as with onsite representatives of Andra. Available written materials were consulted, including the numerous information brochures distributed by Andra and thematic articles published by the local press. On the basis of these empirical data, we attempt a prospective analysis of communication practices, seeking to describe what they 'reveal rather than the accounts they attempt to settle, and what they provoke rather than what they produce in the immediate' (Borzeix, 1987).

This study is divided into two parts. We first describe the installations and actions designed to meet the Act's public information requirements. This will lead us to analyze the new communication policies orchestrated by Andra as managers of the laboratory site evaluation process. In this manner we can trace the move from legitimization on the basis of scientific authority to that of social legitimization through legal and administrative procedures (Mays and Poumadère, 1996). Parallel to this policy actively proclaiming its 'new look', the local information commissions, independent of Andra, carry out their own formulation of information and communication practices. The LIC are seen here as institutional arenas created to delineate debate and contain controversy.

The second part of the study seeks to analyze the ambivalent dynamic created locally by these formal information frameworks. When scientific research processes are made transparent, a certain form of democratic control is made possible by the requirement that the implementers of the technical project justify their actions. At the same time as they explain themselves to their potential neighbors, the implementers however gather information and position themselves to influence the evolution of local attitudes. The high visibility of the siting process thereby serves the different stakeholders in different ways, and moreover allows new stakeholder voices to emerge. In the end, this discussion dynamic contributes to unsettling the careful framework laid out by the Act.

1 ORGANIZATION OF A LOCAL INFORMATION FRAMEWORK

Local information and communication practices are forged in two types of institution. By setting up local agencies, the national management organization Andra carries out an active communication policy proclaiming a break with the secrecy that characterized the prior siting period of the 1980s. A heavy accent is laid on the close proximity and availability of Andra's representatives, along with strong reference to the mission imparted to the agency by the Act. At the same time the LICs are set up on each candidate site, and style themselves as information relay stations as well as public fora in which radwaste management policy is presented and debated.

Andra's New Policy: The Symbolism of Change[8]

The Act of 30 December 1991 made a first step towards giving Andra a new face. Created in 1979 as a simple department of the *Commissariat à l'Energie Atomique* (CEA), Andra was transformed by the law into an independent Industrial and Commercial Public Establishment. As such the agency is under the supervision of the Ministries of industry, research and environment. One of Andra's principal missions is to carry out investigations under the second research direction defined by law, that concerning possible deep underground storage of HLNW. From an organizational point of view, Andra appears to be independent of the waste producers upon whom it nevertheless is dependent for financing. This statutory modification is accompanied by a change in personnel; the entire top management staff turned over in the first four years.[9] These changes appear justified in light of the fiasco produced by the prior repository program, carried out at the end of the 1980s under the old regime of opaque expert authority and institutional subordination to the 'nucleocrats' of the CEA. In order to create fresh credibility, Andra's new management elevates change to the status of a guiding value. Top management does not hesitate to openly condemn the practices of the old regime:

> If, in the past, technical decisions could be made in the name of public interest, without being offered to public debate, recent experience in the area of radioactive waste disposal has shown that this method is no longer applicable, and that decisions must be based not only on technical criteria, but also on a true democratic process resting upon social, political and moral considerations. It is in this spirit that the 1991 Act was written and in this same spirit that its terms are applied and indeed that the research is carried out. (Kaluzny et al., 1996)

Some Andra engineers experienced the failure of the prior research period as an unmerited 'trauma', but all in all the new management exploits it as a rich learning source. The principal shift made from old communication practices is to treat information policy as a continuous process tightly linked with the decision process itself. This is a break with traditional institutional use of information to explain, persuade, or orient behaviors after a decision is taken (see Barthe et al., 1997). Such post hoc communication practices had but reinforced opposition and accentuated conflict in the prior phase. The contrast had been strongly felt between the secrecy or opacity of decision-making, and the subsequent information campaign was apparently designed solely to counter opposition by affected populations. At the time, such public relations efforts had been carried out by a commercial concern subcontracted by Andra. In the new period after the moratorium and the development of the Act, communication is no longer seen as an add-on. A new Communications Directorate is created, well integrated in strategic decision making and enjoying a significant budget. One action undertaken in the context of laboratory site search is to take out advertising space in several major national dailies, to argue the necessity of assuming responsibility for 'our wastes'. Most importantly, the strategic attention accorded to the local scene is highlighted by the creation of permanent decentralized information structures.

Andra's continuous organizational integration of communication may be seen in the tight links created with the local site evaluations, via decentralized information structures or 'local agencies'. In this way communication is tightly linked to centralized decision, but responsive as well to the research process in the field.

The construction of Andra's local agencies from the very start of feasibility studies is an illustration of the shift in method described above. Each local agency counts about ten permanent employees, recruited by the Paris headquarters, and who have subsequently taken up residence in the immediate area. About half the team are trained public relations specialists. Their role is to second the geologists who supervise drilling operations, setting up interface with the interested public. With these agencies, Andra attempts to blend into the countryside and become a 'natural' part of the local scene.

'We are set up in the heart of the village, in buildings with an historical past. The people who work for Andra live in the area, and I think that all this is appreciated by the local population'.[10]

Andra's strategy is hardly covert: the goal is to 'occupy the field', and to embed the agency policy in local territory.

'The communication strategy is localized. It's clear, we don't hide it. Above all we have to succeed in becoming implanted locally'.[11]

Beyond the creation of decentralized offices with strategic autonomy, each site receives a 'local information space' or visitors' center that displays Andra's determination to be visible. This high profile policy is seen as indispensable to the performance of site research activities. The visitors' centers are exhibit spaces open all day long to the public. A visitor can move from poster to poster, or consult detailed models. These present the experiments that must be carried out in the projected laboratories, the major research directions taken in the area of radwaste management, radioactivity, and the administrative procedures set up by the Act. Andra scientists and communication personnel working together designed each display, and a geologist is available to answer questions. In the same manner, guided site tours are available to visit the actual drill works.

Two rationales are given for this approach: tangibility and openness. First, Andra's research work must be rendered *tangible*. The exhibit center heads state that the models are there to allow visitors to visualize the lab project, to become familiar with geological questions and the geology of the local area, and so forth. For instance, 'visitors can touch an actual granite core sample'. Information materials guide the construction of the visitor's view of Andra. 'See and know' ('*voir pour savoir*') titles a rubric in the site information newsletter. The spectator is transformed into a 'witness'. Every interested person can come in and judge for himself. This invitation highlights the will for *openness*, which, it is hoped, will ensure credibility by giving an identifiable face to the institution. These visits furnish direct interaction between the management agency and the population; they are the occasion to make personal and informal contact with Andra employees.

This 'friendly neighborhood' communication takes the form also of sponsorship for local groups. Football, rugby and bicycling clubs have signed sponsorship agreements, and Andra supports a number of trade associations (the Town Center Trade group in Bagnols-sur-Cèze, Gard, for example). These organizations thereby are effectively recruited as information relays.

'The shopkeepers, the club presidents are becoming fundamental for us. They may run into the town mayor, and tell him they are working with us. It's micro communication, in the best sense of the word; we're creating our own network'.[12]

This definition of communication as a 'political' activity is a clean break with traditional 'good neighbor' actions carried out by any industrial organization. Unlike advertising practices, which direct messages across sports club tee shirts at an undifferentiated audience, Andra's activities contribute to identifying interest groups, and securing anchorage points for targeted messages. This strategic vision reflects the underlying goal of developing allies for the later period when local elected officials will definitively accept or refuse the laboratory offer. Another way to state this alliance is in the words of a staff member: '*encourage synergy among different interests*'.

In parallel to the direct contacts made in local information meetings or sponsorship events, the communication policy makes use of written and pictorial media: brochures, comic strips, documentary film cassettes, all distributed at the visitors' center or during events, as well as advertising blocks in local papers, etc. Several thousand readers or viewers may be reached by this combination. Each site has its own monthly newsletter, distributed to residents' homes. The layout of the newsletter is standard across the three sites, but each has its own title. The content is adapted to the local context, recounting events on both the scientific and communication fronts in site territory.

Andra's high profile policy thus stands out as a break with the prior site search period in which there was apparently no conception that decisions or even actions should be visible to the public. By developing the theme of openness and availability, Andra prevents conflict that could be nourished by a perceived shortcoming in that area, even before a definite decision is taken on where to install the required laboratories. That choice will depend not only upon technical criteria but also on the degree to which its future neighbors will welcome each lab and Andra as a long-term industrial presence. This transparency is identified by Andra, in the context of international practices, as an appropriate response to today's public demands on risk management. Andra's high profile and neighborhood outreach are also strategic in developing the social networks of allies and initiates on whose support the project will stand or fall. As project implementer, Andra enjoys unusual conditions: its actions are legitimated not by commercial interest, nor even by its own interpretation of the public interest, but by the management framework stipulated by national law.

We described above the signs of a change in the organization of Andra's information and communication practices. The message content, we will now argue, shows how the grounds for legitimacy are shifted from scientific authority toward procedural authority. Traditionally, technical sectors like radwaste management have put forward their reference to scientific method. French nuclear policy has been analyzed as relying upon 'euphoriant discursive strategies' (Delavigne, 1994). Institutional statements to the public convey an image of science as the protector and source of progress and safety. Messages can be shaped as popularization of science, with an accent on the institution's positive role in promoting science.

Traces of such reassuring content may be found in Andra's public information. For instance, less focus is made upon HLNW than upon geology and the geologist's profession. The visitor to the Vienne information center is welcomed by the following text: 'Welcome to Andra-Vienne. By following this pathway, you will cross 350 million years and discover the granite of South Vienne'. Andra emerge as a group of scientists and technicians whose mission is to produce neutral knowledge and to share their discoveries with the public. Still, scientific knowledge is less the focus of information than is the process itself of scientific research in which Andra are engaged.

The site evaluations that bring Andra to the locality are justified by the scientific uncertainty surrounding the feasibility of a deep geological repository. This uncertainty and the notion of accompanying risk are thereby implicitly recognized, which in itself is a break with the traditional discourse of the nuclear establishment. Valuing research, whose results by definition are unforeseeable, functions as a guarantee that repository siting is not a foregone conclusion; only by performing prior research in an underground laboratory will it be possible to make an enlightened decision as to whether a repository is a viable management solution. The staged mission confided to Andra by law (laboratory candidate site evaluation, and then experiments in the actual lab), may thus be interpreted as a guarantee offered to the potential neighbors of a laboratory. A candidate site will not necessarily become a laboratory site, and similarly, the chances that a laboratory will later become a repository are formally unknown. In the context of this mission, Andra's information efforts are not simply scientific pedagogy performed while an inexorable technical project moves forth. The chosen information strategy seeks less to transmit scientific knowledge than to stress the experimental approach, the uncertainty surrounding future decisions, and the importance of data gathering to support those decisions. Radwaste management policy is translated as a large-scale scientific experiment whose progress laymen are invited to follow in real time.

More important than this scientific reference for Andra's credibility, however, is probably the accent put upon the respect of the legal framework for this research. In the traveling exhibits set up by Andra in neighboring townships, or in the permanent visitors' centers, posters stating the principal edicts of the 1991 Act are centerpieced. Rare are the agency brochures that do not open upon a reminder of the mission set out by law. With this explicit inscription of all its activities in the legally defined process, Andra presents itself as the emanation of democratic political will. The image of an organization responsible for geological investigations is put into the background. Andra seeks thereby to be seen as an institution primarily occupied with fulfilling a mission dictated by the national legislator, a mission thus remaining under democratic control. The fact that radwaste management policy is embedded in regulatory procedures is stressed with as much insistence as are the scientific verifications accompanying each step of research. In other words, the legal framework, and explicitly its definition of a specific research program, give *meaning* to Andra's pursuits.

For these reasons it can be said that a significant shift is made in the type of legitimacy sought. Science and technology, as primary instruments of legitimation, are joined by legislated procedures. In this context, the local information commissions are neither an 'add-on' nor an opponent to Andra, but an integral part of the fulfillment of a mission.

Local Information Commissions

Article 14 of the Waste Act requires local information commissions (LICs) to be created when a laboratory begins construction. However, on the basis of his tour of candidate regions conducted after the vote of the Act, the Mediator suggested that LICs be instituted from the very start of candidate geological evaluations by Andra. This initiative is coherent with openness built into the legislated process as a primary guarantee. The LICs thus function from the earliest moment as a vital part of the 'continuous democratic control' of the laboratory process demanded by the Mediator (Bataille, 1993). Beyond their mission to provide information, these organisms correspond to the peculiarly French system of institutionalizing – and thus containing – dialogue by organizing debate among designated partners.

The creation of LICs is not an innovation on the French industrial scene. A ministerial circular by the brand new socialist government in 1981 instituted such commissions for major accident hazard sites and other risk producing installations such as large power plants. However, the 1991 Act institutes LICs for the first time as a *legislated* organism. The LICs created at the Mediator's demand to accompany preliminary geological evaluations at candidate sites thus prefigure the organisms that by law must operate at the time of actual lab construction. The candidate site LICs are heterogeneous, grouping local elected officials, environmental protection group members, spokesmen for unions and trade associations, state representatives, and local scientific experts. This diversity is designed to allow consideration of all angles associated with the industrial project. The participants are chosen by the regional Prefect who presides over the commission, and are supposed to represent the major forces involved in each *département*. In that the choice is left to the judgment of the Prefect, as the decentralized representative of the state in each *département*, the number of participants is quite variable (from 30 to 80 members), in each case considered sufficient to represent a wide variety of interests. The LICs' mission is to 'inform itself on the basis of serious, objective and scientific data, to transmit this information to the populations concerned locally, to analyze and forge an opinion on the precise nature of the project, deadlines and procedures, issues, risks, the safety measures to be taken, (and) the possible impacts on the human and natural environment'.[13]

The essential contribution of the 1991 Act is to ensure the feasibility of this mission by endowing each LIC with funds and the power to produce counter-expertise (Prieur, 1992). However, given that the pre-selection project is limited to preliminary geological sampling and given the significant resources that would be required to lead a counter evaluation, this activity at the time of writing (1997) remains hypothetical in each LIC. In reality, the commissions mainly meet on specific themes (the first themes were suggested by a national consultant):[14] radiation risks, the repository concept, and administrative procedures. In addition, Andra representatives and independent experts come before the commission to testify periodically on the advancement of the geological evaluation. The Prefect, sometimes with the help of a restricted guiding council designated by the full commission, sets the agenda for each bimonthly meeting. The LICs are seen by the Prefects as a working mechanism whose role is to *produce* solid information through argument and counter argument, and to *disseminate* the outcome to a broad public, through different media: reports by elected officials to municipal councils, distribution of a commission newsletter, newspaper articles by local journalists who are invited to sit in on commission meetings. The heterogeneity of the LICs today, however, make them resemble scenes of latent conflict more than efficient instruments of information production and broadcast.

To understand the role played by the LICs in the process sparked by the 1991 Act, it is necessary to go beyond the dichotomy of 'opacity' vs. 'openness'. Certainly, the pre-site LICs contribute to and demonstrate the openness of the process; in this they are coherent with the spirit of the law. However, they do not appear to function as vehicles for a broad-based local public debate on the potential lab or other radwaste management issues. Though the LICs were conceived as a means of involving the citizenry in debate up to now reserved to experts, an analytic view sees them as simply *displacing* the debate. By the intermediary of these commissions, new discussion fora are created, but involving only the representatives of established, identified or defined interests.

In fact, these commissions may be seen as part of a strategy of public action meant to defuse conflict by bringing on board partners seen to be inherently influential. This action is another means of avoiding past mistakes: in the prior management phase, local institutions had been kept out of the decision arena, and they had forced entrance as protestors. Here, the significant place given to local politicians in the LICs (more than half the seats on each commission) shows the public authorities' intention to engage their support and thereby ensure the laboratory project's viability. In such a context, it is difficult to distinguish to what degree LICs are fulfilling their disinterested information relay role, or functioning rather as a setting for accord making or negotiation. LICs in this light appear to co-opt[15] elected officials. Indeed the information produced in the LICs is far from just technical. Other aspects appropriate for discussion by custodians of the public interest, and apt to win politicians to the cause, are given good place, as for instance the economic development measures that would be part of a laboratory package. Andra distributes funds of 5 million francs[16] per year and per candidate site, calculated on the basis of the average local tax levied on a working nuclear power installation; the LIC subgroups responsible for their administration are composed solely of elected officials, among all possible candidate participants, and overseen by the Prefect. By facilitating direct relations between elected officials and project implementers, the LICs permit compromises to be found, concerning e.g. financial compensations, and this in a discrete setting. It must therefore be observed that the characteristics of these information commissions are highly dependant upon the *use* their participants agree to make of them.

Such differentiated uses of the information framework hint at the power plays that may take place within LICs. At least once a year, each candidate site commission hears a status report from Andra. This meeting is the occasion for project opponents to nourish debate within the commission, but also to feed controversy outside. The technical information delivered provides the opportunity for opposed members to contest the project point by point. The project managers are obliged to defend their research choices, and to 'confess' the uncertainties that surround the feasibility of a laboratory. The high profile given to research undertakings in the strategy discussed above, results in highlighting numerous questions that in the current state of knowledge must remain unanswered. While scientific uncertainty is unavoidably part of the radwaste management file, it can be exploited in such a setting to question the credibility of the research efforts. Rather than contesting the authenticity of the data presented by the experts, and without need for counter expertise, opponents may question the scientific foundation of the methods chosen to evaluate those data, or focus on whether agreed procedures have been scrupulously respected.

The open reporting of research information to this manner of citizen board is a legitimization of the program on procedural grounds. However, it also exposes the research program and its implementers to attack. In this light the LICs may be seen as a forum that favors the voicing of objection.

To the extent that conflicting interests may confront one another in the LICs, these become potential battlegrounds. In this way they appear to conform to the 'conflictual' profile described by Blancher et al. (1996) in their study of similar commissions attached to working power or chemical plants (the four profiles identified are 'convivial', 'involved', 'dominated' and 'conflictual'). However, the voice of opponents in the LICs we study appears to be too isolated to bring the debate to outright controversy within this confined space. The Prefect, as state representative, can be seen to control debate by insisting that it be dispassionate. The exchange of argument and counter argument is confined to a delimited institutional space in which the wind often turns to the advantage of project supporters. As an example, newsletters are published after each meeting by the Gard and Vienne LICs, and distributed to 'all the households in the sector concerned by the project and to numerous organisms and decision makers in the *département*'[17] to a total of 12,000 copies. These publications do not always recount the conflicts that may emerge during the proceedings. Interviews performed with LIC members, in contrast, reveal the diversity of positions that exist within the commissions. Despite this diversity, the newsletters deliver only a consensual report. Their articles are written but unsigned by prefecture employees, producing a homogeneous picture of the however heterogeneous members of the LICs. This process is pronounced to the point that some local journalists have distanced themselves from reproducing the information disseminated by the commissions: 'We're no longer part of the LIC, whereas we were before. That was a choice made by our bureau chief. We resigned to keep our neutrality. When we're invited, sometimes we do go, but we obtain less information, it's too institutionalized'.[18]

The LICs both provide a place for criticism to be voiced, and channel it. The formalisms placed on taking the floor appear to channel opposition. Conflict is contained by bending it to formal group procedure. LICs then can be seen in their ambivalent nature, as fora in which information and public debate are produced, but which at the same time confine discussion and block heated exchange that could potentially turn the tide of opinion. These fora can be considered as fragments of public space, in which the integration of new partners, such as elected officials, renders binary opposition between implementers and 'the public' a thing of the past.

The local rooting in of the process initiated by the 1991 Act is thus accompanied by information and communication development. Whether carried out by Andra as the major implementers of the law, or by such institutions as the LICs, the communication practices tend to legitimate policy by constant reference to its legislative origin. The decision process does not make a direct appeal to public participation; instead, it is more or less carried out 'in public' rather than 'by the public' (Wynne, 1980, p. 191). Information in this context intervenes as an instrument of public action, containing and channeling controversy.

2   A DYNAMIC PROCESS

We have described above the concrete interpretation given to several measures of the Act, and the forms given to Andra's communication policy and to the LICs. However a case study cannot be complete without examining the effects of placing the high profile research process in a local setting. This part of the study will look at the new pressures put on local stakeholders by the arrival of the laboratory preproject. Andra's communication, to be effective, must follow the evolution of the local debate, meaning that the project implementers must keep tabs on public reaction and attempt to anticipate it. While the LICs seem to be run in a manner that contains debate, the visibility of the research process nevertheless leads stakeholders to define their positions. Controversy thus takes on its own dynamic drive that reveals the instability of the LIC framework.

The Ambivalent Nature of Communication Actions

The observations presented in the first section of this study showed that Andra's communication policy tends to substitute the openness of the process for the 'natural' legitimizing authority of science. This approach is a source of pressure. Whereas traditional forms of authority invoke solidity and permanence, the use of communication introduces a 'legitimacy of the ephemeral' (Rangeon,

1991), never acquired, ever to be renewed. The existence of a 'political and social consensus' in favor of possible laboratory construction was put forth by the Mediator as a principal criterion for the selection of the three candidate sites. Still, his report specified that such a consensus had to be considered 'from a dynamic perspective, that is liable to evolve in one direction or another over time. The same goes for opposition to the project' (Bataille, 1993, p. 31). Communication actions therefore must target the legitimization of a dynamic process, rather than defend a foregone conclusion. The credibility of information and communication actions thus requires continuous adjustment to the current claims heard for or against the project. 'In this dossier, the essential thing from our point of view is to be reactive. Things change over the course of 24 hours. We can hear bad news in the morning, that becomes good news by noon, and then in the evening receive other news. Does this impression result from the fact that we are too deeply involved in the subject? In any case, we're into something very alive. Thus, responsiveness is really the important element'.[19] In order to be 'reactive', Andra thus has equipped itself with procedures to monitor and predict the evolution of public concerns, as well as its own image.

At each public information session (organized by Andra, separately from and outside the LICs), and in each informal contact, Andra representatives attempt to answer all the recurrent and sometimes embarrassing questions raised as to the reversibility of an underground repository, the risks it poses, and the criteria that guide research. The primary task for communication delegates is to construct a clear message; they must thus anticipate the questions that may be posed by visitors. For this reason, an internal brief is produced after each traveling exhibit or public meeting. These reports are feedback for Andra scientists who get together over the questions raised and attempt to develop responses. During the formal public inquiry that took place around each laboratory candidate site in 1997, the questions written in official registers by members of the public were systematically analyzed.

'The important thing is to be able to provide answers to the technical questions. Thus we have to go through those things [the registers] to know what the questions are. So, we prepared a certain number of responses, we know where things get hung up. Then, at headquarters, there's a pilot group that's supposed to receive as fast as possible the most trivial or the most difficult or the most twisted questions, and try to come up with the answers. (...) We brainstorm to try to figure out what kind of questions will come up, it's the same thing for the public meetings'.[20]

The anticipation of questions, and the process of reflection that they set into motion, enable Andra to develop a more 'robust' presentation of the project. It is tempting to describe this systematic review of questions as a form of technology: public reactions are materialized the better to be treated. This monitoring enables the implementers to 'reframe and refine our discourse'. In sum, Andra has equipped itself to adjust its message in response to concerns that may emerge. The briefs allow the effect of the prepared message to be evaluated and stumbling blocks to be identified. Is this primarily a dedication to integrating public concerns, or simply a monitoring device? In any case, these procedures permit Andra to be up to date and on the spot when there is a drift in the tone of argument or modification of public attitudes, and to anticipate them.

On this basis it can be said that Andra's local visitors' centers and meetings function not only to provide information to the public, but to produce information on the public and the local milieu. These neighborhood information actions must thus be grasped in their ambivalent character. On the one hand, they put pressure on Andra, linked not only to the need to justify its research, but to the very visibility of its undertakings. The guiding proposition that the public 'see and know' can turn against the implementers. The visibility given to Andra exposes it to the critical regard of citizens taken as witnesses. It is significant that the campaign launched by laboratory opponents in the Gard in May 1997, at the time of the public inquiry, titled itself '100,000 Witnesses' (reported by *Le Monde*, 24 May 1997). On the other hand, though, Andra can exploit neighborhood communication actions for the information they provide upon local populations. Communication in this context is thus far from the model of a predetermined message, emitted, possibly deformed, and received. On the contrary, exchanges take place, with each interaction providing information for each partner.

Framework Instability

Andra's monitoring procedures are not sufficient to control the dynamic produced by the visibility of the research process. The high profile given to its undertakings can trigger defiance and the emergence of new spokespersons for newly defined interests, who perpetually reinstate controversy and displace the debate. These displacements lead to new definitions of the very notion of 'risk'. To illustrate such an effect, we will explore the project opposition mounted by the wine growers of the Gard.

The very first French nuclear complex, performing basic and military research, was born in the Gard, in the early 1950s. The nuclear industry very soon set up cohabitation with the dominant agricultural activity, wine growing. The symbol of the easy relationship remains the famous 'Cuvée Marcoule', a Rhone Valley wine that carries the name of the nuclear site. Nothing, it seems, foreshadowed the negative reactions of the wine producers when the Gard was preselected for the new phase in nuclear development: radioactive waste management. Indeed the city council closest to the potential laboratory site, in which actual growers held the majority of seats, had expressed a favorable opinion, reassuring to project implementers. A spontaneous council vote was held in 1993 on the issue of lab candidature, with a positive outcome.

Little heard until the end of 1994, the wine community took their first official position on the project during the annual meeting of the Côtes du Rhône syndicate: the president expressed their 'refusal to see their vines grow on top of a nuclear dump'. The opposition by producers went on growing to reach its summit at the public inquiry in spring 1997. This sudden positioning appeared to surprise most local politicians and leaders. However, Andra gave the following interpretation: '(The wine growers) said it very clearly at the time (i.e. from 1994): "When you do your research, don't talk about it much and we won't be bothered by it. It's not in the interest of our product image for us to talk about it much either". When the CEA and the military landed in Marcoule (in the 1950s) and it was all secret, it didn't bother anybody. Since it was secret, no one was concerned by it. Whereas Andra arrived with the resolution to get the message across, to show off openness, meaning we organized exhibits, presentations, all sorts of things like that. And every time, the growers were obliged to say they had image problems'.[21]

This interpretation shows the paradoxical and unexpected role placed by information procedures. The main trigger for positioning by the wine community is not the fact of radwaste management research, but the visibility of the research caused by Andra's successive public information campaigns. It must be remembered that the growers' position may have been reinforced by the negative impact France's military nuclear testing had upon wine exports in late 1995, and by the 'mad cow' affair in 1996, which demonstrated the potential commercial and economic impacts of an image crisis.

A new stakeholder finally was sent to center stage: the Côtes du Rhône *Appellation d'origine contrôlée* (AOC) Vineyards. This new player would radically modify the terms of the debate and the grounds for controversy. Despite the fact that the *de facto* partnership between wine producers and nuclear industry had worked well for thirty years, it was unsettled by the prospect of a waste repository. The local press titled in 1997: 'Côtes du Rhône *vs.* nuclear waste'.[22]

The center of debate thus moved from the health and environmental risks that may be associated with radwaste, to the risks for wines product image posed by the semantics of the word 'waste'. It was as if uncertainty shifted ground. On a technical plane, the question is one of whether deep geological layers can contain HLNW, and project implementers further faced the political uncertainty of whether local populations would welcome or reject the various stages of the project. But in regard to exchanges over the future of the *appellation contrôlée*, the most important uncertainty appeared to be whether the wine and nuclear industries could continue to coexist in the Gard. By the sole expression of this discord, the formulation of issues, risks and necessary risk reduction measures was radically transformed.

Faced with the emergence of this unexpected player, certain information measures were taken by Andra and by the LIC, in the objective of containing controversy. Rapidly, the central organism for concerted action and information instituted by law, the LIC, attempted to take a mediating stance. The discussion bore on what sort of pacifying action should be taken toward the Côtes du Rhône syndicate. 'Should we propose to the wine growers a seat on the LIC? Should we send a letter to the heads of the syndicate to invite them to dialogue with us?'.[23]

This first stage of response terminated by allowing entry to the growers' fears. Representatives of two organisms were soon made part of the LIC: the Federation of cooperative cellars and the Winegrowers' syndicate. The LIC thus displayed its intention to bring potential opponents quickly into the fold and to waste no time in developing a strategy. This integration would then allow the growers to set out their complaints. One new delegate stated to the commission[24] 'wine is 40 percent liquid and 60 percent dream. That's the source of our fears'. The clay shield, the waste containers, homeowners, elected officials and scientists were thus no longer the sole elements brought together in the waste management formula: from now on, wine export data were part of the risk analysis. This new variable was integrated by expanding the range of experts consulted; these were no longer strictly of scientific bent. Indeed, the Côtes du Rhône syndicate clearly claimed a monopoly on expert knowledge of the international wine market: 'The wine growers are resolutely opposed to the project of creating a research laboratory by Andra on the Marcoule site. It must be stated without ambiguity that this opposition is not based on technical considerations linked to the safety of the proposed installations. We have no competence to judge such matters. However, we consider ourselves to be competent and authoritative in judgement as to the image that buyers and consumers have of our wines'.[25]

The LIC would contribute to producing a new type of information in response to the grower's concerns. The LIC ordered a study by the Chamber of Agriculture on the possible stigmatization effects upon wine that would be produced by the construction of an underground lab. This study, produced by a consultancy, was made public in March 1996 and confirmed the wine community's fears. Far from pacifying debate, the results of the study only reinforced the grower's position. On the basis of the results of that marketing evaluation, the LIC would go on to mount an institute whose mission was to collect data on all food market risk factors (producing a map of pollution sites in the region, collating scientific articles bearing on the impacts of agricultural chemical additives, etc.). Pertinent data also included the analysis of food market risk 'precedents' like the 'mad cow' affair and rumors of food contamination. In sum, an observatory was created, producing by the way a network of scientists who could be called upon to intervene with reassurances in case of 'media alert' on the wine and waste issue. The LIC thus expended significant effort on setting up the means to tame the unpredictable and unstable element of food stigma risk. These means, appropriately, involved information management, in the form of monitoring and crisis preparedness, and were centered in an identified institution set up by the LIC.

Andra, on the other hand, would seem outpaced by the wine growers' strong mobilization. It reacted with a counterstudy of 95 pages that 'shed new light' on the impact by industrial establishments upon agricultural product image. The conclusion states: 'To the extent that the Andra underground laboratory is a scientific research establishment which entails no risk to the environment, the fears for harm to wine's brand image are without real basis. This reassuring analysis should lead to a new taking stock by all parties, in the goal of reinforcing agricultural brand image'.[26]

Andra brochures too would be put up to date with the wine controversy. These stressed the problems posed for agricultural product image by any risky installation. In February 1997, in a press kit entitled 'Brand image: *Appellation contrôlée* and waste', a Champagne grower working near the surface waste storage facility run by Andra, the Centre de Stockage de l'Aube, recounted his reassuring experience: 'Finally, opposition quieted down and we realize today that this installation has had a positive impact on the region's economy. There has never been any problem since Andra's arrival. On the contrary, the people who come to buy Champagne ask where the Center is located'.[27]

Andra put the emphasis on reassuring discourse, but its effectiveness appeared limited. Indeed, with the stage entry of wine growers and the political force they represent, the social networks on which Andra's communication policy was based seemed to break down. The LIC's actions seemed to be no more successful in putting an end to the dynamic controversy, which spilled outside the space carefully set up for it. The fragility of the information frameworks, and their inability to contain controversy, were showed up by the way positions for and against the project became more pronounced, and new alliances were formed in the community. The mounting mobilization of the wine community against the laboratory project produced direct effects upon the local political scene. The principal effect of the controversy was to render fragile the system of alliance that the LIC seemed to epitomize.

The interpretation given to the 1991 Act, we saw above, introduced the major innovation of bringing elected officials into the management process. They become the third party situated between project implementers and opponents (mainly those from environmental defense groups), a third party whom implementers openly try to co-opt[28] and whose positive view on the project is sought. They are indeed in great majority favorable to the project, and are especially interested by the economic incentives that go along with it. However, their position is far from frozen. Inasmuch as they gain entry on their status of representatives of the public (or their electorate at least), they are perpetually at the mercy of swings in the balance of power on the public scene. The wine lobby went to them to seek support for the opposition movement, and pressed them to make a public position statement. Another aspect of risk was thus made apparent: the risk to established political balance. In a region where wine producers constitute both a major economic and a major electoral force, a public statement of disfavor for their syndicate's position could be suicidal. Indeed, the syndicate went on to publish the list of mayors who maintained their support for the laboratory preproject, leaving no doubt as to their intention to place the debate on such a plane.

One of the consequences of the pressure brought by the wine lobby would be that some officials indeed change their minds and reject the preproject. Another consequence was that some players who did not gain entry to the LIC or who otherwise had not been taken into account, rode the wave of contention produced by the lobby. They included most of the elected officials from the neighboring *département* of the Vaucluse, consulted neither by the mediator nor by the LIC. For these players, the wine grower's launch of controversy was a window of opportunity allowing them to state their position.

On the other two candidate sites, in the Vienne and in the Meuse, local politicians opposing the lab project created groups. The public inquiry procedure then put an effective moratorium on LIC business and on Andra communication campaigns, Andra being fully concerned with studying and preparing responses to questions collected in the registers. At this time, the opponent politician groups made their own statements,[29] hanging them on the 'hook' of the inquiry that moved debate out of the space defined by the LIC. A variety of more visible protests were also seen, like street marches. It must be noted that the wine lobby's open opposition also drew counterbalancing statements greatly in favor of the lab project. Professional unions left their habitual reserve to create a 'laboratory support committee'.

With this emergence of new players determined in their opposition, the debate thus took on a new conflictual aspect that could not be controlled or channeled by the LIC mechanism. In such a light it would appear that despite the good intentions expressed in the Act, no forum for real discussion among stakeholders has been created; only a highly goal-centered institution, the

LIC, and the familiar discourse of political posturing have managed to emerge. At the time of writing, it appeared that without the possibility for real engagement with local populations, Andra's communication policy could lose credibility. When conflict of interests reaches the degree of exacerbation seen in, e.g. the Gard, local exchanges, or communication fixes, indeed appear no longer to suffice. It would seem that such conflict should be considered as a learning opportunity (Stern, 1991) and that its resolution be sought on, once again, the national level.

3 CONCLUSION AND POSTFACE

This study looked at the concrete forms given to information requirements set out by the French high-level radioactive waste management Act of 1991. It was seen that a traditional descriptive model of risk communication was inappropriate, in that observed information practices went far beyond the transfer of technical information to the public, and beyond even the defense of a foregone technical decision. The organization of communication by project implementers, and by the local information commissions representing 'permanent democratic control', was seen as targeting the legitimization of, in fact, a political process (that of seeking local support for a technical solution). This legitimization was performed through constant reference to the legislated framework.

It was seen as well that the communication practices were tightly adjusted to the local context, seeking to create networks among players judged influential in the upcoming site decision. The selection of these actors and the provision of an identified space for their exchanges contributed to circumscribing the controversies that may be expected in siting any risk producing installation. Communication in this context is best analyzed as an instrument of authoritative action, part of a general governing style that might most simply be described as 'pragmatic' as it pursues the nation's major technological projects.

But the second part of the case study showed that such an instrument is not without specific and sometimes unforeseen and uncontrollable effects in the field. Despite the asymmetry of authority and power available to the various actors, a wide margin of action remains for the expression of project opposition (or favor) on the margin indeed of the instituted communication space, whose limits and even fragility are thereby demonstrated. The high profile given to the scientific research process renders it visible, and then increasingly meaningful and pertinent in a wide variety of settings. Technical projects led in a 'discreet' manner may be condemned for reserving decision power to a technocratic elite, but at least they do not intrude daily upon the concerns of their neighbors. In contrast, the visibility of today's waste management process exposes it to the critiques of a whole range of players who, allowed a vision of the technical project, may then analyze how its impacts may threaten their interests.

The evolution of controversy in this setting is thus tightly linked to the ability by project implementers or promoters (the radwaste management agency or, more broadly, representatives of the state) to limit debate to a confined setting, and, inversely, to opponents' ability to transfer the debate to the widest possible scale. As this study was written, the deep repository concept itself was indeed encountering challenge on the national level, as three National Assembly members (representing Socialist, Communist and Green parties) denounced the laboratory project. They expressed regret at the overwhelming public emphasis placed on the deep repository option among the three research directions (regret shared by the Mediator himself), and demanded that the Act be modified to guarantee the retrievability of deep stored wastes.[30]

In 1999, only one laboratory site could be designated by the government at the outcome of the phase analyzed here. That was at Bure, the clay site in the East of France (not visited for our study). The rejection of the Gard site has been generally seen as resting upon non-technical grounds (i.e., rejection was based on sociopolitical considerations), while the Vienne site was seen as technically unsuited.

In Spring 2000, a three-man Mission for Information and Conciliation was dispatched by the Prime Minister to the West of France to exchange with publics in localities identified by Andra as technically appropriate for geological evaluation with the view of identifying a granite research laboratory candidate site. This Mission was met by aggressive protestors and a series of large marches (up to 8,000 persons) was set off in various regions of France. The outcome in June 2000 was for ministers to recall the Mission.[31] The language of newspapers and quotes from ministers and regional politicians suggested a disavowal of this phase of the radwaste management program. Andra as implementer finds itself out of alignment with the Act, as it must construct more than one laboratory in order to pursue research on the repository option. The process and calendar of the Act are destabilized.[32]

This study has attempted to describe a number of local communication practices, and their effects in context, giving voice to a variety of players through interviews or quotation of published materials. It is clear that, as the high level radioactive waste management research process and the dynamic it produces are in full swing, our study could only give a view from one moment in time. There is ample matter for study as radwaste management and communication issues continue to unfold in France.

NOTES

1. Based on a national case study within RISKPERCOM or Risk Perception and Communication, European Commission Contract n° F14P-T95-0016 (DG12-WSME, 1995-99), coordinated by L. Sjöberg (Sweden) with partners in France, Great Britain, Norway and Spain.
   The authors acknowledge the support of J. Brenot, IPSN, French coordinator. All analyses
   are the responsibility of the authors. A similar article was published as Y. Barthe and C.
   Mays (2001), 'Communication and information in France's underground laboratory siting
   process: Clarity of procedure, ambivalence of effects', *Journal of Risk Research*, **4** (4),
   411-30.
2. The Commission Nationale d'Evaluation, or CNE.
3. 'High level and long lived' waste according to the French terminology.
4. Commission locale d'information et de suivi, commonly abbreviated to CLI.
5. This Mediator, National Assemblyman Christian Bataille, indeed had authored the Waste
   Act (sometimes refered to in France as the Loi Bataille) after performing a series of national
   hearings (OPECST, 1990; also see Mays and Poumadère, 1996).
6. The procedure followed during that first laboratory site search might jokingly be described
   as 'Decide-Announce-Defend'—without the 'Announce' phase! See Mays and Poumadère
   (1996); Mays (1999).
   A. Faussat, an Andra official much involved in the prior period of site selection, gave his
   point of view on public information history in an interview with the second author (22
   January 1991). 'We did give prior information, I must insist, but the day you give the information people say: 'ah, but why didn't you give it before?'. Faussat also referred to an
   unfortunate event, recounting that Andra held an information meeting for local elected officials in the region of a site pre-selected on technical grounds. The information then was
   leaked to the media as the elected officials left the meeting and went back to their communities, meaning that citizens heard the news on local radio before their own elected
   representatives could deliver it. Faussat recognized that the new Waste Act gave a needed
   framework to all radwaste management activities (constituting in such a way clear prior
   information).
7. This style of assumption is criticized by Beauchamp (1996).
8. This section title is a reference to Marie (1989), who discusses the symbolic use of change in
   governance.
9. Since the time of writing in 1997, both the President and Director of Andra again changed (in
   1999 and 2000 respectively).
10. Communication delegate, Vienne local agency, quoted in *Labo Infos*, the Vienne LIC
    journal, no. 8, July 1997.
11. Communication delegate, Gard agency, interview.
12. Gard agency communication delegate, interview.
13. Préfecture du Gard (undated), Rôle et activité de l'instance locale de concertation et
    d'information.
14. Private communication to the second author by a member of the Mediator's office, 1994.
15. In the sense of 'intéressement', or the process of a 'locking into place' of actors, proposed by
    sociologist M. Callon (1986).
16. A sum described by the Mediator as equivalent to the cost of constructing 5 kilometers of
    highway.
17. *Labo Infos*, no. 1, October 1995.
18. Local journalist, interview.
19. Andra's Communication Director, interview.
20. Andra Gard employee, interview.
21. Andra Gard employee, interview.
22. *Le Provençal*, 25 February 1997.
23. Minutes of the LIC guiding council, 27 January 1995.
24. Minutes of the LIC guiding council, 28 April 1995.
25. Brochure 'Côtes du Rhône A.O.C.: Richesse des couleurs et trésors du gout'.
26. GEM Etudes et Stratégies, 'Impact des établissements industriels à risque sur l'image des

produits agricoles', January 1997.
27. Andra Gard Newsletter, no. 9, February 1997, p. 5.
28. See note 15.
29. See e.g. *Le Monde*, 7 October 1997: 'Des élus locaux relancent la polémique sur la gestion des déchets radioactifs'.
30. *Le Figaro*, 18 September 1997: 'Trois francs-tireurs déterrent les déchets nucléaires; la polémique gagne l'Assemblée nationale'.
31. See e.g. *Nuclear Fuel*, June 2000: 'French government throws in towel on search for granite waste lab site'.
32. The events leading up to and surrounding the granite site search are recounted and analyzed by C. Mays (2004), 'Where does it go: Siting methods and social representations of radioactive waste management in France', in A. Boholm and R. Löfstedt (eds), *Contesting Local Environments*, London: Earthscan.

REFERENCES

Barrère, M. (1991), 'La doctrine nucléaire contre vents et marées', *Autrement*, Paris: Editions Autrement, série *Sciences en société*.
Barthe, Y., J.P. Le Bourhis and E. Rémy (1997), 'Communication in Public Policies', paper presented at the Workshop *'Information policy and information campaigns as tools for improved urban air quality'*, COST 618, Brussels, 2–3 October.
Bataille, C. (1993), *Mission de médiation sur l'implantation de laboratoires de recherche souterrains*, Rapport au Premier Ministre, Paris: La documentation Française.
Beauchamp, A. (1996), *Gérer le Risque, Vaincre la Peur*, Québec: Bellarmin.
Blancher, P., G. Decourt and B. Vallet (1996), *Analyze et propositions d'amélioration du fonctionnement des Commissions Locales d'Information auprès des grands equipements énergétiques*, Rapport pour la Direction de la Sûreté des Installations Nucléaires, premier semestre, 1996.
Borzeix, A. (1987), 'Ce que parler peut faire', *Sociologie du travail*, **XXIX** (2), 157–76.
Callon, M. (1986), 'Some elements for a sociology of translation: Domestication of the scallops and the fishermen of Saint-Brieuc Bay', in J. Law (ed.), *Power, Action and Belief: A New Sociology of Knowledge? (Sociological Review Monograph)*, London: Routledge and Kegan Paul, 196–229.
Delavigne, V. (1994), 'Les discours institutionnels du nucléaire: stratégies discursives d'euphorisation', *Mots*, **39**, 53–67.
Garraud, P. (1980), 'Politique électro-nucléaire et stratégies de l'information', in A. Mabileau and A.-J. Tudesq (eds), *L'Information Locale*, Paris: Pedone, 129–45.
Kaluzny, Y., D. Auverlot, E. Boissac and G. Ouzounian (1996), 'La gestion des déchets radioactifs en France, Un projet technique, un projet responsable pour une gestion à long terme', paper presented at International Conference *'The Environment in the 21st Century: Environment, Long-Term Governability and Democracy'*, Abbaye de Fontevraud, France, 8–11 September (French Environment Ministry).
Marie, J.L. (1989), 'La symbolique du changement', in A. Mabileau and C. Sorbets (eds), *Gouverner les Villes Moyennes*, Paris: Pedone, 109–49.
Mays, C. (1999), 'A value message is worth a thousand words: Impact of management framework on public perceptions of nuclear waste', in Kjell Andersson (ed.), *Valdor: Values in Decisions on Risk, Proceedings*, Stockholm: Karinta-Konsult.
Mays, C. and M. Poumadère (1996), 'Uncertain communication: Institutional discourse in nuclear repository siting', in V. Sublet, V.T. Covello and T.L. Tinker (eds), *Scientific Uncertainty and Its Influence on the Public Communication*

Process, Kluwer/NATO, 137–61.

OPECST (Office Parlementaire d'Evaluation des Choix Scientifiques et Techno-
logiques) (1990), *Rapport sur la gestion des déchets nucléaires à haute activité par
C. Bataille*, Paris: La documentation Française.

Prieur, M. (1992), 'Déchets radioactifs: du laboratoire souterrain à l'enfouissement
irréversible?', *Préventiques*, **44**, March–April, 44.

Rangeon, F. (1991), 'Communication politique et légitimité', in CURAPP (ed.), *La
Communication Politique*, Paris: PUF, 99–114.

Stern, P.C. (1991), 'Learning through conflict: A realistic strategy for risk communication', *Policy Sciences*, **24** (1), (February), 99–119.

Turner, G. and B. Wynne (1992), 'Risk communication: A literature review and some
implications for biotechnology', in J. Durant (ed.), *Biotechnology in Public*, London: Science Museum, 109–41.

Wynne, B. (1980), 'Technology, risk and participation: on the social treatment of
uncertainty', in J. Conrad (ed.), *Society, Technology and Risk Assessment*, London: Academic Press, 173–208.

9. Balancing Risks to Nature and Risks to People: The Coode Island/Point Lillias Project in Australia

Aynsley Kellow

1 INTRODUCTION

This chapter examines a case which involved an attempt by a state government in Australia to relocate a chemical storage and handling facility after a catastrophic fire in 1991. While there was initial strong support for such a relocation, and attempts were made to follow open and consultative siting processes, the fairness of the process was compromised by a decision by the federal government to use the most preferred site for an armaments depot, which made it incompatible with another facility of high explosive risk.

The process thus became essentially one of 'decide-announce-defend' (DAD) as only one other site met the economic and technical criteria for the project, and this site was of some sensitivity on ecological and heritage grounds, as well as involving new risks for residents 7 km away, who were offered few compensating economic benefits. The risks to nature, along with the heritage issues, were able to be invoked by the residents at the new site to resist successfully the proposed relocation, despite the offering of compensation to offset the risks to nature.

This successful opposition, however, meant that the facility would remain at its existing site, meaning a continuation of risks to residents as close as 0.5 km away. These residents were unable to invoke risks to nature to assist their cause, and appear to have made a tactical error in joining a coalition dominated by groups which opposed location at *either* site, apparently not realizing the likely outcome was a 'do nothing' response which would mean the status quo and a continuation of existing risks.

Australia does not have a particularly good record with siting experience (Kellow, 1996). This case had promising beginnings, with consensus on the need for relocation and adoption of a fair, open process, but it ultimately saw repeated most of the mistakes of the past and, in particular, because of the crucial mistake of foreclosing options, provides further support for the importance of decisional fairness in siting processes if risk perception is not to be amplified. In this case, one group of residents was also able to invoke risks to nature, which tipped the balance in their favour but at the expense of those exposed to greater existing risks.

2   THE COODE ISLAND FIRES AND AFTERMATH

At 2.17 pm on 21 August 1991 an explosion and major fire occurred at the chemical storage facility operated by Terminals Pty Ltd at Coode Island in the inner western suburbs of the city of Melbourne in the state of Victoria. The fire involved various hazardous chemicals, including acrylonitrile, phenol, methyl ethyl ketone and benzene (Thomas, 1995).

The 46-tank depot was part of the port storage facility for the Victorian petrochemical industry, which was concentrated at nearby Footscray and Altona further to the west. It took 170 firefighters three hours to control the initial fire, and although nobody was killed in the incident, two firefighters were injured. People in central Melbourne and the western suburbs were told to stay indoors as a cloud of smoke (considered to be potentially toxic) moved across the city, although Environmental Protection Authority testing subsequently revealed the absence of any chemical hazard. Smoke was detected 30 km away from the fire, factories and ships were evacuated, and for a time the Port of Melbourne was closed to all shipping. High winds helped dissipate the smoke, avoiding any injuries among the general public from smoke inhalation (Victoria, 1991; 1991a; 1991b; 1992a; 1992b).

Damage and clean-up costs amounted to about $35m, and the company was later charged under labor and environment laws, with fines totaling about $1.3m being imposed. The government also established a Coode Island Review Panel to recommend an action plan to minimize the risks associated with the facility and make recommendations concerning the long-term storage of hazardous chemicals at port facilities. There had been several other spills and fires in the western suburbs of Melbourne involving hazardous chemicals, the most notable being the April 1985 fire at the warehouse of Butlers Transport Ltd, and there was thus substantial political support for action, even before the Coode Island explosion. A local group, the Hazardous Materials Action Group (HAZMAG) had formed to represent residents' concerns over these risks.

The site involved in the fire was one of three sites operated by Terminals Pty Ltd. Six other companies had facilities on Coode Island under leases from the Port of Melbourne Authority which were to begin to expire in 1995, although most (seven of the remaining eight) leases expired in the period between the end of 2000 and 31 March 2002. This timeline was to prove important later, as delays in site approval began to push up against the limit imposed by the need to renew leases or abandon Coode Island.

While problems have been encountered elsewhere (most notably with the disaster at Bhopal in India) with residential housing subsequently encroaching into the buffer zone established around chemical facilities (Hazarika, 1987), the opposite was the case with Coode Island, because the facility grew incrementally from 1960 in a location only about half a kilometer from residential housing. This lack of an adequate buffer zone was a problem, but despite 47 recorded spills in the preceding ten years the Coode Island Review Panel reported there had been no fires or other serious accidents recorded (Victoria, 1991, pp. 60–62). Consultants engaged by the Review Panel found nothing extraordinary about the Coode Island facility compared with other similar sites around the world, but did recommend a buffer be maintained around any site to which it was to be relocated (Robertson, 1991).

The outcome of the review process was that it was decided in April 1992 to move the storage facility in 1994–95 to a site at Point Wilson, further down the western side of Port Philip Bay, close to the city of Geelong. The existence of a large oil refinery at Geelong meant that there were existing easements for pipelines servicing the area and the site was well-located in relation to the Altona petrochemicals complex, while providing a sufficient buffer from residents and other industry. The cost of this relocation was estimated to be $200m, with $100m of this to be met by the government.

Victoria was the centre of the chemical industry in Australia, with about 50 percent of capacity located in that state, 80 percent of this being on the western side of Melbourne. Industries which would be using the facility had an annual production valued at $1.6b and employed 7,000 people. About 230,000 tonnes of chemicals would be handled and stored at the facility annually. Transport to users of the chemicals would occur mainly by road, although a pipeline connected to the existing line servicing the Shell oil refinery would carry benzene, petroleum, diesel and other fuels. Although the nearby city of Geelong had been hard hit by recession and the collapse of a local financial institution in the early 1990s, the facility would provide only 25 jobs during operation (with another 25 during construction) (Victoria, 1995), so the localized economic benefits provided by the facility were not particularly large.

Chemicals to be stored and handled at the facility included benzene, ethanol, methanol, solvents, chlorinated solvents, propylene oxide, toluene diisocyanate, phenol, styrene, acrylonitrile, methyl methacrylate, acrylate monomers, DTPA, N-paraffin, polyols, oils and miscellaneous chemicals. The major chemical user companies were BASF Australia Ltd (Altona), Dow Chemical (Australia) Ltd (Altona), Geon Australia Ltd (Altona), Huntsman

Chemical (West Footscray), ICI Australia (Laverton) and Rohm and Haas Pty Ltd (Geelong).

The selection of the private sector proponent who would design, build and operate the facility was to be made by the chemical manufacturers who would be the customers for the facility, with the selection process being coordinated by the Plastics and Chemicals Industries Association under the terms of a memorandum of understanding concluded with the state government on 2 August 1994. The Environmental Effects Statement (EES) process was to have been completed only once the proponent was selected, but delays in selecting the company necessitated completion of the EES by the government, increasing the extent to which it was seen as actively promoting the project, rather than facilitating it. This undoubtedly contributed to a perceived lack of voluntariness on the part of residents, a factor known to amplify risk perceptions and contribute to failure in siting controversies (Slovic, 1987; 1993).

A Safer Chemical Storage Taskforce was established to implement the recommendations of the Coode Island Review Panel and undertake preparation of an Environmental Effects Statement (required under the *Environmental Effects Act 1978*) to examine in detail the suitability of West Point Wilson commenced in September 1992. In January 1994 the Taskforce was replaced by a Project Committee which reviewed a number of sites previously examined by the Review Panel.

This reconsideration of sites was necessitated by the plans of the Commonwealth government, which had an existing armaments storage site at Point Wilson and was seeking to relocate its armaments depot from the naval base at Sydney. Point Wilson had been listed as a possible site for a new East Coast Armaments Complex (ECAC), and was confirmed as the preferred site for this complex in April 1994. At the same time the Victorian government announced Point Lillias, about 6 km west of Point Wilson, as the new site for the chemical storage depot. The Victorian government also announced that it would provide the port, roads, and services infrastructure for the project at an estimated cost of $30–40m, while a private company would be sought to build, own and operate the new storage facility.

The Project Committee included two members of the former Taskforce, and was supported by a Point Lillias Project Unit located within the Ministry of Industry Services. The preparation of the Environmental Effects Statement was required to be carried out in an open and transparent process in which full community participation was encouraged. To achieve this, an EES Consultative Committee was established, with members from several government departments, community and environmental groups, and companies with operations in the area.

It is important to note that the government was playing an important facilitative role here, not only to relocate the facility from Coode Island, but to ensure the state benefited by securing the relocation of the armaments complex from New South Wales. By making the siting decisions and then seeking to find a private sector builder-operator, the government was using the power of the state to overcome any opposition to siting which might have thwarted attempts by a private contractor to find a suitable site. And by opting for Point Lillias rather than West Point Wilson it was maximizing the chances that the state of Victoria would secure the ECAC and its associated economic benefits.

While final selection of the Point Lillias site was subject to this EES and public consultation process, it was clear that this was the strongly preferred site. Nevertheless, the EES was required to consider a number of options: West Point Wilson (in case the ECAC did not proceed), Point Lillias with ECAC at Point Wilson, Point Lillias without ECAC at Point Wilson, and several other sites. With Point Wilson effectively ruled out by the selection of that site for ECAC, Point Lillias was clearly favoured on most criteria (see Table 9.1) (Victoria, 1995a). This made the siting process essentially one of 'decide, announce, defend'.

3   THE ENVIRONMENTAL EFFECTS STATEMENT PROCESS

The preparation of the EES was guided by a consultative committee of about 40 representing community, environment, industry, trade union and government interests. This committee met monthly, and in addition an extensive program of community consultation was conducted (Wicks, 1995). Briefing sessions were held at nearby Geelong and in other centres of population, with extensive advertisements accompanying the release of new material, and a portable display used to explain the project to the population. Residents most affected were written to directly, with 13,000 letters being sent (and 616 responses being received). In addition, regular information bulletins were mailed to 2,500 people.

One noteworthy feature was the fact that the opponents of the project were incorporated into the consultation process, but this incorporation meant ultimately that diverse interests were subsumed within a single group, the Statewide Environment Groups (SWEG), which compromised the effectiveness of HAZMAG as a representative of the interests of the residents at Coode Island. The Point Lillias Project Unit distributed with their information bulletins an information bulletin prepared by the Statewide Environment Groups. In addition, the Statewide Environment Groups were invited to send a representative to all the public meetings organized by the Project Unit.

SWEG represented the main environment groups active in Victoria: the Australian Conservation Foundation, Environment Victoria, Friends of the Earth, and Greenpeace. These groups represented interests much broader than those related to location, with some of them having larger agendas in opposition to the chemical industry *per se*. Such opposition was related more to questions of 'whether' there should be a chemical industry and thus a storage facility. Greenpeace, for example, had a global 'toxics campaign' directed at phasing out the element chlorine, central to many modern chemical products. The Coode Island-Point Lillias dilemma presented them with an opportunity to advance this agenda by making the siting of any facility problematic, and using the case to raise community concerns about chemical hazards.

Other organizations opposed to the project included the Geelong Environment Council, Geelong Field Naturalists Club, Geelong Residents Against Hazardous Materials, HAZMAG, Port Phillip Conservation Council, Royal Australasian Ornithologists Union, Victorian National Parks Association, and the World Wide Fund for Nature. Several of these were locationally-specific, particularly related to the Geelong region where Point Lillias was, or to the risks to birds, which was again a Point Lillias issue. It is worth noting the basis of the opposition from these groups. They based their opposition mainly on the presence of Aboriginal archaeological sites of significance at Point Lillias, the claimed lack of adequate buffer zones, the impacts of dredging for the port facility on seagrass beds, cumulative impacts of the facility and the armaments complex, and the possible impact of the facility on migratory birds using wetlands in the area and which Australia had a duty to protect under the Ramsar Convention (on wetlands), the Bonn Convention (on migratory species of wild animals) and bilateral agreements on migratory species with Japan and China. The most significant species affected was the endangered Orange-Bellied Parrot of which less than 200 individuals are thought to remain. The Orange-Bellied Parrot made a powerful symbol invoked by opponents to Point Lillias in protests in Geelong.

The natural coalition which emerged – indeed, was facilitated by the co-optation of opposition into SWEG – was between those concerned with the threats to nature in the form of rare or migratory birds and wetlands which were the subject of international agreements and the residents of the Geelong region who were concerned about chemical and catastrophic risks. The residents from Coode Island, represented by HAZMAG, were marginalized as a result, especially as there were no risks to nature they could invoke to bolster their cause, since the environment at Coode Island was a severely degraded industrial one.

It is important to note that in opposing the facility at Point Lillias, the Statewide Environment Groups not only decided to become part of the process in order to provide a critical assessment of the proposal, they quite explicitly acknowledged the need to close down the Coode Island facility. The question of *whether* a facility was needed was therefore not acknowledged as being at issue, even for the project's strongest opponents, but this joint framework in the SWEG mechanism diluted the effectiveness of those such as HAZMAG who had been primarily motivated by the need to close Coode Island, and this was ultimately to cost them dearly.

The Statewide Environment Groups' preferred alternative was to locate the facility at West Point Wilson, adjacent to the ECAC (as recommended by the Coode Island Review Panel, although before the announcement that ECAC would be located at Point Wilson). The West Point Wilson site was more distant from the city of Geelong, the major population centre in the region, and did not include any Ramsar-listed wetlands. The Australian Nature Conservation Agency, a Commonwealth government agency, opposed the Point Lillias site on the grounds that it did not consider the facility to be a wise use of a wetland designated as being of international importance. If this was accepted, the facility could only proceed if the site was excised from the listed area, which (under Ramsar) was permissible only if this was in the urgent national interest, and if comparable habitat could be provided as compensation. Placing the facility beside the armaments complex would undoubtedly increase the catastrophic hazard associated with both facilities, and the government had required only a broad comparison of this site with Point Lillias.

The Environmental Effects Statement, a planning amendment to the Greater Geelong District Scheme and an EPA Works Approval application were exhibited to the public between 15 February and 28 March 1996 and then referred to an Independent Panel, which submitted its Report to the Minister for Planning and Local Government and the Environment Protection Authority on 3 June 1996.

The Panel neither endorsed nor rejected the project, but made a number of recommendations for further investigations and other actions prior to approval being considered by the government. The Minister rejected this advice and, noting that the Panel had not identified 'substantive impacts' arising from the proposed development which would render the Point Lillias site unsuitable, proceeded to approve the project on 20 June (Victoria, 1996). The DAD character of the process was thus further reinforced.

The Panel was not satisfied with the risk assessment methodology in the EES and recommended that the facility not be approved pending the conduct of a Quantitative Risk Assessment. The minister noted that a QRA had to be undertaken before the facility could be licensed under the *Dangerous Goods Act* 1985, that this would focus on internal design detail and operations and that this process, not the EES, would confirm the safety of the proposed facility and the measures required to be implemented.

The Panel was especially concerned about the absence of a quantitative risk assessment of the risks posed by the operation of Avalon airport, a concern the minister dismissed with a good grasp of the Gambler's Fallacy: 'Whether the statistical risk of an aircraft hitting the facility is once in 19,000 years or once in 4,000 years is of limited significance in the context of the nominal 30 to 50 year life of the facility' (Victoria, 1996, p. 3) Such statements did little to assuage residents' concerns over risks, but neither did the deferral of the QRA until the detailed design stage, *after* the decision had been made. This detracted from perceived decisional fairness, and thus probably served to amplify risk perception.

The Minister for Planning and Local Government decided, however, that final approval by the Victorian government should await a decision of the Commonwealth Minister for the Environment to recommend to the Ramsar Bureau the excision of the site from the Ramsar-listed area on the grounds of 'urgent national interest', and he recommended that the Minister for Conservation and Land Management should prepare necessary documentation and seek this approval. The 'urgent national interest' basis was indicated as being the need to relocate Coode Island to meet community expectations after the fire and the economic significance of the chemical and dependent manufacturing industries.

4 COMMONWEALTH APPROVAL AND FINAL DECISION

The Commonwealth government approved the Point Lillias project on 14 March 1997, when the federal cabinet accepted the Victorian government's argument that the project was in the urgent national interest (*Age*, 15 March 1997). The Commonwealth agreed to excise 20ha from the 5460ha Ramsar-listed wetlands in order to allow the project to proceed. The Commonwealth agreed to a compensation package which involved increasing the Point Lillias wetland reserve by 240ha, creating a 500ha buffer between the reserve and the new facility, and a 120ha reserve on Snake Island for the Orange-Bellied Parrot.

Ironically, the compensation package would have provided more resources for Orange-Bellied Parrot conservation than were currently available, including fencing to prevent access by foxes and other predators. Officers working to conserve this endangered species apparently had mixed feelings after the subsequent cancellation of the project, since this also meant an end to resources for conservation, and with project cancellation, political support for parrot conservation evaporated.

There was apparently some controversy over the Victorian government's behaviour in the decision process, with the Commonwealth environment department believing the Victorians had withheld a report by an international safety group which found that Coode Island was a reasonably safe facility and met health and safety standards. There was, however, perhaps, more than just the persuasiveness of the Victorian government behind Commonwealth acquiescence. The Commonwealth might have been liable for compensation had it not approved the relocation, because of its decision to site the armaments depot at Point Wilson, since the Australian Constitution specifies that the Commonwealth can acquire property only on 'just terms'.

Commonwealth approval was condemned by both the federal opposition shadow environment minister and by conservation groups, which (according to the Victorian National Parks Association) were considering a legal challenge. Both Friends of the Earth and the Australian Conservation Foundation also criticized the decision. Residents near Coode Island were also critical of the decision. Despite their wish to have Coode Island closed, they questioned the appropriateness of the Point Lillias site. The broadening of the issue away from a NIMBY response by these residents to a wider consideration of the issues of chemical storage weakened the strength of their demands for relocation. The spokeswoman for the Hazardous Materials Action Group, the NGO which provided the most effective vehicle for representing the concerns of residents near Coode Island, stated that the Commonwealth decision created a moral dilemma because it was forced to consider environmental factors at both Coode Island and Point Lillias. Inevitably, this compromised the claims of the Coode Island residents.

Environmentalists regarded Point Lillias as the last piece of 'wilderness' left along Corio Bay, but this was a bold claim. The site was close to a functioning airport, contained a salt works, Aboriginal middens and had a boat ramp and several fishing shacks. If wilderness is quintessentially an area untouched by human activity (see Goodin, 1994), it was difficult to accept the Point Lillias was wilderness. It was nevertheless of some importance in terms of ecological and heritage values, although the wider region provided similar habitat for most species. Its strongest claim for preservation came from its association with the endangered Orange-Bellied Parrot, but even this connection was tenuous, as there had been only one sighting of a parrot at Point Lillias, and that came in 1995 after the selection of Point Wilson as the armaments depot site the previous year made Point Lillias the sole option for chemical storage, and that individual was feeding rather than nesting.

Significantly, the representative of the Department of Natural Resources and Environment had told the Review Panel that one sighting after an extensive period of no visits being recorded was not necessarily justification for international significance being accorded to the site, and that there were other habitats for the Orange-Bellied Parrot in the area of more importance than the site for the facility (Victoria, 1996, p. 85).

Another opponent of location at Point Lillias was the salt company which operated the 1267ha of salt evaporation ponds at the site and feared that any chemical accidents would contaminate the purity of the sea water it needed its make its 100,000 tpa product. (These fears were to be addressed by the provision of a new inlet for salt water to the east of the project site, to be provided before any work commenced which might stir up silt.) Ironically, the wetlands of such importance to be listed under the Ramsar Convention were the company's salt evaporation ponds, again, hardly 'wilderness'.

The salt company was joined by the Wathaurong Aboriginal community which was concerned about the effect of the project on the archeological sites in the area. These were middens, which while of substantial scientific interest, were essentially rubbish heaps filled with the remains of old fires and abalone, oyster and mussel shells. The 'footprint' of the facility had been moved to avoid disturbing these middens. While these 'feasting areas' were of some significance, it was drawing a long bow to suggest that they had the same importance as Aboriginal sacred sites, but the attempt to give them equivalence gave rise to possible action to block the project under the *Aboriginal and Torres Strait Islander Heritage Protection Act*, which prevents construction on 'significant' indigenous sites.

5   REJECTION OF POINT LILLIAS

After the Commonwealth had decided to request excision of affected wetlands from the Ramsar register, the ball was back in the court of the state government, but it decided it had little to gain by continuing with the project. To put it bluntly, there was no political advantage and considerable financial cost for the government in meeting its share of the costs, and it announced in June 1997 that the storage facility would remain at Coode Island.

The local government most affected by the decision, the City of Maribyrnong, was outraged at the decision. Its mayor, Mai Ho, attributed blame for the decision to the 1994 decision on the Commonwealth government to locate the armaments depot at Point Wilson, forcing the storage facility to the more sensitive Point Lillias. Mai Ho threatened legal action would be taken against the Victorian government if another chemical disaster eventuated at Coode Island (*Australian*, 26 June 1997). Also hinting at legal action was the proposed builder of the Point Lillias facility, Fletcher Marstell Consortium, which (although no contracts had been signed) had spent millions of dollars developing the project and was 'considering all options'. The consortium had been told of the decision only two hours before it was announced publicly.

Residents and environmentalists vowed to pursue a vigorous campaign of 'harassment and embarrassment' against the government, accusing it of endangering lives. The Hazardous Materials Action Group spokeswoman, Ms Colleen Hartland, said residents were in a 'blind fury' over the decision to leave the plant at Coode Island. HAZMAG was supported by the ACF and Greenpeace in what they saw as an environmental and social disaster, continuing to prefer West Point Wilson. Adopting this position of preferring a site which had been formally ruled out enabled SWEG to maintain a coalition which included both HAZMAG and the opponents at Geelong, but it was not a viable negotiating stance and it could only ever produce an outcome which favoured one location or the other, and those who wished to attack the chemical industry *per se*. The invoking of the risks to nature at Point Lillias helped ensure that it was the Coode Island residents who would lose.

It is clear, however, that the opposition of environment groups to Point Lillias played a large part in the decision to abandon plans to relocate the Coode Island facility. Victorian Premier Jeff Kennett stated that the prospect of 'years of litigation' if relocation had proceeded had been an important factor in the decision (*Australian*, 27 June 1997). Kennett perceived that the 'people who were opposing it remaining at Coode Island are the same people opposing it going down to Point Lillias', lending support to the suggestion that HAZMAG's involvement in the broader issues rather than acting as a voice of the Coode Island residents weakened their influence. He denied that politics played a part (Coode Island is an area which supported the ALP opposition, while Point Lillias was near some marginal government seats), insisting that 'The reason in the end was that we didn't have full confidence that we were able to deliver the product in a reasonable time'. The threat of delay had implications for the date of completion, which could not be guaranteed before the leases at Coode Island required renewal.

Safety levels at Coode Island meantime had to have been upgraded to allow the safe operation of the facility during the project appraisal period, which had been extended by nine months by the Commonwealth approval process. Time had therefore worked against the whole project. The Coode Island fires had receded in public consciousness and the group which should have been pushing strongly for relocation tempered its position with a concern over wider issues, including the suitability of Point Lillias. Environmental approvals had delayed Point Lillias, increasing its costs, and further delays were threatened by litigation from the environment groups. Meantime, more and more was being spent to upgrade Coode Island and decisions on renewing the leases would have to be made before a new facility could be commissioned at Point Lillias.

Opposition to Point Lillias was considerable. It included aboriginal interests, the salt works and the larger environment groups which, in pushing for West Point Wilson (somewhat idealistically, given it had been committed to an incompatible use) and opposing Point Lillias, appear to have over-looked the appeal of the 'do-nothing option' in the face of the opposition they had created. (Ironically, developers themselves are frequently criticized by environmentalists for failing to consider the 'do-nothing' option.) This opposition was not counterbalanced by substantial support in the Geelong region, despite its economic vulnerability, largely because the number of continuing jobs and other economic benefits was small. And resistance to Point Lillias was not countered by a strong push from Coode Island. Given the fact that the government could save money by doing nothing, the decision in favour of the status quo was not surprising.

The decision not to relocate Coode Island impacted negatively not only on residents, but on the $2 billion Docklands project, an urban renewal redevelopment at the eastern end of the Melbourne docks which was to include a new sports stadium plus commercial and residential building. The retention of Coode Island as a chemical storage facility a short distance from the site diminished its appeal as a location for planned luxury housing (*Weekend Australian Property*, 28–29 June 1997).

In the words of Premier Kennett, the Orange-Bellied Parrot – which he had once described as a 'trumped-up corella'[1] – had triumphed. But had it? The Orange-Bellied Parrot would probably have fared better had the Point Lillias Project proceeded, with funding for conservation programs which would have been provided as part of the compensation package. Endangered species require active (and often costly) management, rather than benign neglect (Budiansky, 1995). Indeed the one individual sighted at Point Lillias was the result of a breeding program. The cancellation of the project meant a return to the status quo for the parrot, with less funding for conservation than would have been provided as part of the project and little political attention. What was important was the political significance of the parrot as a symbol which could be invoked by one set of residents and which the residents of the working class suburbs near Coode Island could not counter.

Ironically, by 1998 there were moves afoot in a committee in the Commonwealth Senate to change the site of ECAC back to Jervis Bay, the original site before it had dislodged Point Wilson as a possible site for a chemical storage facility in 1994.

6 DISCUSSION

Many siting decisions involve the selection of sites for *new* facilities which, because of the risks they pose or because of some detraction from amenity, constitute LULUs— locally undesirable land-uses. Perhaps unusually, the Point Lillias case involved the relocation of an existing facility, and this gave the issues some peculiar characteristics.

In particular, the 'Do Nothing' option meant the continuation of existing risks at one site. This might give the appearance of uniqueness to this case, but reality it was perhaps not so different, since all 'Do Nothing' options carry similar consequences: the blocking of LULUs within one jurisdiction inevitably mean their siting elsewhere, often in another jurisdiction, or carry other consequences such as the provision of energy or chemical products, or the storage or treatment of waste by some other means, which carries its own set of risks. It is the reduction of our frame of analysis which often allows us to ignore this reality, although the indeterminate nature of the 'opportunity cost' of successful NIMBY opposition means that those who must bear these consequences (in a locational sense) are not organized into politics at the time of the decision. Only when NIMBY movements in separate locations make common cause at the same time is opposition driven to a higher level, where the justification for *any* proposal comes under critical scrutiny. Such coalition-building can succeed, but the success usually comes in displacing the risks in space or into other technological settings, not all of which are socially desirable.

Coalition-building in this case proved fatal for HAZMAG, the group representing the residents exposed to the risks of Coode Island. HAZMAG predated the explosion and fire in 1991, having been formed in response to a number of chemical spills, and it was the only effective group for representing the residents of the western suburbs of Melbourne. It was essentially a NIMBY group, but it had some wider concerns about hazardous materials regardless of location, and this facilitated its coalition with issue-based (rather than location-based) environmental groups and the residents of Geelong in SWEG, which acted as an umbrella groups for opponents to Point Lillias. As is common with such issues, conflict between the locational, NIMBY groups was subsumed by more general concerns over chemical safety among the established environmental groups. In the case of Greenpeace, this extended to a global campaign against the chemical industry in the context of which Point Lillias represented but one local site where this broader conflict could take place. Such groups can be seen as acting as political entrepreneurs, submersing conflicts between localities in wider, more global issues. Their 'thinking globally' can jeopardize the efforts of those 'acting locally', and this is not the only occasion on which Greenpeace, for example, has jeopardized local action for its international priorities (see Rootes, 1999, p. 302).

For HAZMAG, this broadening of the focus of the campaign ultimately meant defeat, since the larger, more effective SWEG coalition blocked the relocation of the facility and, since there was no prospect of this action contesting successfully the continued operation of the chemicals industry in

Victoria or the location of ECAC at Point Wilson, this meant continued operation at Coode Island, where terminal operators were all the time having to sink more and more capital. The prospect of legal challenges promised further delays to the project which made it highly unlikely that the facility could be relocated before the leases over the Coode Island sites expired and decisions had to be made over renewal. With the government committed to tens of millions of dollars to fund the relocation if it proceeded, the campaign against Point Lillias made the option of allowing the facility to remain at Coode Island all the more attractive.

Not only that, the opposition made the status quo politically attractive, and released the government from an undertaking to relocate which it had made in the aftermath of the Coode Island fires. The residents at risk from Coode Island were in the safe Labor Party seat of Maribyrnong, occupied at the time of the 1991 fires by the then Premier, Joan Kirner (which helped the relocation decision), while the marginal electorate of Geelong had been won by the Liberal-National coalition government at the 1992 election. Maribyrnong was thus unwinnable, while Geelong was more sensitive electorally speaking. Kirner, as Premier at the time of the fires, had promised relocation, a promise which had been matched by the then opposition environment shadow minister. But by 1997, this politician was in government, and a government which had subsequently been reelected with a comfortable majority at that. The risks to nature – to the 'jumped-up Corella' – absolved the government from its promise in a way which a decision not to relocate without going through a site approval process could not have.

This was reinforced by the differing risk perceptions of the participants. The Coode Island residents had a high perception of risks: the 1991 fires simply amplified earlier concerns associated with spillages and fires. But the 'objective' risk (or, perhaps more accurately, that perceived by government authorities) was substantially less, due partly to the fact that, in a sense, Coode Island had 'fired its best shot'. The explosion and fires were about the worst that could happen at the facility. They created a dramatic image which would amplify risk perception among nearby residents and those at Geelong who witnessed the graphic television footage, but damage from the explosion was confined to the site and EPA monitoring revealed minimal resulting hazard through air or water pollution. Improvements required in the regulatory clamp-down after the fires had improved safety.

The risks to Coode Island residents had, therefore, already improved, whereas for Geelong residents they would go from zero to what they saw to be a significant level with the relocation to Point Lillias. Further, the removal of the Point Wilson option by the selection of this site for the armaments complex, meant that the element of voluntariness (often of central importance in achieving successful siting outcomes) was lost. Not only did

Point Lillias become the only realistic alternative to Coode Island, it had already been identified as an inferior site to Point Wilson. Neither was this additional risk to be imposed rather involuntarily on Geelong to be offset by any substantial compensation, economic or otherwise. Most of the compensation was directed toward nature conservation, and the regional economic benefits from the construction and operation of the facility were negligible. Ironically, the Orange-Bellied Parot would perhaps have benefited most.

The ability of the Geelong residents to resist the siting of the facility at Point Lillias was also enhanced by the 'whirlpooling' together of the threats to nature and threats to aboriginal heritage with the risks to the environment and human health posed by toxic and explosive chemicals. The building of a common environmental position in opposition to Point Lillias including these factors essentially condemned the Coode Island residents to endure a continuation of the status quo. Strong linkage of resistance to siting to other issues made siting the facility at Point Lillias more difficult, but it simultaneously advantaged the status quo.

What was significant here was not so much what the realities of wilderness, nature conservation and aboriginal heritage were, because the claims made on these grounds were relatively weak. What counted was that the issue could be 'framed' as one which posed unacceptable risks to nature and heritage rather than just to people. Point Lillias is close to a large oil refinery, with a fertiliser plant and grain elevator a little further away. It is across the water from an aluminium smelter and has on site an operational salt works, several fishing shacks and a boat ramp. As we have seen, describing it as 'wilderness' was drawing a rather long bow, but it was a claim which the Coode Island residents could not make at all. Similarly, Coode Island did not host any endangered species, and was not listed as a Ramsar site of wetlands of international importance.

One might think that its existing industrial use would rather obviously rule it out as an important site for nature conservation, because the notion of wilderness sits more comfortably with nature conservation, but in reality industrial sites have been found to provide significant ecological niches for all kinds of species (Budiansky, 1995), often including endangered ones, and this was the case with Point Lillias and the adjacent area. The evaporation ponds at the saltworks are teeming with wading birds, and to the north are further ponds which attract such abundant birdlife they are an attraction for ornithologists. These are not part of an untouched wilderness, but instead the ponds of the Werribee sewage treatment works which services the city of Melbourne.

The Geelong residents were able to construct a discourse the Coode Island residents could not match. They were able to invoke the threat of risks to nature – to wilderness, to wetlands of international importance, and to the

highly endangered Orange-Bellied Parrot – not just to make their claims
more numerous, but to translate them into claims which transcended the
narrow self-interest of NIMBY-ism, and which were therefore all the more
persuasive and (significantly) unable to be matched by the Coode Island
residents. They succeeded in framing the issue in such a way that they won at
Maribyrnong's expense. Such framing is important for building support in
social movements because participants are arguably drawn to social movements which frame issues in ways which resonate with their values and experiences (Snow et al., 1986). Environmental politics in Australia is framed
more as 'nature protection' than 'protection of humans from risks' (Doyle
and Kellow, 1995), so this framing of Point Lillias as presenting risks to
nature was important in building political opposition, thus resulting in Geelong winning out over Maribyrnong.

The loss of decisional fairness resulting from the pre-empting of the best
site at Point Wilson made this whirlpooling together of risks to nature and
risk to people all the more likely. This outcome meant *less* protection for the
Orange-Bellied Parrot and the continuation of an older facility 0.5km (rather
than 7km) from significant population numbers. The desire of the Commonwealth to find a new site for the armaments depot, and the Victorian
government's desire to secure its economic benefits, meant the considerable
effort to improve the siting process was ultimately wasted, the process became one of DAD, and siting in Australia remains poorly practiced.

NOTES

1. Unlike the rare Orange-Bellied Parrot, the Corella is a common and somewhat undistin-
guished parrot.

REFERENCES

Age, 15 March 1997.
Australian, 26 June 1997.
Australian, 27 June 1997.
Budiansky, Stephen (1995), *Nature's Keepers: The New Science of Nature Management*, New York, The Free Press.
Doyle, Timothy and Aynsley Kellow (1995), *Environmental Politics and Policy Making in Australia*, Melbourne, Macmillan.
Goodin, Robert E. (1994), *Green Political Theory*, Oxford, Polity.
Hazarika, Sanjoy (1987), *Bhopal: The Lessons of a Tragedy*, Harmondsworth, Penguin.
Kellow, Aynsley (1996), 'The Politics of Place: Siting Experience in Australia', in Daigee Shaw (ed.), *Comparative Analysis of Siting Experience in Asia*, Taipei: Academia Sinica.
Robertson Australia and Cremer and Warner (1991), *Coode Island Review Panel:*

Chemical Terminal Facility Review.

Rootes, Christopher (1999), 'Acting Globally, Thinking Locally? Prospects for a Global Environmental Movement', *Environmental Politics*, **8** (1), 290–310.

Slovic, P. (1987), 'Perception of Risk', *Science*, **236**, 280–85.

Slovic, P. (1993), 'Perceived Risk, Trust and Democracy', *Risk Analysis*, **13** (6), 675–82.

Snow, David A., E. Burke Rochford Jr, Steven K. Worden and Robert D. Benford (1986), 'Frame Alignment Processes, Micromobilization, and Movement Participation', *American Sociological Review*, **51**, 475.

Thomas, Ian F. (1995), 'The Coode Island Fires – An Appraisal of the Coroner's Report', in R.E. Melchers and M.G. Stewart (eds), *Integrated Risk Assessment: Current Practice and New Dimensions*, Rotterdam, A.A. Balkema.

Victoria. Coode Island Review Panel (1991), Information Paper (1991).

Victoria. Coode Island Review Panel (1991a), Issues Paper (December 1991).

Victoria. Coode Island Review Panel (1991b), Phase 1 Report (December 1991).

Victoria. Coode Island Review Panel (1992a), Review of Options (March 1992).

Victoria. Coode Island Review Panel (1992b), Final Report (March 1992).

Victoria. Environmental Effects Act (1978).

Victoria. Office of Planning and Heritage, Department of Infrastructure (1996), Assessment and Panel Report: Point Lillias Port and Bulk Liquid Chemical Storage Facility.

Victoria. Point Lillias Project Unit (1995), Point Lillias Port and Chemical Storage Project: Progress Report.

Victoria. Point Lillias Project Unit (1995a), Proposed Port and Storage Facility for Bulk Liquid Chemicals at Point Lillias: Information Paper.

Weekend Australian Property, 28–29 June 1997.

Wicks, Wendy (1995), Point Lillias Project Unit, Personal Communication, 16 November.

10. Visions of the Future for Facility Siting

Daigee Shaw

1 LESSONS FROM THE PAST AND THIS VOLUME

This volume is concerned with the management of siting locally-unwanted facilities that involves decision processes with high transaction costs. Its major purpose is to develop more robust and effective policies and institutions for managing this increasingly intractable problem.

The facility siting management policy has evolved over time. The first phase of this management policy applied traditional scientific management approaches, i.e. the technically-based site-screening and selection process, and the decide-announce-defend approach as Kasperson notes (Chapter 2) or the hierarchical approach as Linnerooth-Bayer notes (Chapter 3). However, it became clear that this approach was in numerous cases incapable of achieving the stipulated goal of siting the facility. The best strategy that the communities had in response to these approaches was to stage NIMBY protests so that they could avoid a situation where their communities became worse off by not accepting the facility, and they had nothing to gain if they accepted it.

In response to this situation, the second phase of the facility siting management policy involved the introduction of market-based instruments such as compensation, economic incentives and bargaining characterized as the bartered consent approach in Kasperson (Chapter 2) or the voluntary, market approach in Linnerooth-Bayer (Chapter 3). In some cases the facility siting was achieved, but in most cases, however, developers still are unable to win local communities' approval to build facilities. Compensation was viewed as a bribe by communities in some cases or has induced communities to take stronger positions strategically in the bargaining process in other cases. Many communities still refused to cooperate and negotiate siting deals with developers even with the addition of compensation and economic incentives. Frey, et al. (1996) attributed the failure of compensation schemes to the bribe effect and the crowding out of the public spirit, and Oberholzer-Gee and

Kunreuther (Chapter 5) attributed it to social pressure.[1]

To counter such problems, the third phase in the evolution of facility siting management policy involved the provision of information and making the community an active participant in the siting process, i.e. the voluntary/partnership siting approach as Kasperson notes (Chapter 2) or the egalitarian siting process as Linnerooth-Bayer notes (Chapter 3). Schneider, et al. (Chapter 7) and Barthe and Mays (Chapter 8) have provided two case studies in Germany and France, respectively, of this approach.

The more recent siting cases employ a comprehensive approach that combines the approaches used in these previous three phases. The influential 'Facility Siting Credo' proposed by Kunreuther et al. (1993) (Table 2.3 in Chapter 2) is the most comprehensive list of must-dos for facility siting to date. The 'Sequential Multi-stage Siting Process' proposed by Quah and Tan (2002) is another example of a comprehensive approach. It includes such elements as the study of site selection, environmental impact assessments, benefit-cost analysis, mitigation, public hearings, negotiation, and compensation.

However, the recent experiences of the U.K., France, the U.S., Australia, Japan, Austria and Germany considered in this volume suggest that the extraordinary efforts of the comprehensive approach in general, and transparency of the process and community/citizen participation in particular, have still failed to deliver approved sites. It seems that the long search for a policy framework for siting facilities where transaction costs are high has not been a fruitful one. In actual fact, this result can be expected because the three phases of policy evolution have only moved policy instruments from the more closed and command-and-control end of a spectrum to the more open and transparent one without major changes in the political institutions which structure the decision process for siting a facility. Political institutions in the context of decision process are defined here as a set of formal and informal rules to determine *who* is eligible to make decisions and *how* the decision should be made at each level in the decision process.[2]

This chapter argues that whether or not a policy instrument can be implemented effectively depends on whether or not the context of the political institution in which the decisions concerning the policy instrument are processed can minimize the failures of political institutions. Failures of political institutions range from rent seeking by special interest groups and politicians, agency problem, opportunistic behavior, poor accountability of politicians, voter ignorance, etc. Thus, the evolution of various policy instruments over the past three phases has not touched the very heart of the facility siting decision process, i.e. political institutions.[3]

2 VISIONS OF THE FUTURE: INSTITUTIONAL CHANGE

As mentioned in the previous section, there are two important elements comprising the institution of facility siting management, i.e. *who* is eligible to make decisions and *how* the decision is being made at each level of the siting process. These two elements are identified because they are the keys to the distributional conflicts that determine whether it is possible to reach an effective agreement between the parties concerning facility siting.

In the following discussion, the management of solid waste will be sometimes used as an example. In this case, a local government is responsible for providing services of garbage treatment for households in its constituency by running several incinerators and dumps that are locally unwanted by the community hosting the facilities. All of the households in the constituency are benefiting from the services provided. Thus, there are three players in the management of solid waste: a local government and two groups of communities, the host community and the benefiting community.

In addressing the question as to *who* is eligible to make decisions regarding siting facilities such as incinerators and dumps, the third phase that makes the community an active participant in the siting process is a step in the right direction. However, the basic problem with the community participation process is that usually only the host community is active in participating in the siting process simply because of the high stake involved in the outcome of the process, but the benefiting community, that who benefit from having the facility sited elsewhere, usually remain ignorant on the siting issue and enjoy being free riders. In their place, the government that is charged to successfully site incinerators and dumps plays the role of the agents of the benefiting community, the principals. However, because there are both the infamous agency problem and the rent-seeking problem prevalent in present-day democratic governments and, consequently, the level of trust in governments is low in most countries, the partial participation of only host community makes the transparency and participation approach ineffective.[4]

Thus, a robust and effective institution should call for the participation of both host community and benefiting community. The participation should be full-scale, i.e. it gives both communities not only the right to have their viewpoints being heard in the siting process such as public hearings, but also the right to make decisions regarding whether or not and where the facility will be sited.[5]

This full-scale participation of both communities is based on the Tiebout hypothesis of 'voting with their feet' (Tiebout, 1956). Tiebout (1956) argues that people could vote with their feet, i.e. move from places they do not like to places they like better. If enough people do this, local governments will have to compete, or risk losing key people and human resources to other places. The people who have moved are now in places they like better. Their choice of places reveals their preferences for local pubic goods. The separate decisions made by each local government concerning which local public goods should be provided and how to provide and finance them lead to a Pareto-efficient allocation of public goods.[6] In the case of facility siting, the local public goods under consideration basically consist of the facilities such as incinerators and dumps that are needed by all but are not welcomed by the host communities. Because full-scale participation is another way to reveal people's preferences for incinerators and dumps, the combination of 'voting with their feet' and full-scale participation of both communities would lead to a Pareto-efficient allocation of them too.

This leads to the second question concerning *how* the decision is being made by the host and benefiting communities. If every one in the communities participated in each decision in the government, the transaction costs would be astronomical. Thus, in order to keep the transaction costs of full-scale participation lower, traditionally, both communities elect their own representatives on the basis of one-person-one-vote and delegate the power of governance to governments run by the representatives of this democratic system of governance. However, in this kind of governance system, in addition to the given role of the principals of their elected representatives, both communities play the roles of special interest groups as well. Kellow (Chapter 9) has provided an Australian example of the strategic rent-seeking behavior played by a group of residents in their favor but at the expense of the other group of residents. The residents 7 km away from the new site of a chemical storage and handling facility were able to invoke the risks to nature, along with the heritage issues, to resist successfully the proposed relocation. This successful opposition, however, meant that the facility would remain at its existing site, meaning a continuation of risks to residents as close as 0.5 km away. Barthe and Mays (Chapter 8) present a French case where different groups seek to exert power over others as well.

Thus, the representatives and government officials are not only the agents of both communities, but also, at the same time, the persons from whom both communities would use the political process to seek rents in the siting process. The agency problem and the rent-seeking problem are still inevitable even with the full-scale participation of both communities. These problems cause the principals to have little trust in governments and their representatives because of the strategic rent-seeking behavior on the part of other principals and special interest groups. Therefore, it is very difficult to site facilities in any place even with the transparency and participation approach.

There are two different kinds of reasons for the prevalence of the agency problem and the rent-seeking problem. The first is the traditional thinking that it is difficult for the principals to monitor the actions of their agents and interest groups in the face of asymmetric information. Information is usually asymmetric. In the case of solid waste management, the principals (the host and benefiting communities) usually know less about the environmental impacts of incinerators and dumps than their agents (government officials) because of the high cost of keeping informed, and as a result, it creates incentives for opportunistic behavior on the part of the agents and interest groups.

The policy implications of this are that, first, the principals should be well informed, and second, they should vigorously monitor the behavior and performance of each agent in order to induce the agent and interest groups to act advantageously on behalf of the principal.[7] On the one hand, there have been many attempts to keep the principals well informed. The communication and information procedure for high-level radioactive wastes set up by the Waste Act of 1991 in France is an example of the attempt (Barthe and Mays, Chapter 8). One of the purposes of the commonly used environmental impact assessment (EIA) is to provide the environmental impact information of a proposed facility to the public.[8] On the other hand, however, in facility siting cases, it commonly observed that both host communities and benefiting communities usually are ignorant on monitoring the behavior and performance of each agent and, at the same time, the host community usually is more likely to play the political role of interest groups. What are the reasons behind the two observations?

This relates to the second kind of reasons for the prevalence of the agency problem and the rent-seeking problem. When the principal consists of a group of people who cast votes during various elections and referenda on the basis of one-person-one-vote, the free-rider problem in relation to public goods is inevitable. This is because the benefits of a principal's voting and monitoring the agents are public goods to be shared by all fellow principals and because the probability that any single vote will be decisive is low. Thus, members of the group that makes up the principal would like to be free riders to enjoy the public goods without shouldering the burden of the cost. That is, the people in both host communities and benefiting communities would remain ignorant on monitoring the behavior and performance of their agents.[9] In conclusion, it is not because it is difficult for the people in both communities to monitor their agents (government officials), but simply because they do not have incentives to provide public goods by monitoring their agents.

In addition, in the case of solid waste management, we often observe that a community that is the candidate of siting incinerators and dumps can successfully organize a coherent, unified interest group to effectively resist siting the facility in their community. However, the benefiting community usually remains unorganized and ignorant. This is simply because, compared with the benefiting community, the number of individuals living in the host community is usually smaller, the area of the host community is usually smaller, and consequently, the cost of forming an interest group is smaller. [10] On the other hand, the stake per individual at risk is larger for the host community. Thus, the opposition to siting incinerators and dumps usually goes without opposition from the benefiting community.

Thus, the fundamental reason for the prevalence of facility siting difficulties is the public good nature of the present-day democratic system of governance. Based on this finding, I believe that a more robust and effective political institution for managing facility siting should have the following two characteristics.

The first characteristic comprises the federal system of governments formed by a number of functional, overlapping and competing jurisdictions (FOCJ) proposed by Frey and Eichenberger in a sequence of papers (Frey and Eichenberger, 1995, 1996, 2000, 2001a, 2001b; Frey, 2001). The federal units are referred to as FOCJ according to their four essential characteristics: 1. Functional: The new political units extend over areas defined by the services (functions) with the nature of public goods to be provided. 2. Overlapping: In line with the many different services, there are corresponding governmental units extending over different geographical areas. 3. Competing: Individuals and/or communities may decide to which governmental unit they wish to belong, and they have political rights to express their preferences directly via initiatives, referenda and election. 4. Jurisdictions: the units established are governmental; they have enforcement power and can, in particular, levy taxes.

The FOCJ are based on theoretical propositions advanced in the economic theory of federalism. Frey and Eichenberger have provided many examples of existing FOCJ-like institutions providing such services as public security, natural hazard mitigation, education, environmental protection, management of natural resources, transport, culture, or sports in Europe and the U.S.

In the case of facility siting, an FOCJ instead of the traditional all-purpose jurisdictions can be formed to provide a certain kind of services to its members by operating some locally-unwanted facilities. For example, a solid waste FOCJ can be formed to provide services of garbage collection and treatment by running those locally-unwanted facilities such as incinerators and dumps. Similarly, a water FOCJ can be organized to provide services of water treatment and supply for households, farmers and industries in a certain area. Dams and reservoirs are the locally-unwanted water facilities operated by this FOCJ. In both of these two examples, the members of a FOCJ include individuals in both benefiting and host communities because they all demand the services provided by a FOCJ.

FOCJ have at least two important advantages over the all-purpose jurisdictions.

Take a water FOCJ as an example. First, there should be no free-riders of the water service provided by the FOCJ because the service is financed by the FOCJ members who are the recipients of the service. In addition, there should be no spillovers of the environmental costs of dams and reservoirs because the host communities of these facilities are also members of the FOCJ. In contrast, the problems of free-riders and spillovers related to the water service would be widespread in an all-purpose jurisdiction because the delineation of the area of a traditional jurisdiction is usually different from a watershed that is the natural geographical area of a water FOCJ. Second, the political environment in the FOCJ is much simpler than that in the all-purpose jurisdictions. This is because the FOCJ only need to cater for the interest groups related to water service, e.g. the benefiting and host communities of water service and facilities, while there are much more different interest groups related to every service provided by the all-purpose government. Consequently, the rent-seeking problem would be much more serious in the all-purpose government and would sometimes cause some minor interests or functions be ignored and sacrificed. For example, a housing developer with a strong connection to the mayor may successfully convince the all-purpose government to develop a new town in a beautiful mountain area within a watershed. Thus, the interest of providing clean water for water users that include residents living in parts of the jurisdiction of this all-purpose government and residents of its neighboring jurisdictions is sacrificed.

The second characteristic that a more robust and effective institution for managing facility siting should have is that, in order to curb the ubiquitous free-riding behavior in the one-man-one-vote all-purpose jurisdictions, individuals under the FOCJ can not only vote with their feet, but can express their preferences fully by means of a political system of one-dollar-one-vote. 'Dollar' here means a unit of taxes levied by a FOCJ to cover the costs of providing the service for its members. The one-dollar-one-vote system follows the Principle of Interest-Pay-Participation (PIPP): the person who has higher interests in the outputs of an organization should share higher responsibility for producing the outputs, e.g. by paying more taxes, fees or inputs. In order to take up higher responsibility, he should be endowed with more shares of rights to participate in the decision making and management of the organization.

According to this principle, those who pay a larger share of the cost of providing the service should have a greater share of the political rights to express their preferences and, consequently, a greater share of the aggregate benefits generated by the service. Both of an individual's shares of political right and aggregate benefits are equal to his share of aggregate costs. Shaw et al. (2003) have proved in terms of economic theory that through this kind of institution of jurisdictions the problem of public goods related to the present-day democratic system of governance can be avoided. The rationale behind this is simply that, even though the benefits generated by the outputs of an individual's contribution is still shared by all fellow members of the organization in this kind of institution, the marginal benefit he would receive is just sufficient to compensate him for his last unit of contribution needed to produce the outputs of an organization. This is one of the standard conditions for efficiency. Thus, the people in a one-dollar-one-vote jurisdiction would have strong incentives to pay attention to and monitor the behavior of their agents, interest groups and other fellow members, in addition to not avoiding paying taxes.[11]

Even though it seems FOCJ with PIPP could be politically unacceptable because it runs against the popular one-man-one-vote political system, among many existing FOCJ, there are three famous and successful water management institutions that are not only FOCJ but also employ the PIPP: the Water Associations (Genossenschaft) in Germany, River Basin Agencies (Agence de l'Eau) in France, and the Water Boards in the Netherlands.[12] All these three water management institutions have existed for a quite a while Generally speaking, the members of the three FOCJ are users of water services (the benefiting and fee-paying communities of water services) and producers of water services (the host communities of dams and reservoirs). They elect their own representatives based on a one-dollar-one-vote system. The body of representatives selects and disciplines administers, controls annual budget, approves work plans, monitors the performance of the water management and administration unit.

Carney (1998) has proposed an institution for the public lands that is also FOCJ and follows the PIPP to solve the long-term problems of the tragedy of the commons that has dissipated the resources in the public lands in the U.S. He argues that through transfer of the ownership of the public lands from the government to a publicly owned corporation, decisions will be made in a disciplined way that considers both the interest of today's and tomorrow's citizens, as owners of the corporation.

The FOCJ with PIPP would be welfare-enhancing simply because the members and representatives of a one-dollar-one-vote jurisdiction would have strong incentives to pay attention to and monitor the behavior of their agents and interest groups and would not shirk paying taxes. With strong incentives to monitor on the part of the members and representatives, the government officials of a jurisdiction would not shirk and would pay attention to what their principals say, and not what the interest groups say. Then people and communities would trust the government and representatives of a jurisdiction and their decisions regarding facility siting and management including which policy instruments to be used. In this kind of institutional environment, any policy instrument can be implemented effectively. Thus, the FOCJ with PIPP can not only promote welfare, but can also handle the difficulties associated with facility siting.

Take a solid waste FOCJ as an example. A FOCJ can be organized to provide services of garbage treatment for households in a certain geographical area. This FOCJ usually has several incinerators and dumps that are locally-unwanted. The members of the solid waste FOCJ are users (the benefiting communities) and producers of the services (the host communities of incinerators and dumps). They elect their own representatives based on a one-dollar-one-vote system. The body of representatives (can be called the solid waste parliament) monitors the performance of the management unit (can be called the solid waste government), selects and disciplines, administers, controls annual budget and approves work plans. In this FOCJ, because the political environment would be much simpler, the rent-seeking problem would be less serious than that in the all-purpose jurisdiction. There should be no free-riders of the benefits provided by the FOCJ and no spill-overs of the environmental costs outside its jurisdiction. Most importantly, the members of the FOCJ with PIPP would have strong incentives not to shirk their own responsibility and to monitor their agents and interest groups. Thus, government officials and parliament representatives would pay attention to what their principals say, and not what the interest groups say. As a result, those problems created by opportunistic behavior under asymmetric information, i.e. the agency problem and the rent-seeking problem, would be curbed. In addition, people would have higher trust in the government and the parliament. In this kind of political institutional environment, any policy instrument can be implemented effectively. Thus, the solid waste FOCJ with PIPP can handle the difficult task of siting incinerators and dumps well.

3   SUMMARY

This chapter indicates that any policy instruments or strategies would be useless without improvements in political institutional designs. The fundamental reason for the prevalence of facility siting difficulties is the public good nature of the present-day democratic system of governance where people do not have incentives to monitor the performance of the government. As a consequence, the problems of opportunistic behaviors such as the agency problem and the rent-seeking problem are prevalent. These problems cause the principals to have little trust in governments and their representatives. Therefore, it is very difficult to site facilities in any place even with the transparency and participation approach. Thus, we should go beyond our endless search for good facility siting policy instruments and move to find a robust and effective institution for managing the siting dilemma.

This chapter demonstrates that a robust and effective institution for managing facility siting should have the following two features. First, it should call for a full-scale participation of both the host communities and the benefiting communities of the facilities under consideration. Second, the full-scale participation can be efficiently facilitated by a number of functional, overlapping and competing jurisdictions (FOCJ) and by employing the Principle of Interest-Pay-Participation (PIPP) to elect their representatives of an FOCJ parliament. The FOCJ with PIPP would be welfareenhancing simply because their members would have strong incentives to pay attention to and monitor the behavior of their agents and interest groups and would not shirk their own responsibility such as paying taxes.

NOTES

1. However, Frey, et al. (1996) find a 'compensation cycle' which finally wins the support of host communities with higher compensation in the long run.
2. Generally speaking, there are three levels in the decision process. Rules are made and clarified first for individuals, later for communities, and/or still later for higher-level organizations, such as countries and international authorities.
3. Franzini and Nicita (2002) have made a similar point for environmental institutions and policy. They argue that 'Many cases of institutional failure, ranging from the problem of defining property rights to environmental resources, to the problem of actuating environmental policy in a reasonable time, not only fail to solve the externality, but create inertia in decision-making, aggravating environmental damage and increasing its irreversibility. Among the underlying causes of this inertia in solving the environmental externality or implementing policy is failure to reach agreement between the parties, which in turn is almost always a matter of distributional conflicts' (Franzini and Nicita, 2002, p. 8).
4. Two major sources of institutional failures are raised here. First, the agency problem is present because agents usually do not pursue the interests of their principals vigorously. The agency problem has long been recognized as the central problem of organization. See Smith (1776, Book V, Chapter 1, Part III, pp. 264-5). Fama and Jensen (1983) argue that this problem would arise when the agents who initiate and implement important decisions do not bear a major share of the wealth effects of their decisions. Second, rent seeking is the use of resources by a special interest group in activities directed at increasing the net benefits going to the interest group, e.g., producers, consumers, host communities, benefiting communities, and government officials, but it will also lower net benefits to society as a whole. Rent seeking was first discussed by Tullock (1967).
5. How decisions are made by both communities will be discussed in detail next.
6. A Pareto-efficient allocation of public goods is an allocation such that no reallocation of public goods could benefit the people of any one place without lowering the net benefits for the people of at least one other place.
7. For example, the principals can design a remuneration plan and contract for each agent that could induce the agent and interest groups to act advantageously on behalf of principals.
8. These attempts to solve the problem of asymmetric information are not successful. Shaw (1996) notes that even with the environmental impact information provided by the environmental impact assessment (EIA) regulation, the information required for the residents to understand the issues involved and make a clear decision is either inaccessible or incomprehensible to the lay person and, as a result, people feel threatened and out-matched. They are also mistrustful of the information provided by the EIAs. Barthe and Mays (Chapter 8) also find that the tremendous efforts of communication and information become an adversarial process in a French case.

9. Various manifestations of this free rider problem are often referred to as 'voter ignorance', 'the tragedy of the commons', 'prisoner's dilemma', 'social dilemma', etc. See Olson (1965) and Hardin (1968).
10. See Olson (1965, pp. 9–16, 22–65).
11. Of course, members of FOCJ are subject to FOCJ's authority and regulations. They must pay taxes to finance their FOCJ.
12. See the reviews by Andersen (1999), Dinar et al. (1997), OECD (1996), Uniterkamp et al. (1995), and Shaw et al. (2003).

REFERENCES

Andersen, M. (1999), 'Governance by Green Taxes: Implementing Clean Water Policies in Europe 1970–1990', *Environmental Economics and Policy Studies*, **2** (1), 39–63.

Barthe, Yannick and Claire Mays (2005), 'Communication and Information: Unanticipated Consequences in France's Underground Laboratory Siting Process', Chapter 8 in Hayden Lesbirel and Daigee Shaw (eds), *Managing Conflict in Facility Siting*, Cheltenham, UK: Edward Elgar.

Carney, W. J. (1998), 'From Stakeholders to Stockholders: A View From Organizational Theory', in Peter J. Hill and Roger E. Meiners (eds), *Who Owns the Environment?*, Lanham, Md: Rowman & Littlefield.

Dinar, A., M. W. Rosegrant and R. Meinzen-Dick (1997), *Water Allocation Mechanisms – Principles and Examples*, World Bank, Available from http:// www- wds. worldbank.org/.

Fama, Eugene F. and Michael Jensen (1983), 'Separation of Ownership and Control', *Journal of Law and Economics*, **26**, 301–25.

Franzini, Maurizio and Antonio Nicita (2002), 'Economic Institutions and Environmental Policy: An Introduction', in Maurizio Franzini and Antonio Nicita (eds), *Economic Institutions and Environmental Policy*, Aldershot: Ashgate.

Frey, Bruno S. (2001), 'A Utopia? Government without Territorial Monopoly', *Journal of Institutional and Theoretical Economics*, **157** (1), 162–75.

Frey, Bruno S. and Reiner Eichenberger (1995), 'Competition among Jurisdictions. The Idea of FOCJ', in Lüder Gerken (ed.), *Competition among Institutions*, London: MacMillan, 209–29.

Frey, Bruno S. and Reiner Eichenberger (1996), 'FOCJ: Competitive Governments for Europe', *International Review of Law and Economics,* **16** (3), 315–27.

Frey, Bruno S. and Reiner Eichenberger (2000), 'Towards a New Kind of Eurofederalism', in Boudewijn Bouckaert and Annette Godart-Van der Kroon (eds), *Hayek Revisited*, Cheltenham: Edward Elgar.

Frey, Bruno S. and Reiner Eichenberger (2001a), 'Federalism with Overlapping Jurisdictions and Variable Levels of Integration: The Concept of FOCJ', in Jürgen von Hagen and Mika Widgren (eds), *Regionalism in Europe: Geometries and Strategies after 2000*, Boston: Kluwer Academic Publishers.

Frey, Bruno S. and Reiner Eichenberger (2001b), 'A Proposal for Dynamic European Federalism: FOCJ', in Ram Mudambi, Pietro Navarra and Giuseppe Sobbrio (eds), *Rules and Reason: Perspectives on Constitutional Political Economy*, Cambridge: Cambridge University Press.

Frey, Bruno S., Felix Oberholzer-Gee and Reiner Eichenberger (1996), 'The Old Lady Visits Your Backyard: a Tale of Morals and Markets', *Journal of Political Economy*, **104** (6), 1297–313.

Hardin, Garrett (1968), 'The Tragedy of the Commons', *Science*, **162**, 1243–8.

Kasperson, Roger E. (2005), 'Siting Hazardous Facilities: Searching for Effective Institutions and Processes', Chapter 2 in Hayden Lesbirel and Daigee Shaw (eds), *Managing Conflict in Facility Siting*, Cheltenham, UK: Edward Elgar.

Kellow, Aynsley (2005), 'Balancing Risks to Nature and Risks to People: the Coode Island/Point Lillias Project in Australia', Chapter 9 in Hayden Lesbirel and Daigee Shaw (eds), *Managing Conflict in Facility Siting*, Cheltenham, UK: Edward Elgar.

Kunreuther, Howard, Lawrence Susskind and Thomas Aarts (1993), 'The Facility Siting Credo: Guidelines for an Effective Facility Siting Process', Philadelphia: University of Pennsylvania, Wharton School, Risk and Decision Processes Center.

Linnerooth-Bayer, Joanne (2005), 'Fair Strategies for Siting Hazardous Waste Facilities', Chapter 3 in Hayden Lesbirel and Daigee Shaw (eds), *Managing Conflict in Facility Siting,* Cheltenham, UK: Edward Elgar.

Oberholzer-Gee, Felix and Howard Kunreuther (2005), 'Social Pressure in Siting Conflicts: A Case Study of Siting a Radioactive Waste Repository in Pennsylvania', Chapter 5 in Hayden Lesbirel and Daigee Shaw (eds), *Managing Conflict in Facility Siting*, Cheltenham, UK: Edward Elgar.

OECD (1996), 'The Efficiency and Effectiveness of Water Pollution Charges in France, Germany and the Netherlands: A Synthesis of Available Evidence', *ENV/EPOC/GEEI* (95) 14/REV1, Paris: OECD.

Olson, Mancur (1965), *The Logic of Collective Action*, Cambridge: Harvard University Press.

Quah, Euston and K.C. Tan (2002), *Siting Environmentally Unwanted Facilities: Risks, Trade-offs, and Choices*, Cheltenham, UK: Edward Elgar.

Schneider, Elke, Bettina Oppermann and Ortwin Renn (2005), 'Implementing Structured Participation for Regional Level Waste Management Planning', Chapter 7 in Hayden Lesbirel and Daigee Shaw (eds), *Managing Conflict in Facility Siting*, Cheltenham, UK: Edward Elgar.

Shaw, Daigee (1996), 'An Economic Framework for Analysing Facility Siting Policies in Taiwan and Japan', in Paul Kleindorfer, Howard Kunreuther and David Hung (eds), *Energy, Environment and the Economy: Asian Perspectives*, Cheltenham, UK: Edward Elgar.

Shaw, Daigee, Chiung-Ting Chang and Yen-Lien Kuo (2003), 'A New Institution for Environmental Management: Beyond the Political Boundaries' (in Chinese), *Taiwan Economic Forecast and Policy*, **34** (1), 1–38.

Smith, Adam (1776), *An Inquiry into the Nature and Causes of the Wealth of Nations* (Edwin Canaan (ed.), 1976), Chicago: University of Chicago Press.

Tiebout, C. M. (1956), 'A Pure Theory of Local Government Expenditure', *Journal of Political Economy*, **64** (5), 414–24.

Tullock, G. (1967), 'The Welfare Costs of Tariffs, Monopolies and Theft', *Western Economic Journal*, **5**, 224–32.

Uniterkamp, S., J. F. Leek and A. F. de Savornin Lohman (1995), *Waste Water Charge Schemes in the European Union*, Amsterdam: Institute for Environmental Studies.

Index

and hierarchical siting approach 40,
41, 43–4, 54, 56, 155
information from 139, 140, 143, 145,
148–9, 152, 166
lectures by 121
site assessments 33, 162–3, 181

facility need 13–14, 29, 68–70, 78
facility siting
acceptability 68–70
approaches 4–5
(*see also* bartered consent;
egalitarian siting approach;
hierarchical siting approach;
robust siting approaches;
voluntary/partnership siting
approach)
costs 85, 181, 188, 189
'do-nothing' option 190, 191
failures 5, 36–7, 40–41, 44–5, 66, 98,
103, 175, 197
and old plants 85
participation 198–9
policies 3, 78–9, 200
policy instruments 5–7, 197–205
Facility Siting Credo 8, 27, 197
faculty siting credo 8–9, 27
fairness
and Cooperative Discourse 144, 149,
152
decision-making 179, 186, 194
and hierarchical siting approach 5,
41–3, 55
and poor communities 96–7
and robust siting approach 60
and values 5
and voluntary/partnership siting
approach 5, 47–8, 55, 96, 98
and waste management 135, 144
farmers 46, 114, 120
fear 26, 120–22, 127–8
federalism 201
fires 180, 181, 189, 191, 192
fisherman 46, 120, 127–8, 130
fishing cooperatives 112, 117–18
fishing rights 117–18, 130
FOCJs (functional, overlapping and
competing jurisdictions) 9, 201–2,
203–4, 205
framing 193, 194

France
Andra 156, 158–63, 165, 167–9, 170,
171, 172, 173, 174, 175
Gard nuclear development 166,
169–74, 175
high-level radioactive waste law
155–9, 163, 164, 173–4, 200
LICS (local information commissions)
7–8, 155–6, 163–7, 171–4
nuclear reactors 110
nuclear research facilities 79–80, 155,
159–63, 166, 169–70, 171
free riders 198, 200, 202, 204
Frey, Bruno S. 79, 93, 95–6, 196, 201

Gard, France 166, 169–74, 175
genetically altered material 14
Genossenschaft 203
geology 156, 160–61, 162–3, 170–71
Germany 7, 66, 109, 136, 142–52
Gerrard, Michael B. 51–2
governance system 199
government
compensation 56, 118–20, 122
and cost-benefit analysis 42–3
decision-making 39, 59
distrust of 16, 26, 33
and hierarchical siting approach 38–9
public consultation 39, 115
talks 115
trust in 39, 50, 56, 57, 58, 59, 199,
203, 204
see also central government;
Commonwealth government;
FOCJs (functional, overlapping
and competing jurisdictions);
local government
Granovetter, Marc 87
Gregory, Robin 64
groundwater 14–15, 85

Hamaoka, Japan 46, 55
Hartland, Colleen 189
hazardous chemicals
environmental effects 183–6, 187–8,
189–90, 191, 193–4
fires 180
and heritage 179, 184, 187, 188,
189–90, 193
laws 182, 185–6